LOUISIANA

The Pelican State

Louisiana

THE PELICAN STATE

BY EDWIN ADAMS DAVIS

Louisiana State University Press

Baton Rouge

For
DEBORAH CLAIRE, my granddaughter,
BOB and BILL, my nephews,
and
ANNA REEVE and ANDY

PREFACE

The story of Louisiana is a fascinating and fabulous saga, filled with romance, drama, and achievement, for Louisiana is a state where the romantic past, the dynamic present and limitless future are happily combined. It is the author's hope that from this book Louisianians of the present and of the future will gain knowledge and appreciation of their state's history and that this book will assist in the development of a strong pride in the Louisiana heritage.

The author secured his factual material generally from secondary historical books and monographs, newspapers, family manuscripts, business records, and state and local governmental archives; his affection for and his understanding of the complex civilization of Louisiana gradually developed over many years through acquaintanceship with citizens in all sections of the state.

Dean Joseph G. Tregle, Jr., Louisiana State University in New Orleans; Otis Hebert, Graduate Assistant, Department of History, Louisiana State University, and Associate Editor of *Louisiana History;* Dr. Raleigh Suarez, Head, Department of Social Sciences, McNeese State College; Dean F. Jay Taylor, Louisiana College; Lionel O. Pellegrin, Director of Elementary Education, State Department of Education; and Dr. John A. Hunter, Dean of Student Services and Professor of Education, and president-elect, Louisiana State University, read the entire manuscript, were generous with professional advice, and were co-operative and uninhibited critics in noting errors of omission and commission.

Several public school educators working in the field of Louisiana history read the manuscript and made valuable suggestions which were incorporated into the finished work: Mrs. Margaret M. Bradbury of Shreveport, Mrs. Opal M. Shea of Lake Charles, Mrs. Elva G. Marks of New Orleans, Mrs. Helen Bankston of Hammond, and Mr. Watt Black of Baton Rouge. Professor Dorris Joseph, Supervisor of Elementary Teachers, University of Southwestern Louisiana, gave counsel on numerous practical problems.

Mrs. Griselda Richardson edited and stylized the manuscript,

while Mrs. Sam P. Mistretta typed the several drafts and did additional editing. Miss Marion Ware, former graduate assistant in
the Department of History, Louisiana State University, compiled
the index. La Verna Rowe Davis, the author's wife, was an active
collaborator and critic at all stages of the research and writing.

To each of the above unnamed and named persons the author
owes a debt of gratitude.

EDWIN ADAMS DAVIS

TABLE OF CONTENTS

Preface   *page* v

Part One: THE LAND OF LOUISIANA AND ITS EARLY
                        INHABITANTS

1 *The Land of Louisiana*   3
2 *The Indians of Louisiana*   14

Part Two: LOUISIANA AS A FRENCH COLONY

3 *The Founding of Louisiana*   25
4 *Louisiana Under Crozat*   37
5 *John Law's Louisiana*   44
6 *Three French Governors*   54
7 *Economic Life and Government in French Louisiana*   62
8 *Everyday Life in French Louisiana*   70

Part Three: SPANISH LOUISIANA

 9 *Early Years of Spanish Louisiana*   80
10 *Louisiana and the American Revolution*   90
11 *Last Years of the Spanish Regime*   99
12 *Economic and Governmental Life in Spanish Louisiana*   108
13 *Social and Cultural Life in Spanish Louisiana*   119

Part Four: EARLY YEARS OF THE AMERICAN REGIME

14 *The Purchase of Louisiana*   129
15 *From Territory to State*   139
16 *Louisiana and the War of 1812*   150

Part Five: ANTE BELLUM LOUISIANA

17 *A Half Century of Louisiana Government (1812–1861)*   163
18 *Economic Life During the Ante Bellum Period*   173
19 *Ante Bellum Social and Cultural Life*   184
20 *The Election of 1860 and the Secession of Louisiana*   196

Part Six: CIVIL WAR AND MILITARY OCCUPATION

21 *Louisiana and the War for Southern Independence*   206
22 *The Period of Military Occupation: 1862–1877*   220
23 *Everyday Life During the Period of Military Occupation* 229

Part Seven: DAYS OF OLD LOUISIANA, 1877–1920

24 *Problems of Government*   237
25 *Economic Progress*   245
26 *Educational Progress and the Growth of Culture*   259
27 *Life in "Old Louisiana"*   270

Part Eight: MODERN LOUISIANA

28 *Politics Since 1920*   284
29 *Economic Development, 1920–1955*   294
30 *Cultural Progress*   307
31 *Everyday Life in Modern Louisiana*   319
32 *Modern Louisiana*   330
   Index   341

ILLUSTRATIONS

A Typical Louisiana Lake   *page*   4

A Road in the Rolling Uplands   5

"Front Lands" and "Backlands"   8

An Indian Village   17

Bel Abbey, a Koasati Indian   23

Fort Maurepas (Old Biloxi)   31

French Soldiers, About 1710   35

The Building of Fort Rosalie   41

New Orleans in 1719   46

Arrival of the *filles à la cassette*   49

Bienville, the "Father of Louisiana"   56

The Acadian House   72

Restoration of an Old Fireplace   73

Don Bernardo de Galvez   91

Battle Between an English and a Spanish Ship   97

Expulsion of the Acadians   110

The Cabildo, New Orleans   117

Iron Balcony Railings   123

The Purchase of Louisiana   134

The United States Takes Possession of Louisiana   137

General Andrew Jackson   154

Jean Laffite   158

The Battle of New Orleans   160

Home of General Zachary Taylor   166

The Old State Capitol   169

New Orleans During the Late Ante Bellum Period   175

A Louisiana Sugar House   177

The Mississippi River Steamboat *Philadelphia*   182

"The Shadows"   186

The Burning of the Capitol   209

Assault at Port Hudson   210

Confederates Attacking Red River Fleet   212

"Belle Grove"   221
A Twenty-five-cent Paper Bill   228
Louisiana State Seminary of Learning and Military Academy   234
New Orleans During Military Occupation   235
Charity Hospital About 1880   244
Early Oil Field Near Jennings   249
The Steamboat *J. M. White*   252
An Old Oil Field Plank Road   254
Central High School, Shreveport   261
A Class of Cadets at Louisiana State University   263
Creole Home   271
No. 3 Fire Company, Baton Rouge, 1887   274
Louisiana State Capitol   288
Sources of Tax Revenue, 1959-60   292
Distribution of Tax Revenue, 1959-60   293
Harvesting Rice in Southwestern Louisiana   295
A Field of Cotton in Northeastern Louisiana   295
A North Louisiana Lumber Mill   299
Industry Along the Mississippi River   301
New State Library   311
Mardi Gras in New Orleans   323
1958 Louisiana State Tigers   325
"Oak Alley"   336

MAPS

The Land   *page*   7
Major Rivers, Lakes, and Bayous   9
Forests   13
Indians—1700   15
Plan of New Orleans, in 1728   52
French Settlements in Louisiana   59
French Colonial Mobile   70
The Louisiana Purchase   140
Parishes—1812   144
British Invasion of Louisiana, 1814–1815   156
Parishes—1860   174
Railroads—1860   181
Louisiana During the Civil War   207
Railroads—1900   253
Agricultural Regions   297
Modern Manufacturing Areas   302
Cities and Towns—1950   305

LOUISIANA

The Pelican State

PART ONE

THE LAND OF LOUISIANA AND ITS EARLY INHABITANTS

1. THE LAND OF LOUISIANA

Introduction. Let us begin by discussing the land of Louisiana—its location, its boundaries, and its shape. The climate must be included, and rivers and lakes, and the surface of the land. Nor can the forests and plants and the animals, birds, and reptiles be omitted. All these things are significant in the story of early Louisiana, for they determine where Indians lived and where later the white men settled. They have in large measure directed the course of Louisiana life in the past, and together with the location of underground resources, they are determining factors in the agricultural, industrial, and general economic life of the state today.

From the earliest colonial days to the present time geography has affected all phases of Louisiana life.

Location and Size. Louisiana lies at the south end of the Mississippi River Valley, and with the exception of Florida and Texas, extends further south than any other continental state. It is bounded on the north by Arkansas, on the east by Mississippi, on the west by Texas, and on the south by the Gulf of Mexico. The Sabine River forms part of the boundary with Texas, while the Mississippi and Pearl rivers help separate the state from Mississippi.

Louisiana is not a large state, having only 48,523 square miles of land and water area. In size it ranks thirty-first among the fifty states. Of this total, over 4,000 square miles are water— nearly 3,500 in lakes and almost 650 in rivers. It ranks sixth among the states with its 769 miles of coastline, being exceeded only by Alaska, Florida, Hawaii, California, and Maine. It is nearly 300 miles, at its widest part, from east to west, and about 275 miles from north to south.

3

A typical Louisiana lake

Like some of the other states, Louisiana has a recognizable shape. If one looks carefully at the map, it appears as a short, wide boot with a very ragged and well-worn sole, heel, and toe.

Climate. Most of Louisiana has a humid, semitropical climate which is remarkably the same over most of the state. The daily variations in temperature are caused largely by the differences in altitude and by the distance from the Gulf of Mexico. Although the summers are hot, the thermometer seldom rises as high as in many of the more northerly states. July and August are the warmest months, when the temperatures average approximately 82° F. in both the southern and northern portions of the state. The days are hotter, however, in the northern sections, the maximum of 100° F. being recorded most summers at Shreveport and other northern

4

A winding road in the rolling uplands

Louisiana cities. In New Orleans and the southern part of the state this temperature is seldom reached, but the humid summer heat is more uniform and oppressive.

Snow rarely falls in the southern part of Louisiana, and when it does, generally just a few flakes reach the ground. Farther north there are only a few light snowfalls a year, which seldom total more than three inches in the northwestern section near the Arkansas line. Frosts sometimes occur during November, more usually in December. January and February can be colder, with frosty and even freezing nights north of the Red River, but in the southern parishes temperatures are seldom severe enough to freeze vegetation. There are delightful days during the winter months when houses need not be closed for comfort.

It rains frequently in Louisiana. The rains are usually gentle showers or steady, heavy downpours, without high winds. The average yearly rainfall is a little over 57 inches. In the southern part the total rainfall averages about 60 inches, but in northwestern Louisiana it is only about 41 inches. While the rainfall is generally fairly well spread over the entire year, February marks the beginning of the rainy season. During the spring and early summer the rains and thundershowers are sometimes accompanied by vivid lightning and heavy peals of thunder. The least rainfall occurs during the late summer and fall; then, according to one traveler who visited Louisiana nearly one hundred and fifty years ago, the atmosphere is of "that mild and delightful blue, peculiar to a southern sky."

High winds sometimes move into the state from the northwest, and when accompanied by drops in temperature, they are called "northwesters." Tropical storms which originate in the Gulf of Mexico usually miss Louisiana by passing eastward of the mouth of the Mississippi River, and the southeastern coastal areas, therefore, are usually in the weakened areas of these storms.

The Surface of the Land. All of the state lies within a general southern area known as the Gulf Coast Plain. This plain is divided, however, into two subregions, the upland districts and the lowland districts.

There are three sections of Louisiana upland. The first is called the Florida Parishes Uplands and lies east of the Mississippi River and north of Lake Pontchartrain. The second, the North Louisiana Uplands, is in north and northwest Louisiana and lies roughly between the Red River and the Ouachita River. The third, the West Louisiana Uplands, lies southwest of the Red River and north of the southwestern Louisiana prairies.

The rolling uplands range in average elevation from about one hundred to four hundred feet. The highest areas are the Kisatchie Hills in the southern part of Natchitoches Parish and the northern part of Vernon Parish, the Tunica Hills in West Feliciana Parish, and the Driskill Mountains in Bienville and Claiborne parishes. These hill sections are picturesque and beautiful, with bluffs and deep ravines along the river and stream valleys.

The lowlands of Louisiana may be divided into three sections,

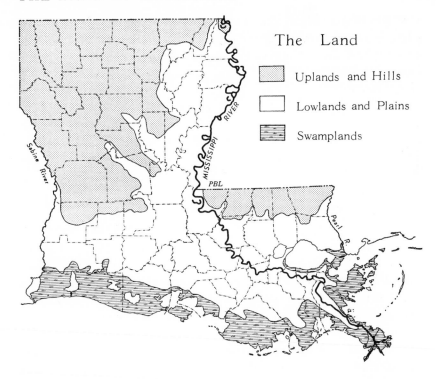

The Land

▨ Uplands and Hills

☐ Lowlands and Plains

▤ Swamplands

which average only about fifty feet above sea level. The Mississippi River Plain is narrow in the north, along the west side of the river. It widens in general triangular fashion south of Baton Rouge. The higher portions of this plain are called "front lands" because they front the Mississippi and other rivers and bayous. Here the waterways have built up leveelike ridges. Behind the "front lands" are the "backlands" and then the swamps. In general, the "front lands" do not drain into the rivers but back toward the swamps, which serve as a sort of catchall for the rainfall and the overflow waters from the rivers.

The Gulf Coastal Plain lies west of the Mississippi River Plain, and the land is similar to it except that it slopes gradually from north to south. The coastal marshes on the south are protected from the Gulf of Mexico by sandy barrier beaches. Sand and shell ridges, called *chénières* and "land islands" are scattered throughout the marshes.

The third region of the lowlands is the prairie section of south-

west Louisiana, which extends roughly some sixty miles north of
a line from Opelousas to Lake Charles. In times past this area was
divided into the Atakapas Prairie, the Mamou Prairie, and the
Opelousas Prairie.

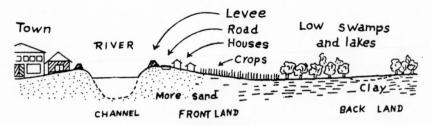

From Russell, *Louisiana: Our Treasure Ground*

"Front lands" and "Backlands"

Soil. The extremely fertile soil of Louisiana is its basic resource
and is generally porous and warm. It is very deep in most sections,
so that after years of cultivation only subsoil plowing is needed to
restore much of its original fertility.

Louisiana's soil may be divided into two general divisions: the
upland and the lowland soils. Each of these two, however, may
be many times subdivided. The alluvial soils of Louisiana were
deposited by the overflowing of the rivers and bayous. Few regions
in the world have as much alluvial soil as Louisiana, roughly one-
third of the state being covered with this type.

Rivers and Lakes. The rivers have been the great architects of
Louisiana, for much of the land was gradually built up by their
deposits. These were greatest along both sides of the rivers and in
time raised the level of the "front lands" until the rivers overflowed
only during times of high flood. In recent years levees have been
constructed to protect the land from flood waters.

The Mississippi is Louisiana's most important river and many
names have been given to it, like the Indian name *Michi Sepe* and
the Spanish name *Río de Flores* (river of flowers). The French for
a time called it "La Salle's River." Generally it has been called
"father of waters," although the Choctaw Indians called it the
"old-big-strong river." This great river and the other Louisiana

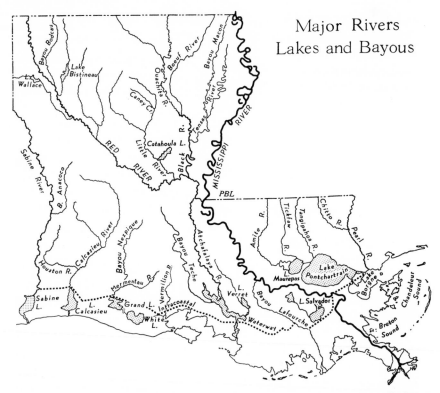

Major Rivers
Lakes and Bayous

rivers and bayous determined the paths of settlement, and until the arrival of the railroad and the hard-surfaced highway, they dictated the routes of Louisiana commerce.

There are some strange facts connected with the Mississippi River in Louisiana, for with the exception of the Red River, no streams flow into it from the west, and the same is true south of Baton Rouge on the east side. The "front lands" built up by the river have caused the streams to flow away from it to the lower lands behind. The levees which have been constructed along the entire west bank of the river and along the east bank south of Baton Rouge have also blocked off the bayous.

The Red River is the second largest Louisiana waterway, and there are many other important rivers and streams. In the northeastern section of the state is the Ouachita–Black River system, so called because the Ouachita and other streams join to form the Black River. In southwest Louisiana is the Sabine River, which separates part of Louisiana from Texas; here also are the Calcasieu, the Mermentau, and the Vermilion rivers, all of which flow into the Gulf of Mexico. Further to the east are Bayou Teche, the Atchafalaya River, and Bayou Lafourche. The Pearl River serves as part of the boundary between Louisiana and Mississippi on the east side of the Florida Parishes.

The words "river" and "bayou" are used interchangeably in Louisiana. "Bayou" really means a sluggish inlet or outlet of a lake or bay, or one of several mouths of a river. Therefore, if one follows the definitions, Bayou Teche is a river, and the Atchafalaya River is a bayou, for it is one of the outlets of the Mississippi and carries about 20 per cent of its waters to the Gulf. From 1904 until recently Bayou Lafourche was cut off from the Mississippi by the levee and was a river; now it is a bayou again, due to the construction of a large pumping station at Donaldsonville which pumps in water from the Mississippi.

Another frequently misunderstood physical feature of Louisiana is the "Isle of Orleans," which is not an island at all. The land that makes up the Isle of Orleans is bounded by the Mississippi River on the southwest and the Gulf of Mexico on the east. Going from west to east, its northern boundary is Bayou Manchac, the Amite River, Lake Maurepas, Lake Pontchartrain, Lake Borgne, and Mississippi Sound. But this area was called the Isle of Orleans long before Louisiana was purchased from France.

Louisiana's lakes are of three types. There are coastal lakes, only slightly above sea level, such as Pontchartrain, Maurepas, Borgne, Grand, Calcasieu, and others in south Louisiana. The flooding of the Red River in years past caused a second class of lakes, which include Catahoula, Caddo, Bistineau, Wallace, and several others. The third class was caused when the Mississippi River cut across its own big bends. The "front land" then built up and the water in the old river bed continued to live as a "lake." There are many of these half-moon-shaped, "oxbow" lakes along the west side of the Mississippi north of Baton Rouge.

Vegetation. The plant and forest areas achieve striking contrasts in Louisiana. It is these contrasts, together with the luxuriant growth of all types of vegetation, which give the state much of its beauty. Over one hundred and fifty species of trees are native to the state, and shrubs, vines, and smaller plants grow in profusion.

The live oak is perhaps the most spectacular tree, for, clad in Spanish moss, it is a sight not easily forgotten. It is native to the coastal regions and grows naturally as far north as the Red River, but transplanted live oaks grow fairly well still farther north. The cypress tree, which grows best in swamp and lowland areas, is distinguished by a sort of feathered green foliage and wide, cone-shaped base. Its roots frequently grow above the surface of the water or swampland for air and are called "knees." The magnolia, another native tree which grows best in south Louisiana, produces large, fragrant flowers and is transplanted in all parts of the state. Many types of pine grow in the uplands.

Numerous ornamental trees are native or have been imported to Louisiana—pride of China (chinaberry), tallow tree, banana, bitter orange, sweet olive, palm, camphor tree, and mimosa, to name only a few.

Shrubs and flowers include the honeysuckle, clematis, spirea, camellia, azalea, crape myrtle, jasmine, and hyacinth, while lilies, irises, and other bulbed flowers are found in many varieties.

When Alexander Campbell, the noted Protestant minister, visited Louisiana in 1839, he described one of the planter's homes. "He literally resides in the midst of gardens . . . with flowers that bloom in January."

Animal Life. Louisiana offers an attractive home for many forms of animal life, and quadrupeds of numerous species inhabit all sections. The rivers, lakes, and Gulf waters teem with both fresh- and salt-water fish. The southern coastal region is probably the most important winter resort in North America for wild geese and ducks, as well as being the year-round home of sea and fresh-water birds.

Only a few large quadrupeds survive in Louisiana. The buffalo, for example, which used to live in the northwestern part of the state, were all killed years ago. Deer and a few black bear are found in the wooded swamps along the lower Mississippi and Atchafalaya rivers and in the Tensas Basin, while a few cougars, or panthers (sometimes called catamounts), are still seen northeast of the Red River. Mink, raccoon, skunk, and opossum are found in the entire state, chiefly in the lowland wooded districts. A few timber wolves and many foxes live in the timbered uplands. Colonies of beaver inhabit some of the more rapidly flowing streams, whereas the otter usually prefers the sluggish lowland waters and bayous. Wild hogs, though almost extinct, are sometimes hunted in the lowland swamps, and squirrels are common in all sections where hickory and oak trees are found.

Louisiana is the home of many different kinds of birds. The Eastern Brown Pelican, the state bird of Louisiana, nests in the salt-marsh areas along the Gulf Coast and in the Mississippi Delta country. These sections are also the homes of ducks and geese and many smaller birds, including gulls, terns, sandpipers, black skimmers, herons, bald eagles, marsh wrens, seaside sparrows, egrets, and wood ducks. The wooded uplands and the less swampy lowlands also have their share of bird life: woodpeckers, warblers, quail, cardinals, southern whippoorwills, mockingbirds, Baltimore orioles, sparrows, redbirds, snipe, and numerous others. Wild turkeys are occasionally found along the rivers and in the swamps and pine-wooded uplands.

Gulf game fish include tarpon, jackfish, king mackerel, sharks, giant rays, and jewfish. Flounder, Spanish mackerel, redfish, trout, croaker, and sheepshead are the most important marketable varieties, but turtles, shrimp, crabs, oysters, and Gulf menhaden are also of great commercial value. Commercial fishing provides a living for many people from Atchafalaya Bay eastward, past Terrebonne Bay, Barataria Bay, the peninsula above the mouths of the Mississippi, and northward to Mississippi Sound.

The most important fresh-water game fish are bass, trout, crappie ("perch" to many Louisianians), and sunfish. Catfish is the most important of the fresh-water commercial varieties. Louisiana bullfrogs live in such numbers and are of such size as to make the state a national leader in the provision of frog legs as a table delicacy. Crawfish are found along the bayous and streams and in the lakes.

Louisiana's reptiles are numerous but mostly harmless. The alligator is the most spectacular reptile and is found in the swamps

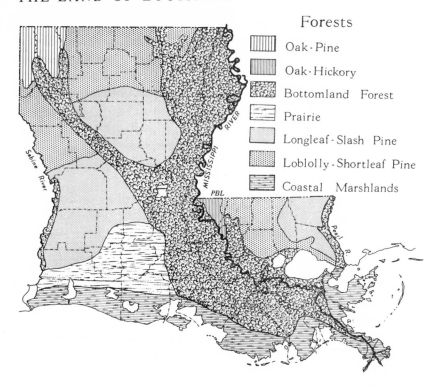

Forests

▦ Oak-Pine

▨ Oak-Hickory

▧ Bottomland Forest

☰ Prairie

▢ Longleaf-Slash Pine

▤ Loblolly-Shortleaf Pine

▤ Coastal Marshlands

and along the bayous in the southern part of the state. Poisonous snakes include the rattlesnake and the water moccasin, or cotton-mouth, a dark-colored, stump-tailed, venomous reptile whose cousin, or it may be a close relative, is called the copperhead or "highland moccasin." The coral snake is even more poisonous and is sometimes found in timber or canebrake areas.

Underground and Timber Resources. Louisiana's most impor-tant underground resources are petroleum, natural gas, sulphur, and salt. The principal oil fields are situated in the Gulf Coast and northwestern sections, though scattered fields have been discovered in virtually all parts of the state. The largest natural-gas fields are in the northeastern parishes. Sulphur occurs in the Gulf Coast region, with the principal deposits near the mouth of the Mississippi River in Plaquemines Parish. Salt is found chiefly in Iberia, Iber-

ville, Winn, and Cameron parishes. Fresh water is a major resource, and the state has enough of it to furnish every citizen of
the United States with several thousand gallons each day.

The forests fall into several groups. Pine timber of various
varieties is most important in the upland portions of the state.
The hardwood forests of ash, elm, oak, and red gum grow in the
basins of the Red and Mississippi rivers, while cypress and tupelo
trees grow in the swamp areas. However, most of Louisiana's
timber areas have been cut over and are now in the process of
regrowth.

In natural resources Louisiana is one of the richest states in the
Union. Except for iron, coal, and a few other basic minerals,
Louisianians could live very well on what they produce within their
own state.

2. THE INDIANS OF LOUISIANA

Introduction. When the first Europeans visited Louisiana there
were about 15,000 Indians living within the present boundaries of
the state, which was a very small population for an area so rich in
natural resources. If the Indians had been evenly settled, each one
would have had more than three square miles of land.

Over two-thirds of the Indians lived in the south and southeast
sections. In these regions there was more game and fish and fowl,
and the grains and fruits and vegetables grew faster and with less
cultivation. The pine-forest regions had the smallest population.

The Indian Groups and Where They Lived. The Louisiana
Indians may be divided into six general families or groups, each
of which can be subdivided into tribes. Each group lived in a
definite area and spoke the same basic language.

The *Caddo* occupied the northwestern quarter of the state, with
most of their important villages along the Red and Saline rivers,
Bayou D'Arbonne, and the upper part of Little River. Unlike the
other Louisiana Indians, the Caddos moved around a great deal,
for they used horses as domesticated animals. The two most important tribes of this group were the Caddo and the Ouachita.

Indians - 1700

△ Indian Villages
☐ Language Areas

After   Kniffen

The *Tunica* lived in northeastern Louisiana, east of the Ouachita River and north of the modern town of Harrisonburg.

The civilization of the *Atakapa* family who lived in southwest Louisiana along the Calcasieu, Mermentau and Vermilion rivers was generally lower than that of the other tribal groups.

The country east and northeast of Alexandria was the home of the *Natchez* group, who possessed a high degree of culture. The most important of their villages were near present-day Natchez, Mississippi, and in Concordia Parish. Other important tribes of this group were the Tensas, who lived near Marksville, and the Avoyel, for whom Avoyelles Parish was named.

The *Muskhogeans* occupied practically all of southeast Louisiana north of the Mississippi, part of present-day Pointe Coupee Parish, and a strip of land a few miles south of the Mississippi. The Tangipahoas, who had villages on the northern shores of Lake

Pontchartrain, and the Acolapissas, who lived just west of Pearl River, were the most important tribes. The Houmas lived in the Feliciana parishes and the Bayougoulas lived near the present village of Bayou Goula in Iberville Parish.

The *Chitimacha* group lived east of Bayou Teche and south of the Mississippi River. Along with the Muskhogeans, they were great fishermen, and their most important villages were located on the shores of the numerous lakes of this region and along Bayou Lafourche.

The Atakapa was the largest group and had about 4,200 members when the French first settled Louisiana. The Muskhogean group was second with 3,500 and the Chitimachas third with 3,000. The Caddos numbered about 2,500. The two smallest groups were the Natchez with 1,200 and the Tunicas with only about 500 members.

The land occupied by these six tribal groups had no specific boundaries, though it was understood that one group should not settle or hunt or fish in the area where another group lived. The rivers of Louisiana, therefore, did not mark the boundaries of the lands of the Indian tribes or groups.

Tribal Warfare. In general the Louisiana tribes were peaceful. The Tunica was the most warlike of the Indian groups, and the Koroa tribe, who belonged to this group, the most cruel. The Assinais, a member of the Atakapa group, was probably the most warlike individual tribe.

Shortly after the arrival of the French in Louisiana there were two important Indian wars. In 1700 the Quinipissas went to live with the Bayougoulas, but after a short time the latter suddenly killed most of the Quinipissa men and adopted the women and children into their tribe. In 1706 there was a war between the Tunicas and the Houmas.

Most of the Louisiana Indians cruelly tortured and killed their prisoners. The Assinais were probably the only Louisiana Indians who practiced cannibalism as a part of their religion. One of the early settlers who visited the tribe later wrote that "neither my comrades nor I could eat until after we had quit those cruel cannibals."

Houses, Tools, and Weapons. The Indian villages were most often built in a large circle, around an open space which was used for dances, games, meetings, and religious ceremonies, but some of the smaller villages were only a row or two of huts set along a river or bayou. There were no palisades or walls around the Indian towns.

The Indians of southern Louisiana built their cabins of wood, canes, or reeds, and roofed them with grass, palmetto leaves, or cornhusks. They were usually round, about fifteen feet high, with

From Kniffen, *The Indians of Louisiana*

An Indian village

small doors but no windows. There was a large hole in the top of the roof to let out the smoke from the cooking or heating fire and to let in light.

In north Louisiana the houses were better made, for it was colder there. Heavy posts were set in the ground and around the posts was woven a kind of framework, which was then plastered with clay or mud. House decorations were uncommon, though the Koroas sometimes adorned their cabins with pieces of shining copper.

The Indians had little furniture. Beds were made by planting four short posts in the ground and weaving on top of them a cane or reed frame, which was then covered with moss, grass, or the skins of animals. There were a few pottery cooking pots, water bottles, and storage jars; some red, black, or yellow baskets made of split cane; and woven mats on the ground. It was the custom to keep a small fire burning in the cabin, for warmth in winter or to drive out the mosquitoes in summer. If the weather was mild only a small torch made of dried canes was needed for these purposes.

The Indians had very few tools and weapons, all of which were crude. Bows were made of wood. The cane arrows had points hardened or tipped with bone splinters, deer horn tines, garfish scales or flints. Blowguns with cane splinter darts feathered with thistledown were used for hunting birds and small animals. They had stone knives, hatchets, and stone-pointed spears. Crude hoes were used for cultivation of their fields. Bone fishhooks, barbed fish arrows, nets made of cedar wood strips and funnel-shaped fish traps were used in catching fish.

While there were a few bark canoes, most of the boats were made by hollowing out large cypress logs. André Pénicaut, one of the early French settlers, describing how this was done, said that they built a large fire at the foot of a tree and "kept it up until the tree fell to the ground. Then they burned it off at the desired length. When they had burned the tree sufficiently for their purpose, they extinguished the fire with moist earth, and scraped out the tree with large thick shells. They then washed the canoes with water so as to give them a fine polish." Some of these large pirogues were thirty and even forty feet long. Cane rafts were used for crossing streams or bayous.

Food. An abundant supply of animals, fish, fowl, grain, fruits, berries, nuts and vegetables made food plentiful. Bear, deer, small animals and alligators lived in the forests, prairies and swamps. Buffalo roamed the northwest and west sections of the state. Three varieties of corn, numerous kinds of roots, plant shoots, grain from native grasses, many varieties of beans, sweet potatoes, cabbage, pumpkins, melons and other vegetables were grown. Peaches, plums, mulberries, persimmons, grapes, and numerous kinds of berries and nuts grew wild or were planted. Bees furnished wild honey. Salt was extracted from either sea water or water from saline springs or dug from near surface deposits.

The Indians generally boiled or roasted their meats. They had separate cooking pots for meats and fish, for they did not like to mix the flavors. Most of their bread was made of corn meal which had been ground with a large wooden mortar and pestle. They made a kind of porridge of ground corn called *sagamite* and to this was sometimes added beans, meat, and even fruits. Bear's fat and deer tallow were used for seasoning. They dried their fruits and vegetables and also smoked and dried their meats for preservation during the winter or summer months.

André Pénicaut described how they lighted their fires: "They take a small piece of cedar wood, the size of one's finger, and another small piece of mulberry wood, which is very hard. They put them side by side between their hands and by spinning them together, like making chocolate froth, they make a little piece of fuzz come out of the cedar wood and catch fire. This can be done instantly."

Clothing. Animal skins were used for clothing by the Indians, as well as cloth woven from grass and mulberry-wood fibers, or from various kinds of feathers. Some Indian men were fully clothed with shirt and pants, some with only pants, and still others with only a breechcloth. The women wore long, fringed skirts and loosely fitting tunics tied at the waist with a belt or cord. Moccasins were worn by some tribes only in winter but by others during the entire year. Children were dressed like their parents, though frequently the smaller youngsters wore no clothing at all.

It was customary for the men's hair to be cut short, but the women left theirs long and it was either coiled around the top of the head or hung in long braids down the back. The men did not wear beards. Pénicaut wrote that they removed the hair from their faces with "shell ash and hot water as one would remove the hair from a suckling pig." Most of the Louisiana Indians painted or tattooed their legs, arms, and faces, and some of them painted their teeth black. They used many kinds of ornaments—necklaces, finger rings, bracelets, nose rings, earrings, and breastplates.

Education. Indian life was simple and centered around the family; the girls were trained in the household arts of cooking, food preserving, sewing, and taking care of the cabin; the boys were taught how to fish and hunt and how to fight in case of war with another tribe. Both boys and girls were given much training in physical fitness. Their diet included raw eggs and a special kind of tea. The boys practiced running, and many wonderful stories are told of their swiftness. It is said that one of the Louisiana Indians could outrun a horse for short distances and that he made his living by running.

Social Life. Many persons believe that Indians were serious people who had very little social life, but this is not true. The Indians had regular rules and customs of behavior, and enjoyed different amusements such as sports, games, and dances.

Most Louisiana Indians were very polite. When the Bayougoulas, for example, met a friend they placed their hands over their own faces and breasts, then over the hands of their friends. After this they raised their hands upward with the palms outward in a form of salute. When an Indian met a Frenchman during the early colonial years he said, "Is it you, my friend?" before stopping to talk. The children were taught courtesy and respect for the older men and women of the village.

The Louisiana Indians had many different kinds of races, running games, and ball games. One of their ball games was called the *tole* game. It was played on a large field about two hundred feet long with a pole set in the ground at each end. The players divided into two sides, and a goal was scored by touching the ball to the pole at the opposite end of the field; thus, it was somewhat similar to our modern game of soccer football. During the summer a favorite sport for boys was the blindfold swimming race. Sometimes boys and girls, wrapped and tied in blankets or skins, were rolled down small hills, and younger children played "tag" and marbles just as they do today.

There were many kinds of musical instruments, for the Louisiana Indians loved to dance, but they were generally used for keeping time rather than for producing music. Horns were made from canes or reeds, and rattles were fashioned out of gourds filled with pebbles. Skins were tightly stretched over wood or earthenware to form drums, and whistles were either carved from wood or molded from clay. A favorite instrument was made from alligator skins. The skin was prepared by exposing the body of the alligator to ants until they had eaten all the flesh and the tender parts of the skin, which was then carefully dried. The sound was produced by raking a stick across the rough, irregular top.

Most of the larger villages had a dance house which was used for social as well as religious dances. The Choctaw Indians of Bayou Lacomb, who had moved to Louisiana from Alabama, had seven different dances which they always performed in the same order. One of these, the "Tick Dance," was danced in this fashion. All the dancers locked arms and formed two lines facing each other. They then began to sing a little song and as they sang they moved forward toward each other. They stamped first the right foot, then the left, at each step looking down at the imaginary little ticks they were crushing beneath their feet.

Most Louisiana Indians loved to tell stories, tales, and legends, some of which were related in a special singsong voice. There was the tale of *Kwanokaska,* a little man-spirit about the size of a three-year-old child who lived in a cave under some large rocks. The story of *Okwa Naholo* told of the "White People" who lived in the deep pools of the rivers, lakes, and bayous. Others included the legend of the hunter who became a deer, the fable of how the opossum got his large mouth, and the story of *Skatene,* an old witch.

A favorite Choctaw story was about a hunter and an alligator. The hunter had been unable to kill a deer for his family, although he had seen many in the forest. Finally he met an old alligator who was lost and weak from thirst. The alligator asked him where he could find water near by for he was exhausted, but the nearest pool was far away, so the hunter carried him to it. When the alligator had quenched his thirst, to show his gratitude he told the hunter how to kill deer, and thereafter the hunter's family was always well supplied with venison.

Medicine. Medicine was considered a part of religion, and many of the medicine men were also the priests or ministers of the

villages. With little knowledge of surgery, if they failed to set a
man's broken leg, for example, they sometimes entertained him
for a few days and then strangled him. No crippled children or
adults were permitted to live. Indians had little resistance to in-
fectious diseases such as measles, diphtheria, or smallpox.

Louisiana Indians were, however, not too far behind Europeans
in the practice of medicine at the time the French came to Louisiana. They used herbal remedies of many kinds. The Louisiana
historian Charles Gayarré says that they discovered and used over
three hundred medicinal herbs. One Frenchman who came to
Louisiana reported that they carefully guarded their knowledge of
these herbs and refused to share it with the French.

Small huts, like ovens, were used for sweat baths and for
boiling a variety of medicinal herbs. For stomach disorders they
used sumac seeds, ripe persimmon pulp, rhubarb, snakeroot, and
sassafras. They treated toothache with a pulp made of acacia wood,
and reduced swellings with a brew of elderberry roots. But their
universal remedy was sweet-gum tea, which they said "gladdens the
heart."

Religion. The Louisiana Indians worshiped many gods, the
Tunicas, for example, having nine gods—the sun, thunder, fire,
and the gods of east, south, north, west, heaven, and earth. They
were very careful not to tell Father Jacques Gravier anything about
their gods when he visited them during the early 1700's. In 1712,
Father Gabriel Marest reported that "Nothing is more difficult
than the conversion of these savages. . . . We must first make
men of them and afterwards work to make them Christians."

The Indians of the Natchitoches region had small round temples,
and every morning, after rubbing their bodies with a white mud,
they entered them, held up their hands, and prayed. In their
many religious ceremonies dancing played an important part.
The Chitimachas had regular dances at different seasons of the
year, the summer dance ceremony lasting six days and being
the longest and most important. All the men were painted red
and wore feathered bands around their heads. The music was
furnished by gourd rattles and rough alligator skins. Dancing
was followed by great feasts in each village.

Their marriage ceremonies varied with each tribe, some, especially those for important people, being long and elaborate. In one tribal ceremony the young man collected a group of his male friends and went to the house of his bride-to-be. Before arriving there they would see the girl with some of her friends, and when the young man tried to catch her, she was protected by them. When she was finally caught, everybody went into the house, and the couple was seated in the center of the group and questioned by the older men. When all of the questions were answered, the marriage ceremony was performed and there was a great feast, after which the people danced until daybreak.

Louisiana Indians Today. In 1940 there were about 1,800 people classed as Indians living in Louisiana, but by 1950 so many of them had intermarried with white people or had left the state that there were only a few over four hundred so classified.

Department of Commerce and Industry

Bel Abbey, a Koasati Indian, near Elton, Louisiana

Probably the largest groups are the Houma, who live in Terre-bonne Parish, and the Koasati, who live in Allen Parish and who moved to Louisiana about a hundred and fifty years ago. Most of the Louisiana Indians today have lost their old ways of life, and are now farmers and trappers and fishermen, living just like white people.

Indians have contributed much to Louisiana life. They gave the white man many vegetables and fruits; they taught the early settlers how to make a living in the forests and swamps; and they gave to Louisiana many of the names of her parishes, streams, and cities. *Calcasieu* is an Atakapa-Indian word which means "crying eagle." *Bogalusa* is a Choctaw word which means "black creek." The Mermentau River was named for an Atakapa chief. In these and other names, the Indian still lives, and will always live, in Louisiana.

PART TWO

LOUISIANA AS A FRENCH COLONY

3. THE FOUNDING OF LOUISIANA

Spanish and French Explorations. Spain explored and settled the islands of the West Indies within twenty years after the discovery of America, and during the next thirty years four Spaniards explored the eastern two-thirds of the South and discovered the Mississippi River.

Ponce de León landed in Florida in 1513 and several years later tried to plant a colony on its west coast, but was driven out by the Indians. In 1519, Alonso de Pineda sailed along the Gulf Coast and found the mouth of a large river, probably the Mobile River. Pánfilo de Narváez, landing in Florida in 1528 to establish a colony, lost most of his men fighting Indians. He built some crude boats and started westward along the coast of the Gulf of Mexico, but near the mouth of the Mississippi River his little fleet was wrecked and only a few men escaped. Álvar Cabeza de Vaca (whose name means "head of a cow") and a few others traveled across the southern part of Louisiana, and after eight years of wandering finally reached Mexico.

In 1539, Hernando de Soto reached the west coast of Florida with some six hundred men. Hearing of a rich Indian nation, he began to search for it, and for four years he ranged from Florida to Arkansas, but never found the gold and riches he sought. He died, probably in southeastern Arkansas, and was buried in the Mississippi River. The survivors of his army, led by Luis de Moscoso, tried to reach Mexico by marching through Texas, but overland travel was too difficult. They returned to the Mississippi River, built boats, floated down the river, and then followed the Gulf Coast to Mexico. For nearly one hundred and forty years after this no other Europeans visited the Lower Mississippi Valley.

25

The French founded Quebec in Canada in 1608, and their explorers and fur traders pushed quickly westward along the Great
Lakes. Nearly fifty years later, Pierre Esprit Radisson reached
the western shores of Lake Superior, where he and his men heard
of a great river which ran southward toward the Gulf of Mexico.
Within the next few years the French had explored the upper
portions of the great river.

At this time a French fur trader and explorer named René
Robert Cavelier, Sieur de la Salle, lived in Canada. He made
plans to explore the Lower Mississippi River country and secured
the aid of another explorer named Henri de Tonti. Tonti was an
Italian whose right hand had been blown almost off by the explosion of a grenade during a battle against the Spanish. Without
waiting for a doctor, he himself cut off the mangled hand, which
was later replaced with an iron one, so that he was called *Bras-de-
fer* (Iron Arm), or "Iron Hand."

La Salle and Tonti started down the Mississippi River early in
1682 with fifty-four French and Indians, including thirteen Indian
women and children. They reached the mouth of the river on
April 7 and two days later La Salle took possession of the country
by planting a large wooden cross in the ground. On it was inscribed: "Louis the Great, King of France and Navarre, reigns,
April 9, 1682." He named the land "Louisiane," meaning the land
of Louis. Two years later, La Salle left France with some four
hundred people to found a colony in Louisiana, but he missed the
mouth of the Mississippi and finally established Fort St. Louis near
Matagorda Bay in Texas. The colony failed and La Salle was killed
by his own men.

Both Spain and France now claimed the land of Louisiana, which
would belong to the first nation settling there successfully.

France Plans to Settle Louisiana. For some years after the
death of La Salle in 1687, France seemed to forget about Louisiana,
though there were some leaders in France and Canada who continued to urge the settlement of the Lower Mississippi Valley.

England, France, and Spain, the three greatest powers of western
Europe, were engaged in a struggle for the control of the entire
continent of North America. Spain had founded St. Augustine,

Florida, in 1565; England had settled Virginia at Jamestown in 1607; and France had established Quebec a year later. France now controlled the St. Lawrence River Valley in Canada, the Great Lakes region, and the Ohio and Upper Mississippi river valleys. She wished to keep the Lower Mississippi Valley from falling into the hands of Spain or England. This could be done by establishing a colony near the mouth of the river. The French especially feared the English.

After the death of La Salle, the Count de Pontchartrain, an important government official in France, became ambitious to expand French possessions. In 1694, Henri de Tonti, the friend and companion of La Salle, offered his services in establishing a Louisiana colony. Three years later, a Canadian, the Sieur de Remonville, proposed the organization of a company to send out an expedition of settlement. The same year Tonti published a book called *La Salle's Last Discoveries in America,* which described the geography, the Indians, and the resources of the Mississippi Valley. It became very popular in France and caused many of her people to begin thinking about Louisiana.

But the English had not been idle. About this time Father Louis Hennepin, who also had been a member of some of La Salle's exploring expeditions, became a subject of the King of Great Britain. In 1697 and 1698 he published two books urging William III to take possession of the entire Mississippi Valley.

The secret agents of Louis XIV of France soon discovered that the English were planning to found a colony in Louisiana. The Count de Pontchartrain realized that he had to take immediate action. He held conferences with French and Canadian leaders. It was decided that there were two possible methods for the settlement of Louisiana. Colonists could either be sent along the Great Lakes and down the Mississippi River under the leadership of a man like Tonti, who knew the country, or they could be sent by ship directly from France. The latter plan was chosen. In their search for an experienced naval commander and a good leader to head the expedition, they considered many Frenchmen and Canadians and finally chose a Canadian, Pierre le Moyne, the Sieur d'Iberville.

Iberville. The Sieur d'Iberville was born in Canada in 1661, the third son of Charles le Moyne, a native of Dieppe, France, who had emigrated to Canada when a young man. Charles le Moyne had married a French girl named Catherine Primot. They had fourteen children. Their sons Iberville, Bienville, Chateauguay, and Serigny were to distinguish themselves in Louisiana.

Reared in Canada, Iberville was an active outdoor youth, who joined the French navy while still in his teens. He became commander of a warship and later a whole fleet, winning victories against the English in Hudson Bay and off the coast of Newfoundland. He was a great hero to the Canadians. The Governor of Canada once remarked of him that he was "as military as his sword and as used to water as his canoe." His experience and success made it obvious that the Count de Pontchartrain and his advisors would select him to make the settlement in Louisiana.

The Voyage of Settlement. Iberville began immediately to organize his expedition. He collected food, clothing, weapons, tools, and other supplies, and secured two frigates called the *Badine* and the *Marin* and two small storeships. Crews of Canadians and other experienced sailors were assembled, a total of about three hundred men.

On October 24, 1698, the expedition put out from the harbor of Brest, France, with Iberville in command of the *Badine.* The little fleet sailed directly to Santo Domingo, where it was joined by a French warship, the *François,* for it was feared that the English might attack. Here, at Santo Domingo, Iberville secured the services of Laurent de Graaf, a celebrated ex-pirate, as a pilot. The ships then sailed past Cuba and up the west coast of Florida. Turning westward, they anchored off Santa Rosa Island, near the entrance of Pensacola Bay.

The Spaniards had settled Pensacola in 1696 and would not permit the French to enter their harbor, so Iberville's fleet moved on westward to Mobile Bay. Exploring the area, they found an island on which was a heap of bones. They named it Massacre Island. As they had seen no English ships, the *François* then returned to Santo Domingo.

Iberville next sailed southwest to the Chandeleur Islands, then northward to Cat and Ship islands. The latter was so named because it had a good anchorage on the land side. Cat Island was given this name because it swarmed with animals somewhat like foxes or cats, probably either opossums or raccoons. Here the little fleet anchored. The next day, February 13, 1699, Iberville and his brother Bienville rowed to the mainland and visited the Biloxi Indians, four of whom returned with Iberville to visit his ships, while Bienville remained with the Indians.

Several days later Iberville, accompanied by Bienville and about fifty Canadians and sailors, set off in two large boats and two canoes to find the mouth of the Mississippi River. Iberville planned to go up the river and choose a place for the new settlement. The fleet was to remain in the harbor at Ship Island, and if supplies should run short or Iberville did not return within six weeks, the *Marin* was to return to France for additional supplies.

Exploration of the Lower Mississippi. Iberville pushed slowly southwestward, threading his way around and between the many islands east of Lake Borgne and west and south of Breton Sound. The wind was usually against him, so the pulling was hard, and fog slowed up his progress. The islands were low and marshy, offering little protection from the winter winds, while wood was scarce and sometimes his men had no fires. Water could be had only by digging into the sands of the low beaches. One night after a stormy day the men had to build a platform on which to sleep, for the water covered the low island on which they were camped.

The storm continued the following day but the party pushed on, and late that afternoon they rounded a sort of cape. The wind drove them toward a series of jutting crags with calmer water between them. Iberville wrote in his journal: "As I neared the rocks, I perceived that there was a river. I passed between two of the rocks in twelve feet of water, the sea very heavy. . . . I found the water sweet and with a very great current." The "rocks" were not rocks at all, but drift logs covered with mud. The river was the Mississippi. It was March 2, 1699.

The next morning the party started up the river, and on the fourth day reached a settlement of the Bayougoula Indians, several of whom offered to guide them up the river. The Indians showed them a letter, which they called "speaking bark," that Tonti had written to La Salle back in 1685. At that time Tonti had come down the Mississippi to assist La Salle in establishing his colony, but La Salle had missed the mouth of the river.

Iberville continued up the Mississippi past the village of the Mongoulacha Indians. He passed the present-day capital of Louisiana, where he saw a red pole with the heads of fish and bear stuck upon it, and so he named the place Baton Rouge, which means "red pole" or "red stick" in French. He passed Pointe Coupee, where the Mississippi was just beginning to cut through the loop and isolate what is now False River, and on March 20 reached the villages of the Houma Indians.

After being entertained by the Indians, Iberville started on his return trip. At Bayou Manchac, below Baton Rouge, Iberville turned eastward with a few men, returning to Cat Island by way of Bayou Manchac, the Amite River, and Lakes Maurepas, Pontchartrain, and Borgne. Bienville continued on down the Mississippi to its mouth, then turned northward to Cat Island. The two brothers arrived at Cat Island within a few hours of each other.

Fort Maurepas, the First Settlement. Iberville now determined to establish a settlement on the Gulf Coast instead of at some point on the Mississippi. The river banks were low and the land behind them swampy. He feared, too, that large ships would not be able to cross the bars at the mouth of the river. If a fort were built on the coast, France would be able to control the mouth of the Mississippi and in addition might gain possession of the entire northern shores of the Gulf of Mexico.

Iberville explored the shores of the Bay St. Louis and the other bays and inlets eastward as far as Mobile, finally choosing the projection of land on the eastern side of Biloxi Bay as the site for his settlement. The little fleet anchored in the bay and the men began immediately to construct a small fort. By May 1, 1699, it was completed and named Fort Maurepas, in honor of the French Prime Minister. It was a small square fort armed with twelve cannon. On each side was a deep ravine and at the back a deep trench was dug to give additional protection. The Sieur de Sauvole was placed in command, with Iberville's brother Bienville

From Fant and Fant, *History of Mississippi*

Fort Maurepas (*Old Biloxi*)

as Lieutenant and second in command. The fort was garrisoned by seventy men and six ship boys with provisions for about six months.

On May 4, Iberville sailed for France with the *Badine* and the *Marin* to get new colonists and additional supplies. He had been successful in rediscovering the Mississippi River and in planting the settlement which was to grow into the French colony of Louisiana.

The Early Years. The early years were filled with hardships for the little colony. Many of the Canadian settlers were hunters and trappers called *coureurs de bois* and did not like to till the soil. Neither did the colonists who had come from France like to farm, much preferring to explore the region in search of gold and other precious metals. They were also unhappy because they had no wives to help them with household duties and make homes for them. No crops were raised the first year, which caused a heavy drain upon the supplies which had been brought from France.

About four months after the departure of Iberville, Bienville, on another exploring trip up the Mississippi, had an adventure which has become famous in the story of early French Louisiana.

On his way down the river, at a short distance below present-day New Orleans, he saw a twelve-gun English ship. The English had decided to establish a colony near the mouth of the Mississippi, and Lewis Banks, the captain of the English ship, was looking for a suitable site. Bienville boldly sailed up to the English ship and informed Banks that he was in French territory. He also told him he had a fleet a short distance upriver and that the English must leave immediately. Believing what he had been told, Banks turned around and departed downstream. This place on the Mississippi is still called "English Turn."

Iberville returned from France in early December, 1699, with supplies and new colonists. Having been told of Bienville's encounter with the English, Iberville ordered him to build a fort on the Mississippi at the first solid ground. Bienville selected a site about fifty miles upriver on the east bank, where he and his eight men built a low stockade, a small blockhouse, and a powder magazine. The blockhouse was a two-story, twenty-eight-foot-square fort, made of cypress logs and armed with two eighteen-pound and four four-pound cannon. A few months later Father Gravier wrote that the twelve-foot-wide moat had not yet been finished but that there were "five or six cabins detached one from another and roofed with palm-leaves." The name Fort de la Boulaye was given to the little fortification, though no record remains of just why it was so named.

Tonti arrived from Canada with ten canoes, fifty men, and a cargo of furs while Bienville was still building Fort de la Boulaye. Having heard of Iberville's settlement, he had brought the furs for export to France. Tonti and many of his Canadians settled in the new colony, contributing much to its success, for they were experienced frontiersmen.

During this period Iberville explored the Mississippi River as far north as Natchez and sent Pierre le Sueur up the Mississippi in search of minerals. Le Sueur returned with some blue and green earth which he thought contained copper; but it contained no minerals and one of the settlers later wrote that "we never had any news of it since."

Iberville again returned to France for supplies and colonists, and on this voyage he went by way of New York, where he checked the harbor and fortifications, believing that France and England would soon be at war again. He returned in December, 1701, his last voyage to the Louisiana colony.

When Iberville arrived, he found only about one hundred and fifty persons remaining in his colony. The rest had died. Supplies had run short and for some months the garrison at Fort Maurepas had had only a little corn to eat. He decided to move most of the colonists to a better location, where the soil was richer and where the harbor was deep enough to float large ships.

Mobile. Early in 1702, Iberville moved the majority of the settlers to Massacre Island, which is now called Dauphin Island. A little later he built another settlement on the west side of Mobile Bay about thirty miles from the Gulf, and only a small garrison was left at Fort Maurepas. Sauvole had died the preceding summer, so Bienville, who was now the second in command to his brother, began the construction of the fort which was named Fort St. Louis de la Mobile.

Fort St. Louis was much larger than Fort Maurepas, being about 375 feet square, and having four batteries of six cannon each. Within the fort were a guardhouse, a storehouse, a residence for the commandant, a house for the officers, and a chapel. The soldiers' barracks were constructed outside the palisade. Near by, homes were built for the settlers.

Iberville left Louisiana for the last time on April 27, 1702. Before leaving he gave some good advice to the French government in one of his dispatches. He wrote that it was "necessary to send here honest tillers of the earth," and not men who came to Louisiana solely with the intention of making a fortune. But he left his colony well supplied and with the first lessons of colonization already learned. He had planned to return, but Queen Anne's War broke out between France and England and his naval duties kept him occupied. He died of yellow fever in Havana, Cuba, in 1706.

Iberville had succeeded where La Salle had failed. He had planted the colony of Louisiana, and though small it was firmly rooted. Not only an inspiring leader, he had also been a practical one. He advocated the extension of agriculture as the colony's chief means of livelihood and urged the emigration of families and of young women to marry and make homes for the young settlers. No French colonizer has a better record of heroism, work, and self-sacrifice. He well deserves to be called the "Founder of Louisiana."

Slow Growth of the Colony. The little settlements at Fort St. Louis de la Mobile, Fort Maurepas, and Fort de la Boulaye grew slowly during the years after 1702. A few farms were established along the Gulf Coast and along the banks of the Lower Mississippi. Voyagers and traders arrived every year from the Great Lakes region or the Upper Mississippi with furs and other trading goods. But disease and famine and storms harassed the settlements. The colonists quarreled among themselves. The home government kept them so busy searching for mines and pearl fisheries, trying to domesticate the buffalo for their "wool," and raising silkworms, that they had to depend upon vessels from France to supply the major portion of their provisions.

Iberville, the other leaders, and the priests had pleaded for the establishment of homes. "With wives," Iberville said, "I will anchor the roving *coureurs de bois* into sturdy colonists." "Send me wives for my Canadians," wrote Bienville. "Let us sanction with religion, marriage with Indian girls," penned the priests, "or send wives of their own kind to the young men." Accordingly, in the summer of 1704, twenty-three young women arrived, girls who, according to the priest, "were reared in virtue and piety, and knew how to work." The same ship, the *Pelican,* also brought seventy-five soldiers, four families of artisans, a curate, and two Gray Sisters.

The colonists looked over the sides of the vessels toward a land which they believed to be one of fabulous riches, where life would be easy and work not too difficult. They were disappointed, "dumped, like ballast," as Louisiana historian Grace King wrote, "upon the arid, glittering sands of Dauphin Island or Biloxi, ill from the voyage, without shelter, without food, without employment." Many of them, unaccustomed to the climate and the hardships, died within a short time.

In 1704, Mobile had only 195 inhabitants; there were 8 officers, 72 soldiers, 14 naval officers and sailors, 10 ship-boys, 40 Cana-

From Winsor, *Narrative and Critical History of America*

French soldiers about 1710

dians, 16 laborers, and 23 women or girls. The two families had
a total of six persons. There were three priests. This year too,
witnessed the first birth in the colony when Jean François le Camp
was born to Jean le Camp and his wife.

The colony was in bad condition. The people were in rags,
and the soldiers wore skins rather than their worn-out uniforms.
The colonists ate acorns, a little corn which they had raised, and
wild game and fowl which were obtained by hunting. Their
wooden houses, roofed with palmetto or straw thatch, were poorly
built. They had made a start, however, in raising chickens and
livestock. A report stated that they had "14 cows; 4 bulls, of
which 1 belongs to the King; 5 calves, 100 hogs, 3 goats, 400

chickens, which the commissary has preserved carefully for breeding."

In September, 1704, a yellow-fever epidemic carried off thirty-five persons, including the gallant and experienced Tonti, whose loss was a severe blow to the colonists. Alcée Fortier, one of Louisiana's noted historians, called him "the most chivalric of the explorers of America."

By 1708 the little colony boasted 279 persons, and in addition "50 cows, 40 calves, 4 bulls, 8 oxen, 1400 hogs, and 2000 hens." But two years later, excluding the soldiers, sailors, and Canadians, there were only 178 inhabitants. The others had died.

Beginnings of Trade. The fur trade with the Upper Mississippi and the western Great Lakes region had begun in 1700 when Tonti had brought the first shipment of furs down the river. During the years that followed, the governors of Canada opposed the trade in furs, hides, corn, meat, and other products, one of them writing that the goods frequently belonged to Canadian creditors. But as it was easy to float boats down the great river, the trade continued.

As early as 1701, Iberville had begun to investigate the possibilities of trade with the West Indies, Havana being, after all, only fifteen sailing days from Biloxi. But the Spanish officials were slow to start trade outside their own possessions. In 1704, however, the French were able to do the Spanish a favor; Pensacola needed flour, lard, and munitions of war, and Bienville sent the needed supplies. Two years later he again sent flour to Pensacola.

By 1708 the trade with Cuba and the other West Indies islands was well established, though it was still frowned upon by some of the Spanish officials. It was upon this trade that the Louisianians depended for much of their supplies during the period of Queen Anne's War, when foodstuffs could not be received regularly from France.

After 1703 the French government maintained a storekeeper at the Balize, near the mouth of the Mississippi. He handled all the supplies, food, ammunition, and other goods sent over from France and was required to keep a strict "account of merchandise and ammunition received and distributed." The early settlers had very little metallic money. For the most part they traded and bartered, or depended upon "bills of credit" which were issued by the governor of the colony.

Bienville and the Louisiana Colony. Until 1712 there were only two important government officials in Louisiana. The Governor, as the representative of the King, was at the head of civil, military, and naval affairs, while a Commissioner served as the auditor, treasurer, and chief storekeeper of the colony. The Curé guided the religious life of the people. There were no courts of law, for the officials decided disputes and punished criminals.

Only three persons served as Governor: Iberville during 1699, Sauvole from 1699 to 1701, and Bienville from 1701 to 1713. Bienville was an able governor, doing the best that could have been done under the circumstances. During the yellow-fever epidemics of 1701 and 1704 he saved his colony from ruin and perhaps from being abandoned. Through both sternness and friendly persuasion, he made the colonists begin raising agricultural products. When the great flood of 1709 overflowed the fort and the town at Mobile, he simply moved them down the river the next year to the present site of Mobile. The fort was renamed Fort St. Louis de la Louisiane.

Though he was to remain in Louisiana for many years, Bienville's first years had been the hardest. By 1712 the Louisiana colony was permanently established, and could boast a population of about four hundred persons, including twenty slaves. It is with good reason that Bienville has been called the "Father of Louisiana."

4. LOUISIANA UNDER CROZAT

Antoine Crozat. There lived in France during the early 1700's a great merchant named Antoine Crozat. He was a peasant's son who had acquired some education and at the age of fifteen had become a clerk in a commercial firm. Twenty years later he was a partner in the company and one of the richest men in France.

Crozat heard that the Count de Pontchartrain was planning to turn Louisiana over to an individual or a company. The English had been very successful with this method of establishing colonies, in Maryland and Virginia in particular, and Louisiana had been a disappointment and an expense to the French government. No precious metals had been found; the silk industry had failed; and the royal treasury was short of funds.

Crozat believed that Louisiana might be turned into a sound, money-making investment. He had made profits from the Guinea Company, which traded in Africa, and the Asiento Company, which imported African slaves to the new world. Louisiana had been described as having splendid opportunities for agriculture and trade.

Crozat's Grant. In September, 1712, Crozat secured a royal charter which granted Louisiana to him for a fifteen-year period. Many rights and privileges went with it. He was granted all the territory called Louisiana south of Illinois. He was to have all the commercial rights formerly held by the King, including the importing and exporting of goods, and the privilege of working mines and searching for precious stones, yielding of course to the King the "royal fifth." He was given all the land that he might cultivate and all the manufactures which he might establish. He was given the use of all property belonging to the King. He was granted the exclusive right to import slaves from Africa. For nine years the King would pay the salaries of the soldiers in the colony, and would give Crozat 10,000 livres a year (about $2,000) for the same period with which to pay the officers.

Crozat in return was obligated to continue the laws of France in Louisiana, and to send two ships from France each year with supplies and colonists. At the end of nine years he was to become responsible for the army expenses.

Governor Cadillac. The colonists learned that Louisiana had been granted to Crozat during the early summer of 1713, when Governor Antoine de la Mothe Cadillac arrived, but it made little difference to them. They were extremely poor and were enduring a hand-to-mouth existence. There were only two companies of soldiers, fifty men to a company, in the colony, while some seventy-five Canadians performed various services for the King. The rest of the population totaled about three hundred persons, but these were scattered along the Gulf Coast west of Mobile and up the Mississippi River about as far as Pointe Coupee. It is quite probable that not more than fifty white persons lived within the present limits of Louisiana.

The new Governor had spent over twenty years in the service of the King in Canada. He had founded Detroit. He was a man of courage, had a great deal of energy, and was rigidly moral and pious. He had lived under frontier conditions in Canada. He also was given sound instructions from the Count de Pontchartrain for governing his colony "with justice and mildness, . . . like a good father."

On the other hand, Cadillac was proud and vain. He wore a "ponderous wig, the curls of which spread like a peacock's tail," and was both quarrelsome and bad-tempered. He was interested principally in making money though he had made little in Canada, while his ancestral castle in France was so run-down that the local wags called it "Cadillac's Rookery." His superiors in Canada had accused him of being "more interested in making money for himself than in the good of his establishment." Other Canadians had said that he was "hated by the troops, by the inhabitants, and by the savages."

Cadillac was very critical of the little colony. He wrote back to France that Dauphin Island "consists of a score of fig-trees, three wild pear-trees, and apple-trees of the same nature, a dwarfish plum-tree, three feet high, with seven bad-looking plums, thirty plants of vine, with nine bunches of half-rotten and half-dried-up grapes, forty stands of french melons, and some pumpkins." On another occasion he wrote that "the colony is not worth a straw for the moment; but I shall endeavor to make something of it, if God grants me health."

With characteristic energy, he went to work.

Work of Cadillac. Acting under instructions of the French government and Crozat, Cadillac first reorganized the government of the colony. An attorney general became his legal adviser and the lawyer of the people, and he organized a court and advisory body called the Superior Council. He put into operation the so-called "Custom of Paris," which was simply the laws and legal customs of that section of France in the vicinity of the capital. Turning his attention to economic matters, Cadillac encouraged agriculture, offered plans for raising tobacco and indigo, and promoted the Indian fur trade. He sent out parties to plant settlements, and encouraged trade with the Spanish in Mexico and the Floridas, with the English colonies, and with the islands of the Caribbean. In fact he tried any sort of economic venture which would make the colony more self-sustaining and give a profit to Crozat.

Extending the Frontiers. In 1714 Cadillac called upon Louis Juchereau de St. Denis to establish a post on the Red River in what is now northwest Louisiana. Spain had been gradually pushing her settlements into Texas and western Louisiana, and the Governor wanted to stop them at the Sabine River.

St. Denis had come to Louisiana with Iberville and was an intelligent and energetic young man to whom the freedom of the Louisiana frontier greatly appealed. He soon became friendly with the Indians and familiar with the entire Lower Mississippi region.

St. Denis, with a sergeant and twenty-five soldiers, took three boats loaded with Indian trading goods, munitions, and supplies, and chose a site at Natchitoches for the new fort. It was well that the French had arrived at this time, for the Spanish had already sent out one expedition to plant a settlement near the same place. Some years before, a few Spaniards had settled near present-day Robeline.

As soon as the fort was completed St. Denis took his trading goods and proceeded southwest to the Spanish post of San Juan Bautista, on the Río Grande. Here the Spanish Commandant made him a prisoner, and during the weeks which passed St. Denis fell in love with the Commandant's granddaughter, Manuela. He was taken to the City of Mexico and later was returned to San Juan Bautista, where he continued his courtship of Manuela. The girl's father at last gave his consent to the marriage, and in 1716, Señorita Manuela de Sanchez y Ramon became the bride of St. Denis.

For several years St. Denis traded with the Indians of western

Louisiana and eastern Texas, and in 1722 he was appointed Commandant of the fort at Natchitoches. He died in 1744. Louisianians during this period maintained that St. Denis deserved to have been made Governor of Louisiana.

In 1716, Bienville completed a fort on the high bluff overlooking the Mississippi at Natchez, which had officers' and soldiers' quarters, a magazine, and storage buildings within the walls. The fort was named Rosalie, after the wife of the Count de Pontchartrain.

From Thompson, *The Story of Louisiana*

The building of Fort Rosalie

At about the same time forts were built on the Alabama River and on the Wabash River, north of the Ohio. These forts, together with Fort Rosalie and those at Mobile and Dauphin Island, gave France several forts with which to protect Louisiana from the English and the Spanish.

Agriculture and Commerce. Cadillac, acting under orders from Crozat, did what he could to encourage agriculture but the colonists did not like farming. Money could be made from tobacco and indigo but it was very hard work, as was the cultivation of corn and vegetable crops. A few settlers, however, did produce food crops and in some years there was a surplus. For the most part the settlers in Louisiana at this time were Canadian hunters, fortune seekers from France, or those who had been sent to Louisiana instead of to the jails of the mother country. Louisiana cannot boast of the qualities of her early settlers.

In order to secure labor for the fields, Crozat imported Negro slaves from the West Indies. Five hundred were brought over in 1716 and about three thousand the following year, but the West Indian Negroes were troublesome, rebellious, and believed in voodooism, so after this most of them were brought from Africa.

Cadillac had hoped to make a personal fortune for Crozat and for himself from gold and silver mines and from pearl fisheries, but despite the fact that he sent out numerous expeditions, none were discovered.

Gradually the French won the battle with the English for the Indian trade in hides and furs. The overland trade with Texas and Mexico, which was carried on from Natchitoches generally, sometimes ran to several thousand livres a year. The trade with Spanish Florida made a little profit. The colony, however, did not prosper and brought in no profits to Crozat, the proprietor.

Recall of Cadillac. Cadillac's temper steadily grew worse. He quarreled with the officials. On one occasion some of the soldiers sent a committee to see the Governor and complained that they had nothing to eat but corn. The Commissary-Commissioner defended the soldiers, so Cadillac "gave him a good rapping on the knuckles." When the people framed a petition demanding free trading privileges with all countries, the Governor complained that they "have dared to meet without my permission."

Cadillac's daughter fell in love with Bienville, and when he ignored her infatuation, she enlisted the help of her father, who offered her hand to him. But Bienville did not love the young lady, so he told the Governor that he must forever remain unmarried. The Governor then became his enemy, and Bienville later wrote in one of his dispatches that "the cause of Cadillac's enmity to me, is my having refused to marry his daughter."

By the summer of 1716, Cadillac had reached the end of his

patience with the colony of Louisiana. His troubles were constant and he had gathered no riches. He had tried to carry out his orders, but many projects had failed. He wrote back to France in disgust: "Decidedly, this colony is a monster without head or tail."

Crozat had also lost patience with Cadillac. He wrote to the Governor and told him bluntly that the evils present in Louisiana were the result of his inefficient administration, and the Governor and the Commissary-Commissioner were dismissed. The Minister of Marine in France wrote that their intellects were "not equal to the functions with which his Majesty has entrusted them."

Bienville served as Acting Governor until the new Governor arrived.

End of Crozat's Colony. Bienville held his second governorship for a little less than a year. In March, 1717, the Chevalier de Lepinay, the new Governor, arrived. He was a naval officer who had served over twenty years in Canada. Governor Lepinay brought with him a new Commissary-Commissioner, three companies of infantry, and fifty colonists. He brought Bienville the decoration of the Cross of St. Louis, and title to Horn Island, which lies just east of Ship Island off the Gulf Coast.

Lepinay had hardly landed in Louisiana before he and Bienville began to quarrel, and soon the colony was divided, one group supporting Bienville and the other the new Governor.

In France, Crozat's financial affairs had taken a turn for the worse, so he reconsidered his Louisiana venture. He had spent over 1,250,000 livres. What had he gained? There were only about seven hundred people in his colony, including the soldiers of the army. Trade with the Spanish and English colonies had not been successful and several millions of livres worth of goods were still in Louisiana for want of a market. The hoped-for mines had produced no minerals and the pearl fisheries no pearls.

Then he received word that Lepinay, the new Governor, was doing no better than had Cadillac. In early August, 1717, he addressed a petition to the King, begging to be released from the agreement, and the ministers of the King accepted his proposal.

Crozat had failed. Louisiana had not grown in strength as it should have. The colony had to be made stronger. A proprietor or a company had to be found to inject new blood into Louisiana. France had recently lost Newfoundland and Acadia to England, and the English colonies must not be permitted to push west of the Appalachian Mountains. This could be prevented only if Louisiana was a strong colony.

5. JOHN LAW'S LOUISIANA

John Law. The story of Louisiana from 1717 to 1731 is the fabulous tale of a Scottish businessman and financier with grandiose ideas, and of two companies which he organized and for a time controlled. The man's name was John Law. Next to Iberville and Bienville, he contributed more than anyone else to Louisiana's development during the French period.

Law was the son of a wealthy Edinburgh goldsmith and banker. Early in his youth he showed ability in mathematics, finance, and commerce. At the age of twenty he had already gambled away his fortune. He killed a man in a duel and fled to France, where he soon gained another fortune at the gambling tables.

Law studied finance, particularly the methods of the Bank of Amsterdam, and developed the idea that France could greatly increase her wealth by printing huge quantities of paper money. He had little difficulty in selling his scheme to the Duke of Orléans and other governmental leaders. In 1716 he organized the General Bank of France and the following year its paper money was accepted as currency in all France. In 1718 it became the Royal Bank of France, with Law as Director-General.

The Company of the West. The Scotsman conceived the idea of using some of the deposits of his bank for the development of Louisiana. The Company of the West was organized, and shares of stock were offered for sale to everyone in France. Law promised that huge profits were to be made in Louisiana and that everyone who purchased shares of stock would become wealthy. The shares sold at 500 livres each and could be bought on credit with only a 25 per cent down payment. The people became very excited over this prospect of easy wealth, and Law had no difficulty in selling his stock.

In 1717, Louisiana was turned over to the Company of the West on approximately the same terms which had been granted Crozat in 1712. In 1719 all of the French trading and colonizing companies were merged into one large one called the Company of the Indies, and the Company of the West was included in this merger.

The Company of the Indies announced great plans for the development of Louisiana. Large numbers of settlers were to be sent to the colony and new settlements were to be established. Agriculture was to be promoted and trade was to be extended with the Spanish in Florida and Mexico, with the English in their southern colonies, and with the Illinois country. Currency would be sent to Louisiana to give the people more money with which to buy goods.

Government Under the Company of the Indies. The governmental officers and Superior Council were left largely as they had been under Crozat. Each of the more important settlements of Biloxi, Dauphin Island, Mobile, Natchez, and Natchitoches had a Commandant, who was both the civil and military official.

The headquarters of the colony was first at Dauphin Island, but by 1719 had been moved to Fort Maurepas. Shortly afterward a part of Fort Maurepas burned and the capital was moved to New Biloxi, on the other side of the bay. The capital of Louisiana remained at New Biloxi until August, 1722, when it was moved to New Orleans.

In 1721, Louisiana, which then included most of the Mississippi Valley, was divided into nine governmental districts, each under the charge of a Commandant and a Judge. The following year three large religious parishes were created, and turned over to the Carmelite, Jesuit, and Capuchin orders. Except for the Florida parishes, present-day Louisiana was given to the Capuchins.

Bienville became Governor of Louisiana for the third time in 1718. He returned to France in 1725 and left Pierre Dugué de Boisbriant serving as Acting Governor. Étienne Périer became

Governor in 1727 and served until 1733, two years after Louisiana became a royal colony again. Under Bienville and Périer, from 1718 to 1733, Louisiana made steady progress.

The Founding of New Orleans. Bienville had always wanted to build the capital of the Louisiana colony on the Lower Mississippi River, but it was some years before he had the opportunity to found his new city.

In 1717, Bienville wrote the Directors of the Company telling them of a crescent bend in the Mississippi which was safe from tidal waves and hurricanes. The new capital should be built here. A colonist named Le Page Du Pratz, who arrived in Louisiana about this time, commented that "a better choice could not have

From Magruder, *A History of Louisiana*

New Orleans in 1719

been made." He also complimented Bienville by writing: "It is not every man that can see so far as some others."

Early in 1718, Bienville left Mobile with about fifty men, including a few carpenters and twenty-odd convicts, and spent much time that year directing the building work. Progress was slow, but by the end of 1719 a number of huts and storage houses had been built, so Bienville began to move supplies and troops to his new town.

The chief engineer of the colony, Le Blond de la Tour, had opposed Bienville's plans. When an assistant engineer, Adrien de Pauger, arrived in the colony in 1720 he was ordered to draw the plans for the new city. He reached New Orleans in March, 1721, and under his supervision the town soon began to take shape. Drainage ditches and canals were dug, a wharf was built, low levees were thrown up, a cemetery was located, and a church and government buildings were constructed.

The central portion fronting the river was occupied by the church, with presbytery on the left and a guardhouse and prison on the right. In front was the Place d'Armes, or parade ground, to the left of which was a market place fronting the river, while scattered about the river front were government warehouses. Bienville built his home on the site of the present-day Custom House and in front of this building erected a powder magazine. At the other extreme end of the town were the quarters of the soldiers. Today we call the eleven-by-seven-block rectangle, which made up the French town, the "Vieux Carré" or Old Square.

Bienville named his new capital *Nouvelle-Orléans,* New Orleans, in honor of Louis Phillipe, Duke of Orléans and Prince Regent of France.

New Colonists for Louisiana. The Company of the Indies had difficulty in getting settlers to come to Louisiana, so the French government began to release people from prisons and houses of correction on their promise to marry and go to the colony. These men and women were hurriedly married, chained together, and dragged toward the French ports. Others, for whom husbands or wives could not be found at the moment, were also released on their promise to go to Louisiana. These people were driven along the roads of France like droves of cattle. At night they were locked up in barns and when shelter could not be found were forced to lie down in ditches, while guards stood over them.

But still not enough people could be found, so orders were given to kidnap the poor and send them to Louisiana. There was no time to choose or select or examine or ask questions. As Grace King has written, "it was a dog-catcher's work; and dog-catchers performed it. Streets were scoured at night . . . the contents of hospitals, refuges, and reformatories were brought out wholesale, servant girls were waylaid, children were kidnapped." Soon the word "Louisiane" became hated for it meant a place of exile, far from France.

Indescribable hardships were suffered by these immigrants on the voyage to Louisiana. The captains of the ships were paid according to the number of people they brought over, so they packed the greatest possible number into their vessels. Conditions were very bad, the food was moldy and sometimes rotten, and the water was stale and usually impure. Hundreds died. Out of 213 persons who sailed on one ship, only 40 reached Louisiana alive.

Criminals and people of bad character do not make good citizens and soon the Company realized its mistake and adopted a new method of securing settlers. Large grants of land called "concessions" were given to wealthy or noble Frenchmen or other Europeans, in return for which these men agreed to settle families on their lands. Smaller grants of land called "habitations" were given to the less wealthy. But these offers did not attract enough settlers.

The Company then tried another method. The expenses of European families migrating to Louisiana would be paid. Each family would also be given sizable plots of land, horses, and oxen for the cultivation of fields, and pigs, sheep, chickens, furniture, kitchen utensils, and food supplies until the first harvest.

Pamphlets and handbills were published, but the descriptions of Louisiana were not correct. They said that four crops could be raised each year; that the Indians were very friendly and did most of the work; that there was plenty of game, including deer, bear, "whole swarms of Indian hens," and other fowls; and that it was simply "impossible to picture the abundance of this country." Many Frenchmen and other Europeans believed these descriptions and came to Louisiana.

Several thousand Germans arrived, as did many Swiss and smaller numbers of other nationalities. Most of these Germans settled along the Mississippi just above New Orleans, and this section soon became known as the German Coast. Many of them changed the spelling of their names; Trischl became Triche, Foltz became Folse, Himmel became Ymelle, Wehrle became Verlay, and Miltenberger became Mil de Bergue, for example. Their towns were given names which were the French approximation of German words, but they remembered their German origin. Even today many of their descendants say with pride: "We are the descendants of those Germans who turned the wilderness into a paradise such as Louisiana never possessed before."

During those early years most of the settlers lived very hard lives. The Company did not keep its promises. The ship captains turned the supplies over to the soldiers or sold them for the Company's profit. The settlers were dumped off the ships onto the beaches of Mobile or Biloxi or at the landing at New Orleans without shelter and without food. Some of them were forced "to

From Thompson, *The Story of Louisiana*

Arrival of the filles à la cassette

subsist on what they might be able to catch on the beach, standing for the most part of the day in the salt water up to the waist."

No one knows how many settlers arrived during those years after 1717. Over eight hundred came in 1718 and this number more than doubled the population of the colony. In 1722, nine ships arrived with over four thousand settlers. But it is certainly true that more settlers came during these years than at any other time while the French held Louisiana.

In the fall of 1727 the first group of *filles à la cassette,* or casket girls, arrived. They were called casket girls because each of them had a small trunk filled with personal belongings, a sort of hope chest which had been given her by the Company. They were marriageable young ladies of good character and were housed by the Ursuline nuns in a large building guarded by soldiers until they found husbands.

Negro Slaves Sent to Louisiana. Additional slave labor was needed. During the summer of 1719 the ships *Grand Duc du Maine* and *Aurora* arrived from Africa with about five hundred slaves, so the Company built a slave-trading station across the Mississippi from New Orleans where Algiers is today. It was called the "Plantation of the Company." Here the slaves were distributed and sold to the colonists.

The "Code Noir," or Black Code, was written in 1724. While the Code dealt mainly with slaves, it also restricted the activities of Free Negroes, ordered all Jews out of the colony, and forbade "the exercise of any other religion than the Catholic."

Establishment of the Jesuit Plantation and the Coming of the Ursulines. In 1726, Jesuit Father Ignatius de Beaubois went to France to secure permission to establish a headquarters at New Orleans for Jesuits on their way to missionary assignments up the Mississippi and to secure the services of the Ursuline nuns for educational and medical work. He was successful and later the same year the Jesuits acquired a tract of land immediately upriver from New Orleans, where they established a plantation and built a residence and a chapel.

The first Ursuline nuns arrived in August, 1727, and were temporarily quartered in Bienville's house, which thus became the first convent within the limits of the United States. The cornerstone for a permanent convent was laid in 1730, and the building was completed four years later. In addition to their teaching duties, the sisters took charge of the military hospital and ministered to soldiers and citizens alike who needed medical attention.

The Natchez Indian War. On December 2, 1729, a ragged, half-starved, half-dead man staggered into New Orleans. He told the excited people that the Natchez Indians had risen against the

French and had massacred all of the settlers at Fort Rosalie and in the surrounding country. He had been away from the fort and had thus escaped. A few other fugitives appeared within a few days and confirmed his report.

The Natchez Indians had been at peace with the French for some years and many settlers had established farms among them. Several of the red men had already visited France, one of whom had said that in Paris he liked best the Street of the Butchers' Shops, because they had so much meat there. He had seen men who "had their hair done up like women [they were wearing wigs]; that he had a strong suspicion they used rouge and that they smelled like a crocodile."

But a Commandant named Chepart had been sent to Fort Rosalie. He was an iron-handed man who treated his soldiers and the Indians harshly and planned to become rich through the establishment of a large plantation. When the Indians did not want to give up their village of the White Apple or their land, Chepart flew into a rage and said that they must leave just as soon as the harvest was over. Chepart was warned that the Indians were planning to revolt, but he did nothing. On November 26, 1729, the Indians began a massacre and killed nearly three hundred persons.

Some of the Louisiana Indians joined in the uprising and many settlers west of the Mississippi were killed. One settler, however, who lived off the coast of present-day Terrebonne Parish, drove away the attacking Indians in a very peculiar manner. Upon seeing them, Sylvain Filiosa grabbed a kettledrum and banged it so loudly that the Indians stopped and gazed in alarm at the unknown and strange weapon. From this time Filiosa and his island were called "Le Timbalier," the kettledrummer.

The French marched against the Natchez, who asked for peace and promised to release all their white and Negro prisoners, but they soon went to war again. In early January, 1731, the French again attacked them. This time there was no peace. The Indian forts were destroyed and most of the Indians were killed or captured and sent as slaves to Santo Domingo. The few who escaped moved further westward into Louisiana or joined the Chickasaws. The Natchez ceased to exist as an organized Indian nation.

Growth of Towns and Villages. New Orleans grew slowly during those early years. By 1721, however, it was a sizable village, and two years later Father Pierre Charlevoix wrote there were about a hundred rude houses, a church, several warehouses, and other buildings in the town. He predicted that "this savage and desolate place, which is still almost covered with trees and canebrakes, will one day be an opulent city, and the Metropolis of a great and rich colony."

A storm blew down the church and many other buildings in 1723, but the latter were reconstructed and a new brick church soon replaced the old wooden one. Four small forts called St. Jean, St. Charles, St. Louis, and Bourgogne, were built at the four corners of the little town and were connected by a low earthen wall.

In 1727, when the Ursuline Sisters arrived, one of them wrote back to France: "Our town is very handsome, well constructed and regularly built." She continued that the streets were large and straight, the houses well built and whitewashed, and that "the colonists are very proud of their capital."

In 1719 a fort was built on the present site of Baton Rouge, and four years later a stockade was constructed and a trading post

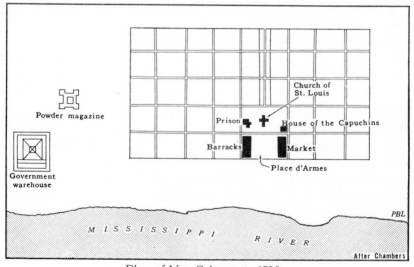

Plan of New Orleans, in 1728

established at present-day Pineville. By 1720 Natchitoches had nearly a hundred inhabitants, who made a good living from agriculture and trade with the Indians. Other villages were established and new settlers opened up farms along the rivers and bayous of southeast Louisiana.

But the pioneers faced many hardships. The land had to be cleared of trees and brush, and they had to learn how to plant crops in the climate of Louisiana, which was different from that of France. Domestic animals were difficult to secure; good prices were not always received for their farm products; there were droughts and storms. "But the greatest torture," wrote Father Paul du Poisson, "is the mosquitoes, the cruel persecution of the mosquitoes. . . ." This little creature had caused more problems since the French came to Louisiana than had any of the animals, other insects, or forces of nature, and Father Poisson continued for two more pages to explain how hateful the little insects were.

Despite all these hardships, however, the Louisiana colony made slow but steady progress.

Company of the Indies Gives Up Louisiana. When the Directors of the Company of the Indies received word of the Natchez massacre and the Indian war they agreed that they could not furnish the money which would be necessary to rebuild the colony. They had tried to make Louisiana a profitable colony, but now all their efforts seemed lost.

John Law's "Mississippi Bubble" had burst in 1720. The stockholders of his bank, suspecting that all was not well with their Louisiana investments, began to withdraw their deposits. Shortly thereafter France was flooded with paper money, and foreign investors also began to withdraw their investments. The government refused to accept the bank's paper money, and the run on the bank continued. Soon it could not pay its depositors. Law escaped from France to Belgium, and died in 1729, in poverty and obscurity, in Venice, Italy.

While most of the people hated Law for the ruin which he had caused, one of the stockholders wrote the following:

> *Monday bonds I bought;*
> *Tuesday gains unthought;*

Wednesday my home to date;
Thursday I rode in state;
Friday I danced with glee;
Saturday—woe unto me!

Early in 1731, the Directors of the Company asked the King to take back their charter. The following November the King issued a series of orders which ended the Company's control of Louisiana.

Work of John Law and the Companies. John Law, the Company of the West, and the Company of the Indies had done great things for Louisiana. Law had found Louisiana a colony with fewer than a thousand inhabitants; the Company of the Indies left it with a population of about 7,500, including Negro slaves. Many towns and settlements had been founded; agriculture was well established, although not all of the needs of the settlers could be supplied; and New Orleans had been built into a town of which the people were proud. Despite the shortcomings of John Law and the impracticability of some of his ideas, Louisiana owes him a great debt of gratitude.

6. THREE FRENCH GOVERNORS

Bienville Governor Again. Périer continued as Governor for two years after the Company of the Indies returned Louisiana to the King, and they were years of constant difficulty. The Chickasaw Indians, who had always been enemies of the French, caused trouble. The colonists were discontented because a hurricane had caused a food shortage. Some of the government officials had grown lax in performing their duties, and there were disagreements among the members of the Superior Council.

Périer lost interest in Louisiana. Though a man of integrity, he was somewhat brisk and harsh, which affected good relations with the Indians and with his subordinates. He finally resigned and Bienville was again appointed Governor.

Bienville had been living in France since his last governorship, but he left there as soon as possible and arrived in Louisiana in 1733 to take over his office.

The Chickasaw Indian War. Bienville was almost wholly occupied with the Chickasaws during his last governorship and had to declare war against them. He ordered Pierre d'Artaguette, a Commandant in Illinois, to gather an army and meet him in the Chickasaw country in May, 1736. He, himself, would raise an army in Louisiana, move up the Mobile River, and join D'Artaguette. Their combined force would have little difficulty with the Chickasaws.

D'Artaguette and his little army of forty-eight soldiers reached the appointed place, but Bienville, who had been delayed because of almost constant rains and a violent storm, was not there. For ten days D'Artaguette searched the area looking for the Governor, and finally decided to attack the Indian villages without waiting for Bienville. He captured one village, but he and some of his soldiers were captured during the attack on the second village. Bienville reached this place a few days later, and believing that D'Artaguette and his men had not yet arrived, he attacked the strong Indian fort but was defeated.

The Indians burned D'Artaguette and fifteen of the soldiers to death. Mathurin le Petit, who was one of the prisoners not burned, reported that the doomed men chanted a prayer, which the Indians called a "song to go above," while they were being led to the two huge fires. They did not "interrupt their singing amid the fire until they fell, half burned or suffocated by the flames."

The Louisiana colonists were much saddened by the deaths of D'Artaguette and his men, and for many years they told stories about him and how he had fearlessly attacked the Indians. These stories gradually became legends, and anyone wishing to speak of something very old said that it was "as old as the time of D'Artaguette."

Bienville never recovered from this defeat. Over a hundred French soldiers had been killed. What had gone wrong? Whose fault was it? The two armies had simply not co-ordinated their movements. Together they could have defeated the Indians; separately they had been defeated. He took the blame upon himself.

Bienville was anxious to avenge the death of D'Artaguette and the other soldiers, but he needed cannon and a larger and better-equipped army. He gathered his supplies, equipment, and men, and moved up the Mississippi to about the present site of Memphis,

From a painting in the Louisiana State Museum

Bienville, the "Father of Louisiana"

where sickness broke out in the camp and the heavy rains prevented his cannon from being moved. In April, 1740, the Chickasaws sued for peace and Bienville made a treaty with them. He explained that "it was not advisable to risk the glory of the arms of the King on the chance of a doubtful success."

Bienville was so disappointed at his failure to subdue completely the Indians that he asked to be relieved of his duties as Governor and to be permitted to return to France. He was getting old, and perhaps had lost the courage and energy of his youth. It is certain that he was a brokenhearted man.

Bienville's Last Years in Louisiana. Bienville spent the next three years engaged in routine matters of administration. He encouraged trade and agriculture. He helped establish a Charity Hospital which had been endowed by a sailor, Jean Louis. He aided in the relief of suffering when two terrific hurricanes hit the Gulf Coast in the fall of 1740. He proposed the establishment of a school in New Orleans where the boys could be taught geometry, geography, and other subjects. He wrote that "young men brought up in luxury and idleness are of little use."

The new Governor arrived in New Orleans on May 10, 1743, and in middle August Bienville sailed for France, after nearly forty years in Louisiana. He had paddled his pirogue over the Louisiana bayous and rivers and had threaded its forests. He had attempted to keep the Indians at peace. He had worked to build the colony into a proud possession of France. Years later, he tried in vain to prevent the transfer of Louisiana to Spain. The "Father of Louisiana" died in Paris in 1768 at the age of eighty-eight.

The Grand Marquis. Pierre Rigaud, Marquis de Vaudreuil, the new Governor, was the son of a Governor of Canada and belonged to a family which was very influential at the French court. He had a genial and kindly nature; he had soldierly courtliness and great dignity and his manners were elegant; and he enjoyed giving magnificent entertainments, formal ceremonies, and military displays. Throughout his governorship, he maintained in New Orleans a fashionable little court which closely resembled the court at the King's palace at Versailles in France.

Vaudreuil's Indian Problems. The Chickasaws had continued to cause trouble, for their peace with Bienville had been only a truce. Most of them preferred to trade with the French rather than the

English, but it was difficult for Vaudreuil to get trading goods from France. So the Indians traded with whichever country had the most goods at the cheapest prices.

In 1747 the Indians made a raid down the east bank of the Mississippi for some distance south of Baton Rouge, and the settlers fled to New Orleans. The next year they again moved down the left bank of the Mississippi, killing and plundering as they went. Some of the settlers escaped by crossing the river, where the militia defended them. In 1752 the Chickasaws again went on the warpath and Vaudreuil led a force of over seven hundred men against them. Their villages were burned and their cornfields destroyed, and without means of subsistence, they sued for peace.

Development of the Colony Under Vaudreuil. Vaudreuil encouraged agriculture, and it was not long before larger quantities of cotton, tobacco, rice, and other crops were being grown. In good years, some of these products were exported. Myrtle wax was produced for the making of candles and for other purposes. Salt, rough-sawed lumber, and bricks were manufactured for home use and for shipment to France or to the West Indies.

A census was taken in 1744, and it was found that the colony had slightly over three thousand white inhabitants, about eight hundred soldiers, and over two thousand slaves. This census revealed that the total population had declined since the Company of the Indies had turned the colony back to the King in 1731. On the other hand there was considerably more prosperity than there had been before.

End of Vaudreuil's Governorship. The Governor was very popular in New Orleans because of his numerous balls and dinners; for the first time the wealthy citizens of the colony had a fashionable social life.

The common people, however, were not so happy with their Governor. They accused him of favoring the soldiers, who bullied and insulted the citizens, and said that he surrounded himself with a small group of favorites who flattered him and who received many economic privileges. They said that the government officials were merely his tools, that his expenses were too high, and that his wife was making large profits from illegal business transactions.

One of the reports sent back to France charged that Madam Vaudreuil "keeps in her own house every sort of drugs, which are sold by her steward. . . . The husband is not ignorant of this. He draws from it a handsome revenue."

However, Governor Vaudreuil remained in favor with the officials in France and he was promoted to a similar post in Canada in 1753. His governorship was long remembered in Louisiana for its splendor and luxury and military display, for its grand balls, and for the refined manners of the upper-class society. During later years, when hard times came, many people enjoyed recalling the good old days of the *Grand Marquis*.

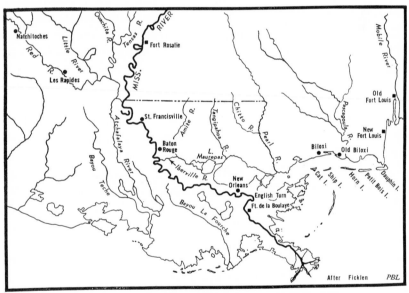

French Settlements in Louisiana

Governor Kerlerec. Louis Billouart, Chevalier de Kerlerec, was a bluff, hearty, honest naval officer with twenty-five years of service to his credit. He was accustomed to discipline, which he insisted should be rigidly enforced. He was not a man of great ability, however, and simply could not handle adequately the many problems which faced the colony during his term of office. The French and Indian War was being fought between France and England during most of his governorship and as a result he faced many difficulties. But he did the best that could have been done under the circumstances, and one of the colonists admitted that he had "qualities of heart very different from those of his predecessor."

Kerlerec's Problems. The Indian trade caused Kerlerec much trouble, for the English had plenty of trading goods and their prices were lower than those of the French. All Kerlerec could do was to play the tribes against each other and to try to trade the goods which he had.

He begged France to send over well-trained, well-disciplined troops and argued that Swiss troops were better than French troops. He strengthened New Orleans by erecting a palisade around the city and by rebuilding the battery at English Turn. In the channel at the entrance of the Mississippi he anchored an old ship which could be sunk to keep out English ships. But during the French and Indian War, Louisiana seemed to have been forgotten, for France could not assist the colony.

Meanwhile, pleasure-loving, indolent Louis XV continued to enjoy the pleasures of his fashionable court. He had the magnificent palace of Versailles built a short distance out of Paris, at a cost of some 150,000,000 francs, and here he lived amidst such splendor that he became the envy of all the monarchs of Europe.

Conditions in Louisiana grew worse, and as they grew worse, Kerlerec's discipline tightened. The Commandant at Cat Island forced his soldiers to cultivate his garden and to do other personal work. He stole their supplies, trading them to the Indians or to the settlers. Finally a few of the soldiers revolted and killed the Commandant. Kerlerec held the trial of the soldiers in New Orleans. Several of them were executed.

The morale of the colony declined. The Jesuits and the Capuchins were engaged in what some of the people called a religious war. In 1761, Kerlerec reported that the Indians "harass us daily, to have supplies and merchandise. They threaten to go over to the English." He also wrote that they "devour the little that remains of our provisions." Agriculture declined and the war prevented foreign trade. One of the officials wrote that the colony was "in a state of complete destitution" and that most of the inhabitants were lazy, insubordinate, and a drunken lot.

Louisiana Ceded to Spain. By 1756, France was spending over 800,000 livres a year on Louisiana and was receiving little revenue from it. The colony had never been profitable. Altogether, between seventy million and eighty million livres had been invested with comparatively little return, and expenses were mounting each year. The colony had a total population of less than 7,500 people. In 1757, Kerlerec wrote that he had not even had a letter from France for two years, and in 1761 the French ambassador to Spain admitted that France had not sent any supplies to Louisiana for four years.

When it became evident during the French and Indian War that France was going to lose Canada to the English, she offered Louisiana to Spain. The Spanish, however, were not interested in acquiring the Louisiana colony at this time. Then, early in 1762, Spain declared war on England and in the following August the English captured Havana. The Spanish wanted to regain possession of this important city and to keep the English out of Louisiana. Perhaps England would trade Havana for Spanish Florida, in which case, Louisiana would be important to Spain. The colony would be expensive, but it might some day develop into a profitable venture and would aid in protecting Spanish Texas and Mexico from the British.

France was much more interested in saving her West Indies islands than in saving Louisiana, for it had been a costly and unsuccessful colony. Only a few Frenchmen wanted to keep Louisiana, and one of these few, the philosopher Voltaire, wrote that he could not conceive how Frenchmen could abandon "the most beautiful climate of the earth, from which one may have tobacco, silk, indigo, a thousand useful products."

On November 3,. 1762, by a secret treaty signed at Fontainebleau, France ceded the Isle of Orleans and the rest of Louisiana west of the Mississippi River to Spain. A few weeks later England acquired Spanish East and West Florida and the French area north of the Isle of Orleans and east of the Mississippi. It was not until

October, 1764, however, that the people of Louisiana found out that they were now Spaniards instead of Frenchmen.

7. ECONOMIC LIFE AND GOVERNMENT IN FRENCH LOUISIANA

Agriculture. Agriculture was not successful during the early years. The French settlers were not farmers and did not like farm work, so it was not until the coming of the German colonists that good farms were established. By the middle 1720's there were many small farms in the vicinity of Mobile, Biloxi, and New Orleans. During good crop-growing years the markets at these towns sold corn, rice, and wheat, and such vegetables as cabbages, peas, onions, sweet potatoes, pumpkins, watermelons, turnips, and greens of all sorts. Fruits included peaches, pears, figs, oranges, and lemons.

On market days and holidays the farmers went to the towns to sell their produce. There was no advertising except by voice, and everywhere men could be heard crying out their wares. Money was scarce and things were more frequently bartered than sold— a pig for so much grain, vegetables for fruits, articles of home manufacture for a chicken or a cow. Everything was labeled "Creole," which meant native to the colony or grown in the colony. There were "Creole" pigs, "Creole" figs, and "Creole" rice. After all, many of the people were themselves "Creoles," for they had been born in Louisiana.

As time passed larger farms were cleared, and after the coming of Negro slaves, plantations were developed. These farms and plantations usually fronted a river or bayou, and a man was granted or bought so many "arpents" (approximately 182 feet) fronting the stream. His holding was ordinarily forty arpents deep, or "the usual depth" as the French said.

At first not much land was sold, for there were great areas of frontier land which was free to all. By the middle of the second decade, however, a few farms and houses were being bought and sold near the villages. In 1717, for example, one small house in Natchez sold for 50 livres and two years later a much better one sold for 1,000 livres. In 1721 a large and well-equipped plantation brought 50,000 livres. As the population increased there was of course much more buying and selling of land.

At first corn and rice were the most important crops, but it was not long before cotton, tobacco, and indigo were being produced also. Sugar cane was first brought to Louisiana by Iberville, but little was grown until 1751, when a better variety from Santo Domingo was introduced. The cane juice was boiled down into a thick mass, for it would not granulate, and this was used for sweetening purposes and for the making of an alcoholic drink called "tafia." It was not until 1795 that Etienne de Boré succeeded in clarifying and crystallizing sugar in Louisiana.

The farmers and planters had many problems. Heavy rains frequently caused the streams and bayous to overflow, and storms blew down the crops. The storms of 1740, for example, were very destructive, and by the end of the year rice had more than doubled in price. Raccoons, opossums, and other animals and insects ate the plants. Weeds were numerous and often grew faster than the cultivated crops.

It was not until the colony had been settled for many years that enough meat was produced to satisfy the needs of the colonists, and sometimes the killing of cattle, sheep, and hogs had to be prohibited in order to save enough animals for breeding purposes. In 1725 cattle sold for 500 to 600 livres each, but the price gradually declined until in 1749 they were worth only about 60 livres. Not many horses were raised, most of them being bought from the Indians or from the Spanish. By the end of the French period there were several *vacheries*, or stock farms, scattered throughout the colony.

Development of Slavery. No one knows the exact date that the first Negro slave was brought to Louisiana. Indian slavery was first tried but was not successful. The Indians did not work well and found it difficult to understand the agricultural practices of the settlers. It is believed that Bienville first brought two slaves from the West Indies about 1708; by 1712 there were twenty slaves in the colony and twenty more were brought in the following year. A small number of slaves were sold during the Crozat period. The Company of the Indies imported many slaves after 1719, and for some years their slave ships arrived nearly every year. In 1724, Bienville enacted a series of slave regulations called the "Black Code." From this time until the War for Southern Independence slavery was an important factor in the economic life of Louisiana.

Industry and Manufacturing. There was very little manufacturing in French Louisiana. The population was too small and the people were too busy growing foodstuffs, trading with the Indians, or working at other industries.

Lumbering was important, for the Gulf Coast and Lower Mississippi Valley were filled with good timber. By 1716 there were at least two sawmills in the colony. The mills increased in number and soon were producing all kinds of lumber for local use and even for export. Most of them were located on bayous or streams so that the logs could be floated to the mills and the lumber could be transported by boat or ship. Cordwood was also cut and sold in the towns for fuel.

Brickmaking became an important industry, because the dampness of the climate caused wood to rot quickly. The bricks were somewhat larger than ordinary bricks, usually being 12 x 8 x 2 inches in size. The brickyards also made floor and roof tiles and some pottery. Many of these clay products were exported to the West Indies and to Spanish Florida.

Most of the manufacturing was done in the home or on the farm, for the settlers made practically everything which they used, including furniture, clothing, leather goods, utensils, a few articles of iron or steel, and farm tools.

Local Trade. The Mississippi River, with its tributaries, was Louisiana's great artery of commerce. All types of boats were used. There were two-place canoes which would carry about 400 pounds of cargo and four-place canoes carrying up to 1,200 pounds. There were "master" canoes, rowed by twelve or fourteen oarsmen and up to about forty feet in length, with a cargo capacity of more than a ton. There were dugouts made of cottonwood or cypress, which were sometimes fifty feet long, used sails, and had a rudder. There were flatboats, called *bateaux plats* or *radeaux* by the

French, made of stout wood planks, some of them carrying as much as fifty tons. Broad horns were flatboats with a sharp bow. Keelboats, large flatboats sixty to seventy feet long and fifteen to twenty feet wide, with a keel, were introduced after 1740.

The Mississippi River trading boats usually left the Illinois country about the beginning of February, when the water was high and the river current was fastest. They generally started the return journey from New Orleans sometime in August or September in order to arrive home before winter set in. The boats usually traveled in "convoys," several boats traveling together for better protection against Indian attacks, the government furnishing a guard of several men and a leader who commanded the convoy.

Pack trains were used by Indians and English traders east of the Mississippi River. Following Indian and animal trails, the long trains of pack horses were driven in regular Indian file, experienced young men leading the procession and older men and boys bringing up the rear. The pack train moved along at a trot and seldom stopped until nightfall.

From the Illinois country came wheat, corn, lard, salt meat, dried meat, tallow, bear's oil, beeswax, skins and hides of all sorts, lead, and other articles. From New Orleans went rice, indigo, sugar and molasses, tafia, tobacco, manufactured goods which had been received from France or other countries, and trinkets for the Indian trade.

The fur and hide trade was very important. By the middle 1740's over 1,500 men were engaged in this trade and its annual value totaled thousands of livres. Owing to the wars which France fought with England, however, the Louisianians were frequently unable to furnish the goods which the Indians wanted in exchange for furs.

Foreign Trade. Foreign trade presented many difficulties. Ships were slow and sometimes badly built so that they sank during storms, and the voyages from the French ports took many weeks and sometimes several months. Sailors were picked up wherever they might be found and frequently were not sailors at all, while the poor food and bad water aboard ship caused diseases. Yellow fever sometimes broke out. Goods were often of poor quality, and smuggling of goods from the West Indies, the Floridas, and Mexico was a general practice.

There was considerable stealing and corruption among ship captains and among Louisiana and French officials. Many cargoes were short when they reached New Orleans. One ship on its arrival was short over 60 casks of wine out of a consignment of 170 casks. The Governor ordered one ship captain to give the colonists an equal chance to buy his goods, but he sold the entire cargo to a public official for 250,000 livres. The official retailed the goods at a profit of 150,000 livres.

Trade with France was the lifeblood of the colony, for the colonists depended upon her for their necessary supplies. During the first twelve years after 1699 more than a dozen ships arrived from France with goods. This number increased to more than twenty-five in the Crozat period. More than a hundred ships arrived from 1717 to 1731, when the Company of the Indies controlled Louisiana. From 1731 to the late 1750's more than 175 vessels brought goods from the French ports of La Rochelle, Bordeaux, Marseilles, Dunkerque, St. Malo, and Bayonne.

These ships brought cargoes of spices, cloth, cutlery, utensils, wines, flour and other foodstuffs, notions of all sorts, and after 1730 many types of luxury goods. When they returned to France they carried skins and hides, indigo, tobacco, myrtle wax, bear's oil, pitch and tar, lumber, and other products.

The West Indies trade was also important. From Louisiana went corn, peas, rice, beans, salted and dried meats, bear's oil, brick, pitch and tar, tiles, and lumber. On their return voyages the ships brought sugar, coffee, cocoa, tanned leather, spices, tortoise shell, fine hardwoods, syrup, and other products.

St. Denis was the founder of the Mexican trade and he continued this work until his death in 1744. The early trade with Mexico was carried overland by way of Natchitoches, but later most of it went by sea to the Mexican ports on the Gulf of Mexico. By the 1740's the Mexican trade had become a significant source of income to the Louisiana colonists.

Louisianians did considerable trading with Spanish Florida. The

Floridians needed foodstuffs, and the Louisiana colonists furnished them with lard, beans, rice, meats, and vegetables.

Much of the trading with the Spanish West Indies, Mexico, and Florida was done illegally. The Spanish usually required all trading to be done with Spain, just as France required all trading to be done with the mother country. Sometimes the Spanish officials seized ships and cargoes. During periods when France and Spain were at war with England, however, the officials permitted trading between their colonies. At the New Orleans wharves could be seen ships from Havana, St. Augustine, Pensacola, Porto Bello, Darien, Cartagena, and other Spanish colonial ports.

The government officials in France did all they could to prevent trade with the English, but Louisiana frequently needed English goods. English ship captains were very adept at making excuses for putting into the Louisiana ports: the ship had "sprung a leak," it had a "broken mast," there was a "shortage of wood and water." In 1735 an English captain entered Mobile Bay on the excuse that he had come to collect some debts which were owed him. A ship which arrived in 1759 brought a cargo of dry goods valued at 600,000 livres, and another which arrived the same year brought flour, lard, beer, hams, cheese, iron, cider, and other goods. During times of war, when English vessels blockaded the mouths of the Louisiana rivers and bays, some trade was carried on with pack trains from Charleston, Savannah, and even Virginia and Maryland towns.

Money. During the entire period the colony depended generally upon paper money of various types, for gold, silver, or copper coins were always scarce and most of those in circulation came from the Spanish colonies. During the period of the Company of the Indies some copper money was sent from France, but these coins soon found their way back to France again. Between 1740 and 1750 hard currency was more plentiful, but after that time there was little in use.

Bills of credit were first issued by Iberville, and afterwards bills of credit and a few bank and treasury notes were issued by the Company of the Indies and the French government. Bills of credit were similar to modern checks, but they frequently declined in value. After 1732 bills of exchange, card money, and other forms of paper money were common.

Most business was transacted with livres, which were worth approximately nineteen cents, or sols, valued at about one penny. Spanish money usually had a more-or-less fixed rate of exchange. One piaster equaled five livres and one real about ten sols.

Barter was the most common method of doing business. Certain goods, as for example bear's oil, tobacco, and corn, had a standard of value which was used as a guide. In everyday matters the people handled their trades so that they came out more-or-less even, or evened matters up when they traded the next time. Ship captains traded their goods for the goods which they wanted and took or paid the difference in bills of exchange.

Laws and Regulations. Simplicity and centralization were the most important features of French colonial government. The Governor, Commissary-Commissioner, two Lieutenant Governors, the Attorney General, and the other members of the Superior Council were the officials of colonial administration. The Commissary-Commissioner was the financial officer and the guardian of the warehouses. He also served as a check upon the Governor, and these two officials frequently quarreled. Bienville had much trouble with the Commissioners during his governorships.

The Commandant of the post or village was the chief local government official. He was sometimes aided by a judge appointed by the Governor.

The laws were the ordinances and edicts of the King, the laws of Paris (called the "Custom of Paris"), and the orders of the French Council of State. These were all "written" laws. "Common," or unwritten, laws were not used in French Louisiana as in the English colonies. Though there was comparatively little crime in the colony prior to 1740, there were many lawsuits over land titles and the settlement of estates.

There were many regulations for everyday living. Landholders along the streams and bayous were required to build roads and levees fronting the waterways. The settlers had to build and maintain small bridges. Food prices were fixed during the times of scarcity. Government officials in towns and villages inspected the meat and fish offered for sale. Weights and measures were standardized. In 1728 the Superior Council decreed that a hogshead (large barrel) must equal 360 pounds; a cask, 240 pounds; a quintal, 180 pounds; and an ancre, 90 pounds.

The selling of liquors was watched very carefully. In 1717 an ordinance prohibited the selling of brandy to slaves or Indians and fixed the penalty at a fine of fifty livres, half the money to be given to the church and half to the hospital. Nine years later an ordinance closed all dramshops on Sunday while church was in progress, and the following year slaves were required to have a permit from their masters before they could purchase any kind of liquor.

By the time of Governor Vaudreuil drunkenness and crime had become so common in New Orleans that he issued the first police regulations and also special regulations for the surveillance of Negroes. All liquor-sellers now had to have a permit. Drinks could be sold only to *voyageurs,* settlers, sailors, and sick persons; they could not be sold to soldiers, Indians, or Negroes. Soldiers had to get their liquor at government canteens where no civilians were permitted. However, these liquor regulations were poorly enforced.

Punishments. Punishments were very severe, but at this time this was the practice all over the world. The death penalty was common, and a person was sometimes put to death by methods which involved torture. Several Swiss soldiers who killed their captain at Fort Toulouse above Mobile were killed by an Indian method of having their heads crushed. A German who had stolen some food from a warehouse was sentenced to be pulled five times through the water under a large ship. This was called keel-hauling. Those who violated the Black Code of 1724 were punished very brutally according to modern standards. First offenders were branded on one shoulder with a fleur-de-lis (the lily flower used on the French flag) and had their ears cut off. Second offenders had the other shoulder branded and the heel tendons cut. Third offenders suffered the death penalty.

Ridicule was the principal punishment for small offenses. One man, for example, was convicted in 1723 of killing some dogs, cooking them, and selling the meat to the patients of the hospital. He was sentenced to be paraded around New Orleans on a wooden horse for two hours wearing a sign reading "Master Eater of Dogs and Cats," and with a dead cat hung around his neck.

8. EVERYDAY LIFE IN FRENCH LOUISIANA

Towns and Farms. There were few towns in French colonial Louisiana. In 1762, New Orleans was the only important town, while Mobile, Biloxi, Baton Rouge, Natchez, Pineville, Natchitoches, and Opelousas were only small towns or villages. New Orleans did not extend beyond the limits of the Vieux Carré, and

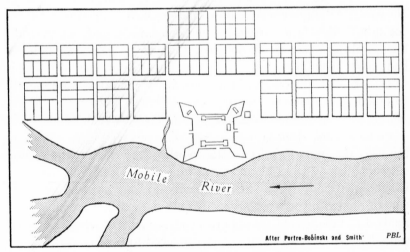

After Portre-Bobinski and Smith·   PBL

French   Colonial   Mobile

not all of its blocks were filled with houses. There were a few scattered houses along the river front above and below the town, as well as some settlers established along Bayou St. John.

The Place d'Armes, present-day Jackson Square, was the center of New Orleans, and behind it and fronting the river was the St.

Louis Church. To the left of the church was the house of the Capuchin Fathers and to the right was the town jail and the guardhouse, while on each side of the square was a row of soldiers' barracks. Most of the houses and other buildings were made of wood. On each side of the streets was a small ditch about two feet wide and a foot deep, and these ditches had little bridges for the use of the citizens. After 1735 a town ordinance forced the citizens to build these little bridges, or pay a fine of ten livres.

Most Louisianians lived on farms, which were generally strung out along the lower Mississippi or other streams, or along the Gulf of Mexico from present-day Bay St. Louis to Mobile. Pole-fenced farmyards held the horses, cattle, or sheep during nights or bad weather, and during the day the animals grazed on pasture land or in the woods and were usually guarded by small boys. A double furrow or ditch separated the farms.

Farm tools were simple and primitive. There were wooden plows, rakes, and harrows. Scythes and sickles were used to harvest the grain, while the threshing was done with a long wooden flail. Every farmer had axes, hoes, spades, hammers, hatchets, and other such tools.

Homes and Home Furnishings. Unlike the English colonist, who built his log house by laying the logs one on top of the other, the French settler stood his on end. He called his cabin a *maison de poteaux en terre,* a house of posts in the ground. The spaces between the posts were usually filled with *bousillage,* a mixture of grass and clay; but if a man could afford a better house, he placed bricks between the posts and called it *briquete entre poteaux,* brick between posts. Gradually houses of sawed lumber and of brick began to make their appearance. They were roofed with straw, grass, or wooden shingles, and the floors were of plain earth or roughhewn boards. A few of the houses had glass windows, but most had only wooden shutters called *contrevents.*

Houses were much alike. The smaller ones had only one room, while the larger ones had two, three, or even four rooms. In most cases the rooms were placed end-to-end, with the front doors opening out upon a gallery, or porch. Frequently there was also a gallery at the back of the house and sometimes on all four sides.

If the householder was a farmer he had a few other buildings— a stable, a henhouse, a barn for the storage of grain and vegetables, and a few Negro cabins if he had slaves.

The combined kitchen and living room was the most important room in the house. It had a large fireplace equipped with andirons, a pothook, and a spit for roasting meat. Near by were the frying

Department of Commerce and Industry

The Acadian House, Evangeline State Park, St. Martinville, a modern replica of Acadian type colonial homes

pan, an iron grill, and several copper or iron kettles and pots. There was a large table in the center of the room and around it some straight chairs. Against the walls were a few benches and large chests which held the family's clothing and other belongings and which also served as seats.

On the wall hung a picture of the Virgin Mary, perhaps the parents' marriage certificate, and the father's musket, powder horn, and bullet pouch. The mantél held some of the family's prized ornaments and trinkets.

The bedroom was sometimes partitioned off into several smaller rooms. The beds were frequently six or more feet square, held a straw mattress or a feather tick, and were covered with buffalo hides, bearskins, or heavy woolen blankets. The beds were sometimes curtained with hangings of red or green serge or other heavy

Department of Commerce and Industry

Restoration of an old fireplace, Audubon Memorial State Park, West Feliciana Parish

materials. If the family did not have enough beds, the children slept on cots or on the floor on pallets.

Food was eaten from earthenware or pewter dishes, but glassware was expensive and so was not widely used. Forks were usually of steel or iron, while spoons were made of pewter. Knives were not generally used by the mother or children, the father cutting the meat with his hunting knife.

When the fire in the fireplace was low or the weather was warm, the family used crude iron lamps or candles made from the wax of the candleberry myrtle.

Travel. Most people traveled from place to place in some kind of boat, for all of the Louisiana settlements could be reached by waterways. During the period before 1732 there were few roads in the colony, but in that year Governor Périer ordered every man who owned land along the Mississippi to build a road in front of his property, and this law was soon applied to most of the streams and bayous in the colony. After this time more people began to travel in two-wheeled carts, wagons, and even some carriages, but the roads were still in such bad condition that most land travelers rode horseback. In New Orleans there were chaises drawn by two horses, and coaches to which four horses were hitched.

But throughout the French period boats were the commonest method of travel, and most families had a pirogue or two as well as a small, flat-bottomed boat or skiff called a *chalan*. Even water travel was difficult, however, for the streams and bayous carried floating trees, had sand bars, and few good camp sites, and the travelers suffered from excessive heat or cold, heavy rains, and storms, from the scarcity of drinking water and food, and from flies, gnats, and mosquitoes.

Clothing. Imported clothing was expensive, so most of the family's wearing apparel was made at home from imported wool, cotton, or other material, spinning wheels and looms being uncommon in French Louisiana. The men and boys wore knee-length pants and loose-fitting shirts. In summer they went barefoot, but when the weather was cold they wore long stockings and soft-soled shoes somewhat resembling Indian moccasins. Some of them owned a knee-length coat, with a sash and a hood, called a *capot*. Over their heads they tied a large handkerchief or wore a tasseled cap.

The women and girls wore ankle-length skirts and short-sleeved blouses. In winter they added shoes and stockings, a bodice over the blouse, and perhaps a heavy *capot*. When they went to church or to a party they put on their bright-colored costumes—"bodices of red and blue stuffs, waists of flowered muslin, skirts of scarlet drugget and printed calico, and starched white caps."

The smaller children were dressed just like their older brothers and sisters and fathers and mothers.

The families of army officers, government officials, and wealthy planters and businessmen imported their clothing from France or bought the cloth and had it made by tailors or dressmakers in the colony. When one Commandant died in 1737, the Governor wrote of him as a "poor man." His clothing, however, included eighty-five "new, trimmed men's shirts," thirty muslin shirts, twenty-five ordinary shirts, twelve pairs of silk and cotton stockings, numerous pairs of pants and dress coats, and one "great coat" trimmed with "gold lace and buttons."

The women washed clothing at that time just as they did in France, dipping it in a wooden tub or stream or bayou, and scrubbing it with a coarse brush or pounding it with short-handled paddles. Soap was made at home of ashes and waste fats. The lye in the soap was hard on the skin, so women rubbed their faces with bear's or sheep's fat to protect and soften it. Only people of means could buy French perfumed soap.

Food. After general farming began, most people had plenty to eat, but there were many times during the early years when the citizens of Mobile, Biloxi, and New Orleans went hungry, for they depended upon France for much of their food supply.

The farmer's breakfast was at sunrise and was a light meal. Dinner was at noon and was the most important meal of the day, at which soups, various meats, vegetables, and fruits were served. For supper the family ate the leftovers from dinner or had a stew or soup. They sometimes ate their stews and soups from one large bowl, each one dipping in his spoon or large slice of bread.

Bread was baked out of doors in large, rounded clay ovens. Meats were salted, smoked, dried, or partially cooked and put into large jars and covered over with hot fat. Butter was usually made by whipping the cream with a spoon, for there were very few churns in French Louisiana. Wild honey instead of sugar was generally used for sweetening. Meats were boiled, roasted over open fires or in the ovens, or fried in hog lard or bear fat. Cucumbers served raw in cream and roasted pumpkins topped with honey were favorite dishes.

During periods when food was scarce, the most common diet was *gru* and wild meats, or *sagamite*. *Gru* was simply boiled corn meal seasoned with a little fat, while *sagamite* was corn meal, fat, and meat all cooked together. For many of the common people the usual diet was rice, corn, and beans.

The larger villages and towns had open-air markets, where during good seasons all kinds of vegetables, fruits, meats, and fish were sold. The Germans who had settled above New Orleans took their produce there on Sundays and sold it near the St. Louis square. At various times food prices were fixed by the government.

Religion. The Roman Catholic religion was the universal religion in French Louisiana. It is believed that the first church was built in 1699 by Father Paul Du Ru near the junction of Bayou Goula and the Mississippi. All of the towns and some of the villages had churches, and there were a few priests who traveled about or acted as missionaries to the Indians.

Daily services were held in the churches, and on Sundays High Mass was sung. During the harvest season vespers were said immediately after Mass so that the men could return to the fields. Everyone had his own pew or bench seat, which he rented by the year, and his social position was indicated by its position in the church. Important people sat directly in front of the sanctuary, near the altar.

More than twenty-five Holy Days besides Sundays were celebrated each year. On some of these days the Blessed Sacrament (consecrated bread, consecrated Host, placed in a sacred vessel called a "monstrance") was carried along the streets and everyone knelt as It passed. Sometimes the Blessed Sacrament was carried to the levee to aid in turning back a flooding river or to a burning building to assist in putting out the blaze.

The church bell was rung on every occasion. It announced each church service and was rung at births and marriages and tolled at funerals. When the bells rang for the Angelus early in the morning, at noontime, and in the evening, the people would pause at their work, bow their heads, and recite a prayer called "the Angelus."

Christmas was celebrated with much revelry. The midnight Mass on Christmas Eve started the holiday, after which the people went to different homes for Christmas breakfasts. On Christmas morning followed another Mass and afterwards dinners and parties in the evening. On New Year's Eve many people dressed in costume, put on masks, and headed by a man playing a violin, paraded through the village. *Le Père Noel* (Santa Claus) visited the children on the Twelfth Night and left gifts, and the next morning everyone had a holiday breakfast and then went visiting his friends and neighbors.

The Catholics of Louisiana were under the jurisdiction of the Bishop of Quebec, who until 1722 permitted the Jesuit, Carmelite, and Capuchin orders to operate churches and missions wherever they chose throughout the entire Mississippi Valley. In that year, however, he assigned the Jesuits the area north of the Ohio River and east of the Mississippi, the Carmelites the country east of the Mississippi between the Ohio and the Isle of Orleans, and the Capuchins the Isle of Orleans and all the territory west of the Mississippi.

This arrangement worked well until the 1750's, when a quarrel broke out between the Capuchins and the Jesuits, who had been permitted to establish a plantation and build a small chapel near New Orleans. In 1761 an investigation of the Jesuits was begun, and two years later the Superior Council banished them from the colony. Their plantation and 140 slaves were seized and sold at auction, their chapel ornaments and sacred vessels appropriated by the Capuchins, and their chapel "razed to the ground." Father Dagobert, a Capuchin, was appointed Vicar-General soon afterwards.

Until about 1730 the members of the various orders were active in their missionary work among the Indians, but after this time they lost their enthusiasm for this difficult and hazardous task. They became complacent and were content to minister to their parishes. At the end of the French period there were many rural areas, small settlements, and villages which were without the services of a resident priest.

Education. It is believed that Father Raphael de Luxemburg, a Capuchin priest, opened the first school in Louisiana in New Orleans in 1725. It was for boys only. About a year later the Ursuline nuns agreed to come to Louisiana to educate the girls, and early in 1727, eleven of them sailed from France, reaching New Orleans after a long and tiresome voyage. Bienville's house was given to them and here they established their school, remaining there until 1734, when their new home was completed on what is now Chartres Street at Ursulines Street. There were few private schools and no public schools in Louisiana during the French period.

Medicine and Health. Yellow fever, malaria, smallpox, mumps, tuberculosis, and disorders of the stomach or intestines were the most common diseases in French colonial Louisiana. On several occasions yellow-fever and smallpox epidemics broke out and carried off hundreds of settlers.

There were few doctors. The first hospital was established in Mobile in 1713 and in New Biloxi eight years later. New Orleans had a small military hospital by 1722, and a new one was built later in the same year. The Ursuline nuns established a hospital in 1734, and in 1736 Jean Louis willed a small sum of money to be used to found another hospital, the hospital which is today the Charity Hospital of Louisiana. But these hospitals were all small and poorly equipped.

Drugs were scarce and expensive and most of them were brought from France or the West Indies. Quinine, rhubarb, spirits of wine, ammonia, and sarsaparilla were the most common drugs used. The people made home remedies of various kinds and used many different types of charms.

When someone died the funeral was held at the church, where a Mass was said for his soul. His casket was then carried on the shoulders of several men along the streets to the cemetery. Once the men started from the church they never stopped until they reached the grave, for it was believed that death would visit any house in front of which they halted.

Amusements. The typical French settler was a gay, spirited person, carefree, kind, and good-humored. He did not read much even if he was able, for he had little desire for learning. He danced on Sunday after Mass, played card games and billiards and loved to gossip, hunted and fished and sang. He organized a *fais-do-do* or a party or dinner at the slightest opportunity.

The wealthier classes were much more formal in their amusements. They gave balls and masquerades and banquets. When Governor Kerlerec arrived in New Orleans to succeed Governor Vaudreuil, he gave an elaborate banquet to which two hundred guests were invited. After dinner there was a display of fireworks, during which two fountains flowed with wine. The dancing then began, and lasted the rest of the night.

PART THREE

SPANISH LOUISIANA

9. EARLY YEARS OF SPANISH LOUISIANA

French Remain in Possession of Louisiana. Although Louisiana was transferred to Spain in November, 1762, the French continued to control and govern the colony until the arrival of Spanish Governor Don Antonio de Ulloa in March, 1766. Meanwhile, in 1763, England acquired Spanish East and West Florida and all of French Louisiana east of the Mississippi River and north of the Isle of Orleans.

After Louisiana had been given to Spain, Kerlerec continued to act as Governor. These were troubled days in Louisiana. General economic conditions were bad, France having neglected the colony for many years. Trade and commerce had declined, and the paper money which had flooded Louisiana had decreased in value until it was practically worthless. The farmers and planters could not sell their products. The Capuchin and Jesuit priests quarreled. The Commissary-Commissioner accused Governor Kerlerec of stealing money from the treasury and of being a dictator, and Kerlerec accused the Commissioner of theft and of neglecting his duties.

Finally in 1763, Kerlerec was recalled to France and thrown into prison, and a new French Governor, Jean Jacques d'Abbadie, was sent to Louisiana. The new Governor, describing his colony in a report, said that Louisiana had been in a state of disorder since about 1737 and that its financial condition was bad. The people were lazy and insubordinate, they drank too much, and about three-fourths of them were bankrupt.

However, D'Abbadie wrote back to France that "everything will again be set to rights" and that the colony would again prosper, and he immediately went to work. Although he had an army of only about three hundred men, he strengthened the defenses of the colony. He permitted English ships to go up the Mississippi to the English ports of Manchac (which was at the mouth of Bayou Manchac), Baton Rouge, St. Francisville, and Natchez. Soon conditions grew better as the English ships brought trading goods and the French were permitted to do business with them.

In September, 1764, D'Abbadie received a letter from King Louis XV, stating that Louisiana had been given to Spain and that a Spanish Governor would soon arrive to take possession of the colony. D'Abbadie was ordered to return to France with all his records and all the soldiers who did not wish to remain in Louisiana. He was also ordered to inform "the people of the colony, of all ranks and conditions," that they now lived under Spain.

The following month D'Abbadie informed the people what had happened. They received the news with dismay, for Louisiana had been a French colony for over sixty years and they considered themselves just as much Frenchmen as if they had lived in Paris. They had lived under pioneer conditions where there was a considerable amount of personal freedom and they had heard that Spain governed her colonies with a tight rein.

Jean Milhet Sent to France. A group of colonists living in New Orleans and its vicinity held a mass meeting and decided to send a messenger to France to appeal to the King to take Louisiana back again. Jean Milhet, the wealthiest merchant of the colony, was appointed to carry the message, and he immediately set out for France.

About this time Governor D'Abbadie died, and Philippe Aubry, the senior captain of the army, became Acting Governor.

Milhet proceeded to Paris and went to see Bienville. Bienville had not been in Louisiana since the end of his term as Governor in 1743, but he still loved it. He and Milhet went to see the King, but Louis XV would not receive them. Finally they were granted an interview with the Duke de Choiseul, the Prime Minister. Bienville made an impassioned appeal but the Duke would not alter his resolution concerning the colony, and after remaining in France for some time, Milhet returned sadly to Louisiana.

At first the people would not believe Milhet when he said that

France would do nothing for them. Then they became angry. The streets hummed and throbbed with the sounds of marching and shouting citizens . . . the King did not know what he was doing . . . his advisers had kept him in ignorance of conditions in Louisiana . . . they had been loyal subjects of France . . . they would not accept the representative of Spain when he arrived . . . after all, it had been over two years since Spain had acquired Louisiana and she had not as yet sent a Governor . . . they would have time to organize . . . when the new Spanish Governor arrived they would be ready for him.

Governor Ulloa. In July, 1765, a letter arrived from Havana. Don Antonio de Ulloa wrote that he had orders to come to Louisiana and take possession of the colony for Spain, but the months passed and he did not appear. The group of leaders continued their plans for a revolution.

Governor Ulloa finally arrived in March, 1766, nearly three and a half years after Louisiana had been given to Spain. He was a small, thin man with an excitable, nervous temperament. He was certainly not impressive in appearance, although everyone knew that he was one of the greatest scientists of Europe. He had founded an astronomical observatory and established a laboratory for the study of minerals, but he was a scholar rather than a practical-minded man. One historian has written that "he was wise where wisdom was study, but foolish where wisdom was action."

Ulloa had brought with him only two companies of soldiers, totaling about ninety men. Did these few soldiers represent the great power of Spain? The French of Louisiana became more confident.

Ulloa made many mistakes during the two and one-half years of his governorship. He showed little respect for the Superior Council and insulted the French soldiers, so that they refused to enlist in the Spanish service when their terms of enlistment expired. He would not attend the social functions which the people of the colony planned for him. When his bride-to-be, the young and beautiful Marquesa d'Abrado, arrived from Peru he went down to the Balize to meet her and had their wedding ceremony performed there by his private chaplain. This made the colonists and the local priests furious, and when he and his bride returned to New Orleans, the wives of the leading citizens refused to call on their Governor's new wife. She, therefore, having been cut by society, kept to her home and even attended Mass in a private chapel. Meanwhile, the leaders continued to plot their revolution.

Ulloa tried to be a good Governor, although he did not publicly assume the authority of one. Aubry still performed many of the duties of a Governor, but he carried out Ulloa's orders in the name of the King of Spain. Meanwhile, Ulloa did what he could to help economic conditions. He made tours of inspection, tried to improve the paper-money problem by paying more for it than had been paid by the French, and prevented overcharging by the merchants. He helped immigrants by giving them land, livestock, tools, and supplies. In general, he tried to carry out his instructions "not to change existing conditions in Louisiana," but to improve its economic life.

Then in the spring of 1768, instructions came from Spain ordering the people of Louisiana to use only Spanish ships in their commerce and restricting their trade only to Spanish ports. Those who had been plotting against Spain believed that the time for revolution had arrived.

Governor Ulloa Leaves Louisiana. In October, 1768, the plotters called a convention to meet in New Orleans. This convention passed resolutions condemning Ulloa, declared him a usurper of power, and ordered him to leave the colony. The Superior Council supported the actions of the convention, though Aubry protested to its members.

Aubry did not know what to do. Some months before he had written back to France: "My position is most extraordinary. I command for the King of France and at the same time I govern the colony as if it belonged to the King of Spain."

A few days after Aubry's protest, the Superior Council declared his protest null and void and ordered Governor Ulloa to leave the colony within three days. Fearing for his life, Ulloa went aboard a ship lying at the wharf.

For years the loyal Frenchmen of Louisiana told this story of Ulloa's departure from New Orleans. On the night of November

1, 1768, a group of citizens who were returning home from a wedding went to the wharf. They sang French songs. They yelled: "Long live the King! Long live Louis-the-Well-Beloved! Long live the wine of Bordeaux! Down with the fish of Spain!" Then a man cut the mooring cables of Ulloa's ship and it drifted down the Mississippi. For a long time historians believed this story, but it is now thought to be only a legend.

Aubry in Control. Ulloa's departure filled the colony with exultation. The rebellion had succeeded, and everyone celebrated: *"Vive le Roi! Vive Louis! Vive la Louisiane! À bas Ulloa! À bas les Espagnols!* (Long live the King! Long live Louis! Long live Louisiana! Down with Ulloa! Down with the Spanish!)." The King had not heard Milhet, but now he would listen to the Louisianians.

A member of the Superior Council was sent to France. He carried with him a copy of the decree expelling Governor Ulloa and a memorial of the "Inhabitants and Merchants of Louisiana" swearing loyalty and allegiance to France.

Aubry was now in a trying position. Should he support the revolutionists, whose rebellion against Spain had apparently been successful, or should he support Spain? After all, Spain might send another Governor with sufficient forces to put down the rebellion and establish Spanish power. Aubry tried to carry water on each shoulder.

In order to satisfy the French government and the colonists he sent a report to France in which he blamed Ulloa for what had happened, admitting that "it is no pleasant mission to govern a colony which undergoes so many revolutions."

A short time later he wrote to the Spanish Captain General at Havana that he hoped that Ulloa had reported the services which he had performed for Spain: "No one venerates the Spanish nation as I do. . . . This revolution dishonors the French in Louisiana. . . . The leaders should be punished as they deserved to be."

Governor Ulloa had gone. Aubry was still at the head of the Louisiana colony. The Louisiana rebellion had succeeded. But what would Spain do?

Governor O'Reilly. On August 17, 1769, a large Spanish fleet, carrying more than two thousand troops, arrived at New Orleans. The expedition was commanded by Lieutenant General Alejandro O'Reilly, who had been appointed the new Governor of Louisiana.

O'Reilly was a man far different from Ulloa. A native-born Irishman who had settled in Spain, he was a professional soldier, and at this time was Spain's best military commander. Suave, courteous and mild of manner, he was nevertheless a man of iron. He had orders to put down this Louisiana rebellion and he was prepared to carry them out.

At five o'clock the following afternoon a signal gun was fired and with military precision the Spanish troops landed. The batteries of artillery and companies of infantry moved to the Place d'Armes and ranged themselves about the square in front of the Church. The sailors and the troops shouted, *"Viva el Rey, Viva el Rey,* (Long live the King, Long live the King)." The guns of the ships roared out a salute, which was answered by the fifty cannon of the batteries. Clad in bright uniforms, O'Reilly and his staff came ashore and with great pomp marched to the square, where Aubry awaited them at the flagpole from which fluttered the flag of France. The French flag came down and up went the flag of Spain, to the roar of *"Viva el Rey,"* and the booming of another cannon salute. Then O'Reilly went into the Church to receive the blessing of the Vicar-General.

The revolution had failed. What chance had a few hundred Frenchmen against the armed might of Spain? O'Reilly had taken the first step in establishing Spanish authority. He had "displayed most effectively the military force under his command, and through the pageantry of his dramatic entry had inspired the respect of the colonists."

Trial of the Conspirators. A few days later O'Reilly arrested the leaders of the rebellion. They were informed that they would be tried without delay for having led the people of Louisiana in rebellion against Spanish authority. O'Reilly issued a proclamation which stated that only the leaders would "answer for their crimes" and that they would be "judged according to the laws."

When O'Reilly asked Aubry who had been the leaders of the rebellion, he named them, further stating that they had plotted "to send away the governor, and to free themselves from the Spanish domination."

The Spanish law read: "He who labors by deed or word to induce any people, or any provinces, under the domination of the King, to rise against his Majesty, is a traitor." The punishment of a traitor was death. There was no question but that the leaders had tried to free Louisiana from the rule of Spain.

The trial was conducted in strict conformity with Spanish laws and lasted about three weeks. The verdict of the court sentenced six of the most important leaders to be put to death by hanging. Several of the others were given prison sentences. The property of all of the men was confiscated.

A hangman could not be found, so five of the six men were shot by a firing squad. One of them had died in prison before the execution day. On the morning of October 25, 1769, the town criers of New Orleans went through the city reading the death sentence to the people, and at about three in the afternoon the men were executed by a platoon of grenadiers.

A short time later Aubry slipped aboard a ship and sailed for France. It was said by some that he carried a fortune with him, but near the coast of France the vessel ran into a heavy storm and sank, and Aubry was not among the few survivors. No one in Louisiana mourned his death.

O'Reilly's Reorganization of the Colony. O'Reilly had turned his attention to the political and economic reorganization of the colony even before the trial of the conspirators was held. He fixed food prices in order that the merchants could not make excessive profits. He reorganized the government of the colony, wherever possible permitting the French officials to continue to hold their offices. He assisted in reviving trade and commerce. He appointed Frenchmen as Lieutenant Governors of the Natchitoches and Illinois districts. He ordered the abolition of Indian slavery, visited the Indian tribes and signed treaties with them, and licensed only those Indian traders who had good reputations.

In December he sent most of his army back to Havana and

organized thirteen militia companies under the command of native Louisianians. He recommended that the Church send more priests to the colony. He aided the farmers by establishing land titles and creating a system of "homesteading" land. In all these reforms, he insisted that the old customs of French Louisiana be kept as much as possible.

By the spring of 1770, O'Reilly had completed the reorganization of the Louisiana colony. In March he departed for Havana, leaving Colonel Luis de Unzaga y Amézaga in charge as Governor.

O'Reilly's Place in Louisiana History. What is O'Reilly's true place in Louisiana history? Most Louisiana historians have condemned him for his punishment of the leaders of the Rebellion of 1768, and some of them have called him "Bloody O'Reilly."

It must be remembered that O'Reilly was a soldier, accustomed to the discipline of a soldier. He had been ordered by his King to punish, "in strict conformity to the laws," the leaders of the rebellion. He carried out his orders, and in so doing only five men were executed, which at this time in history was a mild punishment for a colony which had rebelled against authority.

The French Creoles never forgave Governor O'Reilly. Years later one of them wrote a play called *The Martyr Patriots; or, Louisiana in 1769.* Generations of Louisiana school children recited the lines:

What! sold like cattle—treated with disdain?
No! Louisiana's sons can never bear
Such foul disgrace. And when I'll tell them all,
Of every insult, and the shame which thus
This reckless King would heap upon their heads,
'Twill put a burning fagot to their pride;
'Twill blow their indignation into flame;
And like the fire on our grass-grown plains,
By ravaging winds devouring driven,
'Twill spread, in blazing waves, e'en to the edge
And utmost limit of the land; and then,
Proud Kings, beware! lest e'en within the bounds
Of Europe's slave-trod vales the blaze should catch,
Sweep despots and their thrones away, and like
Unprofitable weeds consume them all.

It must also be remembered that just as Iberville was the founder of French Louisiana, so O'Reilly was the founder of the Spanish regime. His governmental and economic reforms paved the way for the steady growth and progress of the Louisiana colony, which prospered much more under the Spanish than it had under the French. The Spanish, not the French, were the real makers of colonial Louisiana.

Unzaga as Governor. Unzaga had come to Louisiana with O'Reilly. While O'Reilly was the Governor, Unzaga's commission to succeed to the governorship had already been issued. O'Reilly was to turn the colony over to him just as soon as the rebellion had been put down and order restored. This was done on December 1, 1769, several months before O'Reilly left the colony. After this date O'Reilly acted only as a military commander, though everyone knew that Unzaga was under his orders.

Colonel Unzaga had served over thirty years in the Spanish army and had fought in Spain, Italy, and Africa. He had lived in Spain's American colonies for twenty-five years and knew well the problems of colonial administration. Older than O'Reilly, with a mild, easygoing nature, he liked the French Creoles and felt that he would have little difficulty in reconciling them to the rule of Spain.

Unzaga Reconciles Louisiana to Spanish Rule. Unzaga continued O'Reilly's policy of appointing Creoles to governmental positions. He explained the code of laws which O'Reilly had drawn up for the colony, and it soon became evident to the Louisianians that the new Spanish system of government was more efficient than the old French system had been. There were no quarrels among the Spanish officials as there had been between the French governors and their subordinates, and the Creoles who were appointed to office soon discovered that they were expected to show results. Everyone began to realize that Spain wanted Louisiana to be a strong, contented, and prosperous colony, and that there was no desire to oppress the citizens.

It was not long before the Creoles in governmental service were promoted to more responsible positions. As the French and Spanish mixed more socially, the French discovered that the Spanish officials were usually men of merit, good birth, and high moral character. Marriages were arranged between young Spanish officers and the daughters of prominent Creole families, Governor Unzaga himself marrying a daughter of the St. Maxent family. The Creoles became contented with the new government, even though they would give up neither their language nor their social customs.

Unzaga did his best to promote the welfare of the colony. He winked at the illegal trade which was being carried on with the British of West Florida, for the colony needed the English goods. He used government money to purchase tobacco, and soon tobacco plantations were springing up throughout Louisiana. He granted land to immigrants, asking only that they obey the laws of the colony, and he organized the first public school in Louisiana. If Unzaga made mistakes, many of the people said, he made them only on the side of kindness.

However, the Governor had many problems to solve. When the Spanish Capuchins arrived and tried to secure the dismissal of Father Dagobert, he sided with the French and wrote that "Father Cirilo does not possess one particle of prudence." He strengthened the militia when it was rumored that the British were planning to attack Louisiana, and the companies drilled enthusiastically for the defense of their homes and farms. He made treaties with the Indian tribes and licensed traders at the various trading posts, and when the American Revolution began he quietly aided the American colonists by sending them the supplies he could spare.

But by 1776, Unzaga was ready to retire. He was in poor health and his eyes were causing him trouble. He was not a young man any more and he wanted to return to his native Malaga in Spain. But his requests for retirement were refused, and instead he was promoted to be the Captain General at Caracas, Venezuela. He turned the government of Louisiana over to the young Colonel of the Louisiana Regiment, Don Bernardo de Galvez, in January, 1777. The following March he sailed for Caracas on the frigate *La Luisiana*.

Unzaga had reconciled the French Creoles of Louisiana to the rule of Spain. A just administrator, he had constantly promoted the public welfare, thereby winning the respect and affection of the people.

10. LOUISIANA AND THE AMERICAN REVOLUTION

Bernardo de Galvez. The young colonel who succeeded Unzaga, although only in his late twenties, had already proved himself a brave and excellent soldier. Born of a politically important Spanish family, he had entered the army in his teens and won a lieutenant's bars in a war with Portugal. He had served with distinction in Mexico, campaigning along the Rió Grande against the Apache Indians. He carried the scars of several Indian-battle wounds. In one fight he had been "struck in the arm by an arrow and with two lance thrusts in the chest." He had returned to Spain, later serving in North Africa, where he had received another severe wound. He was then sent to Louisiana.

Galvez as Governor. As was customary, Galvez received an elaborate set of orders. He was to take a census of Louisiana. He had to prepare a statement of the yearly expenses of the colony. He must welcome foreigners on the condition that they become Catholics and take the oath of allegiance to Spain. He was to encourage agriculture and take especial care to see that slaves were humanely treated. He was to promote commerce but to take strong measures against smuggling. The friendship of the Indians was to be cultivated. He was specifically ordered to watch the English in West Florida and to reorganize and improve the discipline of the Louisiana militia. And he was to make carefully prepared reports on practically everything—roads, money, the people, mines, the religious situation, and many other things.

Galvez plunged into his work. He reduced the export duty to 2 per cent and permitted trade to be carried on with the British. He called a meeting of the farmers and planters to discuss agricultural matters, and as farm labor was short, he permitted slaves again to be imported. He took a census and found that out of a

From Fortier, *A History of Louisiana*

Don Bernardo de Galvez

total population of nearly eighteen thousand nearly half were Negro slaves.

Perhaps his greatest interest was the encouragement of new immigrants to the colony. Galvez gave to each settler five arpents of land fronting a stream and extending as far back from it as the man would clear his land. He also gave to each family an ax, a sickle, a spade, a hoe, two hens and a rooster, two pigs, and enough food for the first year. It was not long before word of Galvez' generosity spread beyond Louisiana.

Soon hundreds of Spaniards were arriving, as were settlers called *Isleños* from the Canary Islands. A few Germans from Maryland had come to Louisiana as early as 1774, and now, with Galvez' encouragement, many more settled along the Mississippi. English and American refugees from the American Revolution also arrived, and some of these settlers founded, a few miles from the mouth of Bayou Manchac, a town to which they gave the name of "Villa de Galvez" (Galveztown). They asked the Governor not to change the name for it was an indication of their gratitude to him. Francisco Collell, the Commandant, wrote Galvez that "they asked me to give each one of them a Spanish name." So Davis became Deves, Riley became Reeli, Morris became Moris, and so on.

Despite their many duties, Galvez and his officers and officials had time for social life, and more Spaniards fell to the charms of the French Creole girls. Don Estevan Miro, an army officer and future Governor of Louisiana, begged Galvez to secure the King's permission for him to marry Marie Celeste Elenore de Macarty. The King approved the match. Jacinto Panis, another officer, won Margarethe Wiltz, the widow of Joseph Milhet who had been executed by O'Reilly. Galvez himself fell in love, and petitioned His Majesty for permission to marry Félicie de St. Maxent d'Estréhan, a young and beautiful widow. Their marriage was a very happy one and the Governor's wife greatly aided her husband not only in Louisiana but in Mexico, where he later became Viceroy.

Galvez and the American Revolution. The American Revolution began in 1775, but the Englishmen of East and West Florida did not join their kinsmen along the Atlantic seaboard, and Louisiana became a center of war activities for both sides.

Although Spain was neutral, Galvez aided the Americans. He helped their commerce and permitted them to go up and down the Mississippi. He sold much-needed supplies to an American agent named Oliver Pollock, and loaned money to the young Republic. Spanish guns, powder, and other supplies aided George Rogers Clark in his conquest of the Northwest.

In early 1778, an American named James Willing led a raiding expedition down the Mississippi against the English of West Florida. He either destroyed or captured much English property between Natchez and Bayou Manchac. While sympathizing with the Americans, Galvez extended every courtesy to the English who were driven from their homes and who sought refuge in Louisiana. He offered them land, which many of them accepted. After Willing's raid the British strengthened their forces at Mobile and Pensacola and later reoccupied their towns along the Mississippi.

Galvez became uneasy for the safety of Louisiana, where large numbers of Englishmen had settled. He required them to take an oath of allegiance to Spain, and American immigrants were likewise obliged to swear their loyalty. He began to strengthen his military forces, to build gunboats for patrol work on the Mississippi, and to repair the Louisiana fortifications.

Then Colonel Alexander Dickson left Pensacola with an army to strengthen the British forts along the Mississippi, and soon Fort Panmure (Natchez), Fort New Richmond (Baton Rouge), Fort Bute (at the mouth of Bayou Manchac), and other military posts were humming with activity.

In May, 1779, Spain declared war against Great Britain. The English immediately planned an attack on New Orleans. A large force was to descend the Mississippi from the Great Lakes region, while another expedition would sail from Pensacola. Ex-governor George Johnstone of West Florida was excited over the prospects of English success. He wrote: "Thank God that we are all firm and relishing the opportunity to strike a blow against the Dons."

But Bernardo de Galvez had not been idle. Louisiana was ready. He would strike a blow before the English could put their plans into operation.

Galvez Plans an Expedition Against Baton Rouge. Galvez had already planned his campaign against the British in case there was war between the two countries. He kept secret the news of the declaration of war and also his official appointment as Governor of Louisiana. Advertising his work as preparing for the "defense" of New Orleans, he began to gather a fleet of river boats, gunboats, supplies, and munitions, and to equip and drill the militia units.

He set August 23 as the date for the start of the journey up the Mississippi to capture Baton Rouge. On August 18, however, a violent hurricane sank practically all of his boats. This setback would have disheartened most men, but Galvez feverishly renewed his activities. He set August 27 as the new date of departure.

A few days before this date he called a meeting of the people of New Orleans at the Plaza de Armas (the old French Place d'Armes), to tell them that Spain was now at war with Great Britain. He promised to defend the province of Louisiana, but refused to accept the governorship unless the people agreed to help him: "What do you say? Shall I take the oath of Governor? Shall I swear to defend Luisiana?"

Their cheers drowned his words. He took the oath and continued his preparations.

The Capture of Baton Rouge. By August 27 all was ready, and late in the afternoon the little army moved out from New Orleans. It was a small force of only 650 men of many nationalities. There was no engineering officer, and the artillery officer was ill. The men were without tents and other much-needed supplies. The roads were in bad condition.

Galvez hurried on ahead of his little army, calling upon the local militia units to rally to the defense of Louisiana. Soon they began to join him—from the German Coast, from Galveztown, from Opelousas and the Atakapas, from Pointe Coupee. More than 700 men answered the call, increasing his army to over 1,400 men, but by the time he arrived at Fort Bute the number had dropped to less than 1,000 because of illness and the hardships of the march from New Orleans.

Galvez knew that most of the Fort Bute garrison had been withdrawn to Baton Rouge, so he immediately assaulted and captured it. He rested his men at Fort Bute a few days, then moved on to Fort New Richmond at Baton Rouge.

Fort New Richmond had only recently been built. It consisted of an earthen wall, encircled by a palisade, on the outside of which was a ditch about nine feet deep and eighteen or twenty feet wide. It was garrisoned by about 400 regular soldiers and over 150 settlers and Negroes, and was armed with thirteen cannon.

Galvez tricked the British into believing that he was placing his batteries in a grove of trees, at which they then fired all night. Under cover of darkness he moved his guns to the other side of the fort, and when morning came on September 21, the British, too late, realized their mistake. Galvez opened fire with his cannon and by mid afternoon the fort had surrendered. Galvez insisted that the British surrender Fort Panmure at Natchez at the same time.

This campaign is one of the most significant in American history, for it prevented the British from gaining a secure foothold in the lower Mississippi Valley. It paved the way for later American occupation. It established Galvez' genius as a military commander and proved the loyalty and fighting qualities of the French Louisianians.

The news of the capture of Baton Rouge and the surrender of Natchez was received with a tremendous outburst of joy by Louisianians. As Francisco Collell wrote to the Governor from Galveztown: "It is a phenomenon, because it has been said of other generals that they won various victories but have sacrificed many men, but Your Lordship with the loss of only one man has obtained the surrender of 400 and the advantageous result of the evacuation of Natchez. . . . All the people of this town have celebrated this victory with great demonstrations of joy to congratulate Your Lordship. . . . My only regret is that the inhabitants here do not have that which is necessary in order to honor the victory with illuminations."

Galvez Captures Mobile. In 1778, Galvez had sent Jacinto Panis to Mobile and Pensacola to spy on the British, and he had sent back much useful information. After the capture of Baton Rouge, Galvez began to plan an expedition against these two British strongholds. His plans were at first opposed by the Captain General at Havana, but he finally gave his consent.

Galvez pushed forward his preparations for an attack on Mobile, and in January, 1780, he embarked 750 regular soldiers and militiamen on a dozen ships and dropped down the Mississippi toward the Balize. Including the sailors, Galvez had slightly under two thousand men. After waiting about two weeks in order to get all his ships over the bar, he headed for Mobile Bay, where a few days later the expedition arrived.

After many difficulties in landing his troops and his batteries of artillery, Galvez began the siege. The regular troops and the Louisiana militiamen worked diligently. They soon had the heavy battery of eight eighteen-pounder guns in position and began to bombard Fort Charlotte. The English replied with their guns, but the Spanish fire was more accurate and the English ran up the white flag of surrender.

The formal surrender took place on March 14. Captain Elias Durnford, the English commander, wrote the same day to his superior officer at Pensacola: "It is my misfortune to inform you that this morning my small but brave garrison marched down the beach, and surrendered themselves prisoners of war to General Bernardo de Galvez' superior arms."

The following days were occupied in repairing the damage to Fort Charlotte. The buildings were restored, the earthworks strengthened, and additional cannon were set in place. The citizens of the region came to Mobile to take the oath of allegiance to the King of Spain.

Galvez had won another significant victory over the British, and had shown courteous regard for the civilians of Mobile. He was promoted to Major General, publicly thanked by the King, and the King's Minister wrote him that "the capture of an important town, well fortified and defended with vigor, is an act worthy of praise."

The Capture of Pensacola. Galvez now turned his attention to the capture of Pensacola, which was the most important objective of his entire Gulf Coast campaign. Knowing that the Pensacola garrison had over two thousand men and that its defenses were strong, he asked that a sizable fleet and a strong army be sent from Havana to aid him.

Failing to get anything but promises, Galvez went to Havana, and sailed from there in middle October, 1780, with a large army, artillery, and ammunition, but a storm compelled him to return to port. He sailed again in late February, 1781, and arrived off Pensacola in early March. The larger ships grounded when the fleet attempted to cross the bar of the bay. Galvez found a deeper channel, but Don José Calbo de Irazabal, the commander of the Spanish fleet, who was aboard the largest ship, the man-of-war *San Ramon,* refused to try it.

Finally Galvez landed his troops on Santa Rosa Island, to camp

From Winsor, *Narrative and Critical History of America*

Battle between an English and a Spanish ship

there until the fleet could enter Pensacola Bay. A few days later he became impatient, and boarding the *Galveztown,* which was the flagship of the little Louisiana fleet, he ordered the ships to follow him. The guns of Fort George began a tremendous fire but the Louisiana ships went through. Don José, realizing that his reputation was ruined if he did not follow, put his fleet in motion, and it too safely passed the English fort.

Meantime a small force from Mobile had arrived, and a few days after this, Don Estevan Miro came from New Orleans with about 1,350 Louisiana regulars and militia. Galvez' army now totaled over 3,500 men. He could proceed with the siege of Pensacola.

Lines were tightened and batteries of cannon were wheeled into position. The siege began. Finally General John Campbell sent a flag of truce and asked for surrender terms. The formal surrender of Pensacola and the entire British colony of West Florida took place on the afternoon of May 10, 1781.

The Spanish flag of Louisiana now waved from the upper sections of the Mississippi Valley to English East Florida and westward to the Sabine River. The King had been well pleased with the capture of Baton Rouge and Mobile, but he was particularly gratified with the capture of Pensacola. He issued a Royal Proclamation in which he thanked Galvez for the "expulsion of the English from the entire Gulf of Mexico." He renamed Pensacola Bay. Henceforth it was to be called *La Bahia de Santa Maria de Galvez,* the Bay of Saint Mary of Galvez. He promoted Galvez to Lieutenant General and gave him the title of "Viscount of Galveztown." Most important of all, he authorized Galvez to place on his coat of arms the motto '*Yo Solo*' ('I alone'), in recognition of his having led the Louisiana fleet into Pensacola Bay.

Galvez and the Rebellion of 1781. The English who lived near Natchez had surrendered at the capture of Baton Rouge and had taken the oath of allegiance to Spain. Just before Pensacola fell it was rumored that Galvez had been defeated, and without delay they laid seige to Fort Panmure, finally forcing it to surrender.

Then they learned that the rumor had been false and that Galvez had been victorious and had captured Pensacola. Galvez would now certainly lead an army to Natchez and would punish them just as O'Reilly had punished those who led the Rebellion of 1768. Some of the Englishmen decided to retain possession of the fort and fight, while the others decided to surrender.

Carlos de Grand Pré, the Commandant of the Natchez–Baton

Rouge District, sent a militia captain of the Atakapas District, Roberto de la Morandière, from Baton Rouge to recapture Fort Panmure. He did so, and several of the rebel leaders were sent to New Orleans for trial. The others escaped to Savannah, Georgia. Galvez was more lenient than O'Reilly had been. The property of twenty-one of the leaders was confiscated and they were imprisoned for about two years, and then released.

Galvez Leaves Louisiana. After the capture of Pensacola, Galvez was ordered by the King to lead an expedition against the English island of Jamaica. Just as his fleet was about ready to sail from Havana, peace was declared between England and the United States, France and Spain.

Meanwhile the King had joined West Florida to Louisiana and appointed Galvez Captain General of Cuba and Governor of West Florida and Louisiana. In the late spring of 1785 he was appointed Viceroy of New Spain, which included all of Spain's colonies north of Central America. He and his family arrived in the City of Mexico early in 1786 and were received by the Mexicans with "the greatest pomp and jubilee," but he did not live long to enjoy his new honors, for he took a fever and died in the fall of 1786.

Louisianians have never forgotten Bernardo de Galvez. The French Creoles forgot that he was a Spanish Don for he worked hard for the good of the colony and led them to brilliant military victories over the British.

11. LAST YEARS OF THE
SPANISH REGIME

Spain's Plans for the Future. After capturing the Floridas from Great Britain, Spain's plans centered around protecting and perhaps enlarging her Louisiana and Florida territories. The northern boundary of East and West Florida had not been definitely located, and Spain hoped to fix this boundary as far northward as possible. She also planned to develop Louisiana into a strong, self-sufficient colony.

From the end of Galvez' governorship in 1785 until France took possession in 1803, Louisiana was ruled by five governors, each of whom attempted to carry out the plans of the mother country.

Governor Miro. Colonel Don Estevan Miro had been serving as Acting Governor of Louisiana since Galvez organized his expedition against Mobile in 1780. He became Governor shortly after Galvez was appointed Viceroy of New Spain and went to the City of Mexico.

Miro was not as brilliant as Galvez but he was an intelligent and mild-tempered man. He was well educated, was acquainted with several languages, and had a high code of honor. Already well known in Louisiana for his tireless industry and strict standards of morality, he was compared to Governor Unzaga by many Louisianians because of his quiet but progressive governorship.

As was usual with Spanish governors, he issued a *Bando de Buen Gobierno* (Proclamation of Good Government), a sort of inaugural proclamation that listed the improvements to be made in the colony, and issued his civil and police regulations. The people approved, nodded their heads, and said that he would make a good Governor.

New Settlers for Louisiana. Miro's great ambition was to make Louisiana a stronger colony. To do this he had to promote immigration, keep the Indians at peace, and increase trade and commerce.

He immediately offered assistance to prospective settlers, and in order that he might locate them properly when they arrived, he took a new census of the colony.

Miro found that the population of Louisiana had more than doubled in the preceding sixteen years. More people had settled in the colony during that period than during all the years of French control. New Orleans was a city of nearly 5,000. The population of the Tchoupitoulas District, which adjoined New Orleans, totaled over 7,000; the German Coast and the area above it, 4,500; and the Balize and Lower Coast, over 2,000. The Pointe Coupee and Natchez districts each had more than 1,500 inhabitants. More than 1,200 persons lived in the Opelousas District and over 1,000 resided in the Atakapas country. Baton Rouge and the near-by area had nearly 300 citizens. Louisiana was growing up.

Immigrants arrived steadily from France, Spain, and the Canary Islands. Americans received grants of land in the Florida Parishes, in the Opelousas District, and in other sections. The only conditions imposed by the Louisiana government on immigrants were that they swear allegiance to Spain and openly practice only the Catholic religion.

New settlements were soon springing up all over Louisiana. Villages were planned, laid out, and established. One of these was the present city of Monroe, where Don Juan Filhiol was appointed the Commandant of the "Post of the Ouachita." He built a rectangular-shaped fort, 190 feet long and 150 feet wide. The palisades were of heavy white-oak and cypress timbers, twelve feet long and set three feet in the ground. The little village soon became an important Indian trading post.

Miro's Peaceful Indian Policy. Miro pursued a peaceful policy toward the Indians. He frequently called the tribal chiefs to New Orleans, where he entertained them, gave them presents, and secured agreements for fur and hide trading. In 1787, for example, the Commandant of Galveztown wrote Miro that about a hundred Indians would soon pass through his post on their way to the capital and that he would give them supplies and "paints for their dances."

Problems arose, however. Sometimes one tribe would raid another, after which an appeal would be made to the Governor for help and for the replacement of lost goods. The tribes quarreled over their hunting grounds. Occasionally a chief would refuse to come to New Orleans. One chief wrote to Miro: "i am willing to come and see you and take you by the hand if you will appoint to meat me at Mobille for if i was to set of[f] to come to Orleans with ten men i should not Get back with five of them alive upon the account of the sickley cuntrey." The chief's spelling and grammar were poor, but his meaning was clear.

But the Indians kept the peace with Miro and caused the settlers little trouble.

Trade and Commerce During Miro's Administration. After the capture of Baton Rouge, Spain had approved Galvez' recommendations for the promotion of trade and commerce. Louisianians were to be permitted to trade with France for a period of ten years. They were also to be allowed to trade with the French West India Islands. They might purchase slaves free of duty for ten years and duty-free ships for two years. All exports and imports were to be taxed only 6 per cent. Plans were to be made for the building of a custom-house at New Orleans.

These regulations went into effect shortly before Miro became Governor, and greatly aided him in the promotion of trade and commerce. It was not long before the Louisiana trading posts were making a good profit and New Orleans was a busy port city. All kinds of goods came down the Mississippi from the St. Louis region and the Ohio River country. Miro reported that as many as forty river boats at a time could be seen at the New Orleans landing.

Important Events During Miro's Administration. On Good Friday, March 21, 1788, a lighted candle in the private chapel of the treasurer of the colony, Vicente José Nuñez, fell against the lace draperies of the altar. In a few moments the house was in flames. The fire spread rapidly throughout New Orleans and burned a total of over eight hundred buildings. The town hall, the guard-house, the Church, the arsenal, the prison, the Capuchin Convent, and many stores and homes were destroyed.

Two reasons were offered for the rapid spread of the blaze. Many of the French Creoles could not understand the orders for fighting the fire, for the commands were given in Spanish. Secondly, a very strong wind was blowing from the south that day, which prevented the saving of many buildings, except those along the river front.

The next morning one of the citizens wrote, "In the place of the flourishing city of the day before, nothing [remained] but rubbish and heaps of ruins."

Miro immediately went to work to rebuild the city, securing financial assistance from a wealthy citizen, Don Andres Almonester y Rojas. The Church of St. Louis was rebuilt, and the Cabildo, the arsenal, the military hospital, the customhouse, and other public buildings. A new Governor's house was erected. In the space on the lower levee side in front of the Plaza de Armas sheds were built for those who wished to sell fruits, vegetables, meats, and other foods. This was the beginning of the present-day "French Market."

The new buildings were of Spanish, rather than French, architecture, with high-ceilinged rooms, arched windows and doorways, balconies, courtyards, and much handmade ironwork. Many of them were constructed of brick and stone rather than of wood. A few of these buildings still stand today, reminding us that the Vieux Carré is really Spanish and not French in style.

About this time a Capuchin priest in New Orleans named Father Antonio de Sedella was appointed the representative of the Inquisition, which was a Catholic Church court for the apprehension and trial of heretics. Governor Miro soon received a letter from him saying that it might be necessary, in carrying out his work, to have some guards or soldiers placed at his command. "On reading the communication," wrote Governor Miro, "I shuddered." And he continued that "the mere name of the Inquisition" would keep prospective immigrants from coming to Louisiana and might even drive out some who had already arrived. So he bundled Father Antonio aboard a ship which sailed away from Louisiana the next morning.

In 1788, Governor Miro took another census. He found that during the past three years the population of Louisiana had been increased by some 10,000 persons. Now more than 34,000 people lived within what is now the limits of Louisiana.

In 1791 a slave revolt broke out in Santo Domingo, and many of the farmers and planters came to Louisiana to settle.

Miro had asked several times to be relieved of his governorship so that he might retire to Spain. Alternatively, he would have liked a position there, where his knowledge of American affairs would have been useful to the government. He was a tired man. For some time the Americans of the Ohio River country had been causing him considerable trouble, and some of them had been threatening to invade Louisiana. The growth of Louisiana had greatly increased the duties of the Governor. He was satisfied with his army rank, for in 1789 he had been promoted to Brigadier General.

Finally, the Spanish government recalled him to Spain, where he later rose to the rank of Major General. On December 30, 1791, Don Francisco Luis Hector, Baron de Carondelet, succeeded to the governorship.

Carondelet and His Reforms. Carondelet was a prudent, firm man of great administrative ability. Short and plump, with a somewhat thin face, he could be short-tempered when things did not go well. But ordinarily he was in good humor, and he quickly became a well-liked and highly respected Governor. At the time of his appointment he was serving as the Governor of San Salvador.

Early in 1792, Carondelet published his Inaugural Proclamation and listed some reforms which immediately went into effect. He divided New Orleans into four wards, in each of which was to be a combination fire and police chief whose duty was to preserve order in his ward, keep a record of small debts, and in case of fire, to take charge of the fire companies.

Later the same year, Carondelet issued new orders to the Commandants of the various districts. He ordered the Commandant of the Avoyelles District, for example, to be more careful in his administration of justice and more systematic and orderly in the keeping of his records.

In 1796 he organized a regular police force for New Orleans. There were to be thirteen *serenos,* or watchmen, who would patrol the city at night and see that order was kept. At the same time he ordered eighty lamps to be placed along the streets. To meet the costs of the watchmen and the street lights, a "chimney tax" was levied upon every chimney in the city.

Carondelet continued Miro's policies regarding trade and commerce. It was not long before he received specific instructions from the Spanish government to continue the encouragement of American trade in Louisiana, so New Orleans grew in trading importance and her wharves were constantly filled. All types of river boats came down from the Upper Ohio and Upper Mississippi River country. Merchants arrived from Philadelphia and the other American cities.

Young men came to represent manufacturing or mercantile houses or to make quick fortunes in this land of opportunity.

Carondelet and the French Revolution. The French Revolution had started in 1789, causing some of the French Creoles to hope for a revolution in Louisiana. These Creoles marched through the streets of New Orleans yelling "Liberty, Equality, and Fraternity" or "Hang the aristocrats to the lamp posts," and singing the "Marseillaise," the "Ça Ira," and other French revolutionary songs.

In 1793 the French Revolutionists beheaded Louis XVI and Spain declared war on the new French Republic. Carondelet immediately issued a proclamation forbidding Louisianians either to discuss or to read aloud any printed matter concerning political affairs in France. Those guilty of so doing would be sent to prison at Morro Castle, a great fort in Havana. Anyone who permitted "meetings, gatherings, or conversations of this nature" was to be fined two hundred pesos. Some of the Creoles violated the proclamation, but only about seventy of them were expelled from the colony and only a half dozen were sent to Morro Castle for a year's imprisonment.

Carondelet also strengthened the defenses of his colony. He built Fort St. Philip down the river from New Orleans, repaired the fortifications of New Orleans, and reorganized the militia companies.

Carondelet and the Americans. The Governor had trouble with the Americans, many of whom at this time wanted to secure Louisiana for the United States. They plotted to start a revolution in Louisiana or, if this failed, to organize an expedition on the upper Ohio River to invade and capture the Spanish colony. As a defensive measure, Carondelet built a small fleet of river boats to patrol the Mississippi River as far north as the mouth of the Ohio.

In 1795 the United States and Spain signed a treaty which settled many of their differences. One section of it fixed the northern boundary line of that section of Louisiana east of the Mississippi. This line today is the northern boundary of the Florida Parishes. The troubles came temporarily to an end.

Everyday Events During Carondelet's Administration. In a New Orleans courtyard, on the afternoon of December 8, 1794, some boys started a small fire which spread to a feed store next door where some hay was stored. There was a brisk wind blowing, and despite the efforts of the firemen the blaze roared across the city. In about three hours over two hundred buildings, many of which had been built since the fire of 1788, burned.

There was great distress in New Orleans. Within the previous three months three hurricanes had destroyed a great amount of property and now the fire had consumed most of the foodstuffs stored in the warehouses. Carondelet sent to Havana and Vera Cruz for supplies and started to rebuild the city. He wrote that the houses had formerly been "covered with roofs of shingles, and when they take fire they spread it to buildings sometimes very distant." He ordered future buildings to be constructed of brick or adobe and roofed with tile.

Louisiana's first newspaper, *Le Moniteur de la Louisiane* (*The Louisiana Monitor*), was established in 1794. It was a very small paper with four pages, having two columns on each page.

Also in 1794, Étienne de Boré began planting sugar cane on his plantation near the present Audubon Park in New Orleans. The planting of cane had been largely abandoned in Louisiana after 1766, because the Louisiana sugar could not be made to granulate. All the neighbors laughed at De Boré but he replied that his sugarhouse was about completed and that "I am convinced that I am right and that I shall succeed." The next year his sugar did granulate and he made a profit of $12,000. It was not long before his neighbors stopped laughing and planted sugar cane themselves, using his methods of granulation.

Carondelet watched the actions of the Commandants at the various posts throughout Louisiana very carefully, and if they did not perform their duties efficiently he replaced them with men who could do better. Laws were enforced throughout the colony and violators were brought to justice and punished. The Governor continued Miro's mild Indian policies and became friends with many of the chiefs.

In 1797 the Baron de Carondelet was promoted to a high position in the Spanish government at Quito, Ecuador. The people of Louisiana regretted to see him and his baroness leave their colony, for he had protected their rights and had treated everyone fairly. He had conducted a strong and businesslike administration and was one of the greatest of Louisiana's colonial governors.

Three Spanish Governors: Gayoso de Lemos, Casa Calvo, Salcedo. Carondelet was succeeded by Don Manuel Gayoso de Lemos, the Commandant of the Natchez District, whose governorship ended with his death from a fever during the summer of 1799. He liked to entertain his friends with balls and dinners, but as he paid for them himself, refusing to take advantage of his office to secure money dishonestly, he died a poor man. Pleasant and kindly, he was respected and loved by the people.

His successor was the Marquis de Casa Calvo, who was sent to Louisiana from Havana to serve as Acting Governor from the fall of 1799 to the early summer of 1801. Casa Calvo was Governor when Louisiana was again acquired by France through the Treaty of San Ildefonso in 1800. Brigadier General Juan Manuel de Salcedo served until November 30, 1803, when he officially turned Louisiana over to the French.

During the governorship of Gayoso de Lemos, Casa Calvo, and Salcedo there was much unrest throughout the colony. Disagreement existed with the United States over the navigation of the Mississippi River. Many Americans living west of the Appalachian Mountains would have liked to conquer Louisiana for the United States, and some of these people even wanted to secede from the Union and organize a new country which would include Louisiana. Commerce and trade were in bad condition.

Spanish Accomplishments in Louisiana. When Spain acquired Louisiana in 1762 it was a small, unprofitable colony of less than 7,500 inhabitants. Apart from New Orleans, it had only a few small villages along the Mississippi and other streams. The farms and plantations were centered along the Mississippi above and below New Orleans.

At the end of the Spanish regime Louisiana was a large and prosperous colony with over 50,000 inhabitants, over 30,000 of whom lived along the lower Mississippi and in New Orleans. The

Atakapas and Opelousas districts had 12,000; Lafourche, 6,000; Ouachita, Natchitoches, Avoyelles, and Bayou Sara (St. Francisville), 6,000.

Economic progress had been slow prior to 1762. The Louisiana colonists had of necessity used paper money which quickly went down in value, and trade had not been permitted with other colonies or countries. Some of the French governors had been more interested in making fortunes for themselves than in providing good government. The French had scattered their settlements too widely, and their administration of justice had been poor.

In contrast to the French, the Spanish had introduced sound currency into Louisiana. In spite of the fact that Spain had imposed many trade restrictions, she had permitted Louisianians to trade with other countries. The Spanish governors had generally been hard-working, intelligent, and honest, and the Spanish systems of government and administration of justice had been efficient and fair to all. Under Spanish rule settlers from many countries had established farms and villages and towns in Louisiana, and better means of communication had been organized.

From a weak French colony in 1762, Louisiana had grown into a strong and prosperous Spanish colony forty years later. While the French in Louisiana never adopted Spanish ways and customs, they owed a greater debt to Spain than they did to their mother country.

12. ECONOMIC AND GOVERNMENTAL LIFE IN SPANISH LOUISIANA

Immigration. Despite the efforts of the French to promote agriculture, there were periods as late even as the 1750's when the people of New Orleans went hungry. There were simply not enough farmers to raise the staple necessities during years when harvests were poor. The Spanish remedied this situation by rapidly settling much of Louisiana's unoccupied land.

Governor Ulloa offered land to Maryland farmers who wished to leave their English colony. Many British settled in the Florida

Parishes in the 1760's and 1770's when this section was owned by Great Britain. During the 1770's numerous immigrants from the Canary Islands arrived and established farms below New Orleans, along the Amite River, in the upper areas of the Isle of Orleans, and along Bayou Lafourche. During the 1780's several hundred Pennsylvanians came to Spanish Louisiana.

A constant stream of Acadians arrived after 1764. The Acadians were French Canadians whose ancestors had settled the province of Acadia, or Nova Scotia, early in the seventeenth century. Great Britain acquired Nova Scotia in 1713, but the Acadians never became loyal British subjects, refusing to adopt British customs and to obey the laws. Finally, in 1755, the British lost patience, deported several thousand Acadians, and scattered them among their Atlantic seaboard colonies, after confiscating their lands and burning their homes and barns. A few Acadians reached Louisiana between 1756 and 1764 but the great Acadian migration to Louisiana began in 1765, over 1,500 arriving in 1786.

The Spanish governors were sympathetic and kind to them, gave them lands, tools for their fields, supplies, and some money. Governor O'Reilly complained: "The settlement of these poor families is very costly." Yet some Acadians were unappreciative and participated in the Rebellion of 1768 and even accused O'Reilly of having tried to make slaves of them. Their chief areas of settlement were the lower Mississippi section above the German Coast, which they called the Acadian Coast, and the Opelousas, Atakapas, and Lafourche districts, though many settled in small groups in other sections. They were hard-working farmers, herdsmen, and fishermen, extremely conservative and religious, and became good citizens. Some four to six thousand of them came to Louisiana during the Spanish period.

Several large land grants were made by the Spanish during the 1790's. The Marquis de Maison Rouge was given a large tract on the Ouachita River near the present city of Monroe, and the Baron de Bastrop received over thirty square miles of land north and northeast of Monroe. The Baron agreed to settle four hundred families on his land, but was unable to do so.

There were many hardships involved in moving to Louisiana, but the settlers wanted the opportunity to own the land they culti-

From Magruder, *A History of Louisiana*

Expulsion of the Acadians from Acadia

vated. A Carolina farmer who was not too well educated wrote to Governor Miro explaining the problems of moving to Louisiana. He would have to travel through "a howling Wilderness of 200 Miles, infected by hostile Hords and Savages & through a perillous, & irksome River-navigation of nearly 1,800 Miles, which is yet before me."

So, unlike the French, the Spanish found many new settlers for the rich lands of Louisiana. Those who came established farms and plantations and made the colony self-sufficient through their agricultural products.

Agriculture. Governor Ulloa encouraged the raising of wheat for flour, and in 1768 he asked the government to send six horse-drawn mills and six water-driven mills to Louisiana. He stated that there were only two horse-drawn mills in the colony, at Opelousas and Natchitoches, and that they were crude mills and ground only four bushels of flour per day. Wheat production began to improve.

Indigo had become an important product during the French period and it continued in importance until worms appeared which destroyed crop after crop. The farmers and planters then turned to tobacco. Governor Galvez called a meeting of the tobacco farmers, at which they fixed the price and established a system of grading, packing, and shipping the tobacco. The Governor then agreed to purchase the entire tobacco crop. One of the planters wrote that Louisiana had a better tobacco-producing climate than Maryland or Virginia and that the colony could "furnish the world with tobacco." In 1790 the Pointe Coupee District alone produced nearly 75,000 pounds of tobacco.

After Étienne de Boré granulated sugar, the planters began to clear more land, acquire more slaves, and build sugar mills, so that they could produce large quantities of sugar. By the end of the Spanish period there were many sugar-producing plantations in the colony.

General farming, however, was the common practice. The farms and plantations produced hogs, cattle and sheep, corn, rice, wheat, vegetables of all kinds, and different varieties of fruits. These foodstuffs were produced in all sections of Louisiana, and even during periods of drought or too much rain there was enough food for all, with some left over for export.

However, there were many agricultural problems. Cold weather sometimes killed the plants. In the winter of 1784, for example, the temperature went below zero and blocks of ice drifted down the Mississippi as far as New Orleans. Ten years later there was a terrific hurricane. Insects and wild animals destroyed crops. Another problem, particularly in western and southwestern Louisiana, was the stealing of livestock. Despite the fact that the cattle were branded, many were stolen, killed, butchered, and the meat sold.

Agricultural labor was difficult to secure. There were never enough slaves to supply the demand, and white men were hired by the month, most of them living in the homes of their employers. Wages were about twelve dollars a month, and board, which was estimated at six dollars. Parents sometimes signed a contract whereby their sons or daughters worked for farmers for a period of years. In 1796, for example, ten-year-old Alexis la Montagne was contracted to William Walker for ten years. Alexis was to be given a heifer and a mare, and a brand for them. He was to be the owner of their increase and in addition was to be housed, clothed and fed, and "treated as a son."

Not all Louisiana farmers and planters were wealthy owners of extensive property. In 1792, Zacherous Routh, a farmer of the Avoyelles District, made his will. It was a very short one for he was a poor man. "I leave my body to earth, and my soul to God, who gave it to me. I bequeath to my wife the cow, . . . I bequeath and give to my son, Ben Routh, my house, 3 cows, and 2 calves, my horse, my tools, etc." That was all he had to give his family.

Slavery. Slavery had existed in Louisiana since early in the French period. When O'Reilly arrived, he ordered that slaves must be brought only from Africa because he knew that the West Indian Negroes practiced voodooism, and were poor workers. An African Negro could be trained more easily than one from the West Indies. Throughout the period, however, West Indian slaves were smuggled into the colony.

As the plantations grew larger during the Spanish period, slavery became a very important economic institution. More regulations became necessary as slaves began to run away with greater frequency and to commit crimes. The French had issued one set of regulations for the slaves, and in 1792, Governor Carondelet issued another. The code provided that slaves should be adequately housed, fed, and clothed. No slave should be made to work on Sundays unless he was paid. He must not be required to work before sunrise or after sunset, and he should have a half-hour rest for lunch and two hours for dinner. No slave should be punished with more than thirty lashes within a twenty-four-hour period.

The slave insurrection in Santo Domingo in 1791 had caused the Louisiana slaves to become restless and to work poorly. In 1795 some of them in the Pointe Coupee District planned a revolt, but the plotters, including three white men, were discovered and arrested. The white men were banished from Louisiana and over twenty of the Negroes were sentenced to death. They were placed on board a boat, which moved down the Mississippi, and at more-

or-less regular intervals one was landed and hanged from a tree.

Many of the slaves worked hard for their masters and earned their freedom. Many fought in the militia companies under Galvez when he captured the British towns of Baton Rouge, Mobile, and Pensacola. One of these, Santiago, a slave who lived on the German Coast, fought so well at the siege of Pensacola that he was decorated by Governor Galvez.

By 1788 there were about fifteen hundred Negroes who were not slaves in Louisiana. They were called "Free Negroes" or "Free Men of Color." After 1794 many Free Negroes came to Louisiana from Santo Domingo, and some of them had considerable amounts of property and were well-educated, cultured people.

It was not long before the upper-class Free Negroes, who called themselves "Creoles of Color" or "colored Creoles," established a social circle of their own in New Orleans. They gave balls and parties, dressed in the highest fashion, and some of them sent their children to France or Spain to be educated. At first they caused no trouble, but as their number grew many undesirables worked their way into this group. Their conduct finally forced Governor Miro to issue regulations regarding the actions and even the dress of all Free Negroes. They were not to go out at night, nor to wear jewelry or plumes, and the women had to cover their hair with a sort of kerchief, called a *tignon*.

Industry and Manufacturing. There had been little manufacturing in French Louisiana, but the production of manufactured goods increased during the Spanish period. Sawmills grew in number; brickyards were soon scattered throughout the colony; indigo was processed; hides were tanned and mills began making flour and corn meal. Candles were made from tallow and myrtle wax, while pitch and tar were produced as a by-product of the timbering business. Tobacco was processed and packed for export. Syrup was boiled, and considerable amounts went into the making of tafia.

But most of the manufacturing continued to be the production of articles needed in the home: furniture, leather goods, clothing, utensils, and various tools and other implements made of iron.

The Mississippi River and Local Trade. Trading in the villages and towns was usually done in open-air markets or in the public squares, as in the French period, but every village or town now had a few shops. The market in New Orleans was the largest in Louisiana and carried all types of goods.

There were three kinds of merchants at this time: first, the merchant who had a shop; second, the peddler who traveled the bayous and streams in a trading boat; and third, the peddler who traveled on foot, on horseback, or in a hack or carriage. Most of this trading was done by barter, and there was much haggling over the value of the articles to be traded.

Prices were cheap as compared with modern prices. In 1769 fresh beef and pork cost about six cents a pound; fresh butter, about twenty-five cents; and a jar of bear's grease for frying or seasoning purposes, about thirty cents. A jar of milk cost twelve cents and a barrel of kidney beans $3.75. Other items were in proportion. By 1797 prices had risen slightly. Sugar was thirty cents a pound, meat seven to ten cents a pound, and a hat or a pair of shoes cost two dollars.

After 1784 the Spanish tried to close the Mississippi to American traders, but the need for their goods was too great. The trade continued but was subject to close regulation. In 1787 a 25 per cent duty was charged upon American goods. Later the duties were lowered to 15 per cent, and still later to as low as 6 per cent. Though the keelboats, flatboats, scows, and other boats kept coming down the river loaded with flour, whiskey, bacon and salted or smoked meats, furs and hides, bear's oil, corn, butter, and a wide variety of manufactured goods, the trade caused much trouble between the United States and the Spanish governments.

Foreign Trade. Foreign trade presented as many difficulties as it had when Louisiana was under the French, for at that time each nation wanted to control the trade of its colonies. Spanish Louisiana needed to sell its goods and it needed supplies of all kinds, many of which Spain could not supply. In 1769, O'Reilly wrote to an official: "Your Excellency is well aware that this province cannot live without commerce." The Governor then listed the goods which Louisiana needed, and those which she produced, adding suggested plans which, in general, were followed throughout the rest of the Spanish period.

Most of Louisiana's foreign trade during the time of Ulloa and O'Reilly continued to be with the West Indies and British West Florida. Later, however, trade increased with Mexico and even with Texas, despite the fact that Mexico wanted this trade for herself. On several occasions, particularly during the American Revolution, trade was permitted with France. Trade with the United States increased rapidly after 1790.

There had been considerable corruption in regard to trade during the French period, but most of the Spanish officials were honest and forced ship captains to account for all of their shipments. There was little personal graft, and none of them permitted their wives to engage in business or establish monopolies, as Madame Vaudreuil had done.

Luxury goods were imported into the colony at an ever increasing rate, for the colonists, by producing more themselves, had more money to spend. Life was much easier in Spanish Louisiana than it had been under the French.

Money. When Louisiana was ceded to the Spanish, there were over seven million livres worth of French paper money being circulated in the colony at but a fraction of its normal value. The Spanish fixed the trading value of this paper money at one-fourth of its face value in gold or silver. Soon a stream of Spanish gold and silver money came pouring into Louisiana from the Spanish colonies and, as trade developed, from the American colonies and from the countries of Europe.

Thus, French paper money quickly disappeared and Spanish gold and silver took its place. This was a great blessing to the colonists, for the hard money did not depreciate in value as the paper money had done.

Laws and Regulations. In 1769, O'Reilly abolished the French colonial government and created a Spanish political unit called the Province of Louisiana. At the same time he issued a code of laws for the people and a list of rules to be followed by the Spanish officials.

The Code of 1769 was issued in the form of two ordinances, or proclamations, which were written in French and in simple form so that the people could understand them. They followed the various laws then in operation in Spain and her other colonies.

The change in government was a drastic one. The French had been lax in their enforcement of the laws. Now the French Creoles saw that the Spanish intended that their laws should be observed. Aubry soon wrote back to France that "O'Reilly enforced all those wise and beneficent laws" which the French government had failed to enforce for many years. By the end of 1769 the Spanish laws and courts were functioning, and the French Creoles had realized their value. O'Reilly wrote that his political government had been well received and that a favorable impression had already been made "on the minds of the people."

Government. Under the Governor there was an Intendant, who was in charge of the treasury and the revenues. Two Lieutenant Governors were located in the Illinois and Natchitoches districts. There was an Auditor, who also served as assessor, and a Surveyor General. Other officials performed special duties.

O'Reilly organized a *Cabildo,* which was a town council for New Orleans composed of two alcaldes (judges), a prosecuting attorney, a sheriff, and several other members. The *Cabildo* met every Friday and the Governor presided at the meetings.

But the *Cabildo* was more than an ordinary town council. In addition to governing New Orleans, it advised the Governor, made suggestions concerning the general public welfare, and acted as a court of appeals for the entire colony. It was a dignified and efficient body.

Of course it took money to run the government. The colony's expenses were largely paid from taxes on ships and from the duties on exports and imports. Local governmental expenses were paid from the taxation of chimneys, inns, billiard halls, taverns, butcher-shops, liquors, from the rental of government buildings and land, and from the collection of fees and fines by local officials. In 1769 the total income of New Orleans amounted to about 2,000 pesos, and O'Reilly wrote that this sum paid for the city's *fiestas* and for other unusual expenses.

From McLoughlin, *The Jack Lafaience Book*

The Cabildo, New Orleans. The first Cabildo was built in 1770, burned in 1788, was rebuilt and burned again in 1794; the present Cabildo was completed in 1795

The colony was divided into districts, each of which was governed by a Commandant. At first there were twelve districts, the number being increased as the population of Louisiana grew, but they were too large and parishes then became the units of local government.

The Commandant of a district had many duties. He preserved order and examined the passports of all travelers. He registered titles to lands, witnessed contracts, took inventories of property, and acted as the sheriff of his district. He was a judge in all cases which did not involve more than twenty dollars. He performed marriage ceremonies. By the time of Carondelet, justices of the peace were needed, and these officials, whom the Spanish called "Syndics," were appointed.

The citizens had to build and keep the roads, levees, and bridges in good condition. Sometimes they protested. In 1792 Governor Carondelet ordered the people of the Baton Rouge District to rebuild their levees. They protested to Alexander Patin, their local Syndic, saying that their levees were already high enough, that they were busy with their farming, and that there had been "no breaks or crevices." They were forced, however, to comply with the Governor's orders.

Justice was rapid and there was no favoritism. Civil suits were settled, divorces were granted, marriage contracts were witnessed. land titles were made legal, and criminals were brought to justice. Justice was sometimes harsh, torture being permitted as it had been under the French.

All of the Spanish officials had to keep exact records of what they did. Several copies of each document had to be made for recording by the higher officials.

Indian Affairs. The Spanish had little trouble with the Indians. Through a system of councils and gifts and efficient trading methods there was generally peace with the various tribes. Indian slavery was forbidden by O'Reilly, and the Indian was given justice in the courts. In 1783, for example, when Henry Bradly "borrowed" a canoe from an Indian to go to New Orleans and did not return the canoe, he was ordered to pay twenty dollars to the Indian.

Occasionally there were complaints about Indian activities. In 1782, Antonio Maxent wrote to Governor Miro from Galveztown saying that there were over four hundred Choctaw Indians there and about fifteen hundred more expected to arrive on their way to New Orleans. He was having to feed these Indians and they were stealing from the settlers. They had broken into his warehouse and had stolen more than twenty barrels of corn and forty barrels of potatoes. At another time a report came from what is now Sabine Parish, where the Indians had eaten all the corn crop and had consumed almost all the beans, pumpkins, and watermelons. Sugar was getting short because the Indians found it "most pleasing to their appetites."

But the Indians kept the peace because trading was good and because the Spanish gave them many presents each year. At Natchitoches in 1787 the presents included gunpowder, shot, muskets, kettles, rifle flints, beads, knives, mirrors, needles, shirts, blankets, ribbons, small bells, scissors, combs, lace, vermilion dye, and many other items.

It was not without reason, then, that an old chief named Franchmastabbia called himself a friend and brother of Governor Gayoso. He painfully wrote: "Old Friend and Brother This Comes to Let you no that I am well and hope this will find you in the Same This is to Let you no that I am a man of a Strate hart and one talk and dont want to tell you lyes nor to hid any talk from you—I Believe in you and you Believe in me Our Acquaincence is Small but the Chaine of our Frindship is Grate We are bound to hid no bad talks from Each other."

13. SOCIAL AND CULTURAL LIFE
IN SPANISH LOUISIANA

French Creoles Never Became Spanish. The Spanish period of colonial Louisiana began with a rebellion against Governor Ulloa and the Spanish government. The execution of the rebel leaders by O'Reilly caused Louisiana to hate Spain and the Spanish, but O'Reilly and the succeeding governors were men of ability, honesty and extreme tact. They appointed French Creoles to high positions in the army and in the government. They permitted the French to hold the great majority of the local offices, generally to govern themselves, and to continue speaking French.

After a time the hatred for the Spanish began to disappear, and although the Louisianians would have preferred to have remained Frenchmen, they could see the many benefits of the Spanish regime over the old French government. The French who came to Louisiana from Santo Domingo after the Negro Insurrection of 1791 had no such hatred, and as many of them were wealthy and cultured they immediately took a high place in the society of the colony.

However, the Louisianians would not speak Spanish. French was the language of the people, even in the homes of the Spaniards who had married French women and whose children frequently did not know a word of Spanish. In this way, the Spaniards left few traces of their period of colonial rule. They did leave, however, the spirit of chivalry, some of their laws and legal customs, and a few geographic names.

The French of Louisiana did not forget that their life under the Spanish had been peaceful and happy. When Pierre Clement de Laussat denounced the Spanish government in 1803, they answered him: "We should be unworthy of what is to us a subject of so much pride . . . if we did not acknowledge that we have no cause of complaint against the Spanish government. We have never groaned under the yoke of an oppressive despotism. . . . We have become bound together by family connections and by the bonds of friendship."

Where the People Lived. When Spain gave up control of Louisiana most of the area within the limits of the present-day state was occupied. There were over fifty thousand people in the colony. New Orleans was, of course, the most important city; but Natchitoches, Baton Rouge, Opelousas, and several suburbs of New Orleans were growing towns. Villages had been founded throughout the colony.

New Orleans grew rapidly after the Spanish acquired Louisiana. By 1771 it had 3,200 inhabitants and by 1785 had nearly 5,000.

At the end of the Spanish era its population had increased to nearly 10,000.

The rural areas had also gained in population. Farms and plantations lined the Mississippi and most of the bayous in the southeastern section of the colony. The Red River area was settled as far as Natchitoches. Only in the southwestern, western, and northern sections were the settlers widely scattered and few in number.

The People and How They Lived. The inhabitants of Louisiana at the end of the Spanish period were of many nationalities, considerably less than one-half being of French ancestry. Many were Acadians; some were French who had come from Santo Domingo; there were Spaniards, Canary Islanders, and descendants of the Germans and Swiss who had come to Louisiana during the French period; there were Englishmen, Scots, and Irish. Americans who had migrated from Pennsylvania, Virginia, the Carolinas, or other states were settled in towns or in rural areas. A few Scandinavians lived in north Louisiana, and, according to one traveler who visited Louisiana about this time, there were even a few gypsies, almost all of whom were dancers or fiddlers.

New Orleans had been rebuilt following the fires of 1788 and 1794, and in 1803 was a comparatively new city with well-built houses constructed according to the Spanish style. The city was surrounded by an earthwork and palisaded walls. Five forts, which had been allowed to run down during the previous few years, offered some protection in case of attack. Facing the river upstream was Fort San Luis. Directly behind it on the far corner was Fort San José. Facing the river downstream was Fort San Carlos and behind it was Fort San Juan. Between Fort San José and Fort San Juan on the side directly behind the Cathedral was Fort San Fernando. Three gates opened out of New Orleans, the upper-river or San Luis Gate, the lower-river or Gate of France, as the French Creoles called it, and the Bayou Gate which was directly behind the town.

A traveler up the Mississippi passed first the Tchoupitoulas Coast, then the First German Coast, the Second German Coast, the First Acadian Coast, and the Second Acadian Coast. Eastward from the mouth of Bayou Manchac was Galveztown. Farther up-river were settlements at Baton Rouge, Thompson's Creek, Pointe Coupee and Bayou Sara (St. Francisville). Fort Miro, present-day Monroe, was on the Ouachita River, and up the Red River was the village called Les Rapides (Pineville) and the old French town of Natchitoches.

Southward from Les Rapides were the villages of Opelousas and Atakapas (St. Martinville). On down Bayou Teche was a growing Spanish settlement called New Iberia, which means New Spain. There were no sizable villages along Bayou Lafourche or the other bayous in this section, but along all these waterways were farms and plantations, livestock ranches, truck farms, and the homes of hunters and fishermen.

Outside New Orleans and the larger towns, life was much like it had been under the French, for the French influence was very strong. The houses were French, the clothing was French, and most of the customs of the people had been inherited from the days of French rule.

But New Orleans was a Spanish town as far as its houses and other buildings were concerned. The wrought ironwork was just like it was in Havana or the City of Mexico, even though it had been hammered out by slaves who spoke only French. Many of the houses were built of brick with flat roofs of tile supported by heavy cypress timbers which had been cut, according to the Spanish regulations, only during certain phases of the moon. No house was complete without its patio, or courtyard, in the back. The houses were built flush with the street and the sidewalk was right against the front wall.

The great majority of Louisianians now had better household furnishings, for they were more prosperous; except for the houses of the Spanish officials, most of the furnishings were French in style. If the family was wealthy the home was filled with French furniture, French tableware and dishes, French linens and chests, and French-style clothing. If the family was poor the furnishings were homemade without style or ornamentation.

Most small farmers could be compared with Gidgeon Walker, who lived near the Avoyelles Post about 1799. Walker's farm was

Bureau of New Orleans News

Iron balcony railings of exquisite artistry from the Spanish period

six arpents wide and forty arpents deep and was valued at $125. It had a house sixteen feet wide and about twenty-five feet long, covered with split shingles and with a gallery all around it. There was a small barn behind the house. The farmer owned two horses worth $36, an unbroken horse valued at $15, six cows and calves worth $36, and ten or twelve head of cattle in the woods. Walker's tools, household furnishings, and clothing included: three chairs and a table, a chest, a bed, a mirror, several spreads and blankets, some family clothing, an ax, a brace and bit, a file, a pressing iron, a pair of scissors, a Spanish saddle and bridle, a large bucket, a grinding stone, two knives, three hoes, and a spade. It is evident that Walker was a small farmer and that life was hard for him and his family.

There was little more traveling throughout the colony than

there had been during the French period, but there were more towns and villages, and the people who lived in the vicinity usually went to town on Saturday afternoons. They traveled along the poor roads on horseback or in wagons or carts. If they wanted to travel any distance they still used some type of boat along the various waterways.

Religion. The Spanish were Catholics just as the French were, but to them religion was a much more serious matter. The French were inclined to practice their faith in easygoing fashion; if they went to church on Sundays and kept the Holy Days that was about all that was necessary. The Spanish tried to change this situation.

With the Jesuits already gone, Governor O'Reilly, immediately upon his arrival, reorganized the Catholic Church in Louisiana. He first removed the Louisiana church from the jurisdiction of the Bishop of Quebec and placed it under the Bishop of Havana. There being only eight parishes in all Louisiana, including two in the Illinois country, O'Reilly ordered the establishment of new parishes.

The Spanish were very critical of the French Capuchins. Father Cirilo de Barcelona criticized them in reports to his superiors in Havana. They wore a "watch in a fob," had a clock in the refectory which cost $270, had silver spoons and "smaller ones to take coffee with." They "ruled teal duck as fish and ate it on fast days," and "their table is still reputed to be better than any other in the capital." French Father Hilaire de Genevaux criticized Father Dagobert de Longuory. He "rises at six o'clock in the morning, says, or does not say, mass . . . takes his three-cornered hat, a very superfluous and unworthy appendage for a Capuchin, and goes to a somewhat suspicious house, where he plays until dinner,—that meal over, he resumes his occupations until suppertime."

Father Genevaux also criticized the Ursuline nuns: "They live as they always have done, without being cloistered, and as if they were not nuns at all." The Ursuline nuns later proved their loyalty to the Church. They did not approve of the French Revolution nor of Napoleon, and when Louisiana was given back to France sixteen of the twenty-five nuns refused to live under what they considered a Godless France. On Whitsunday in 1803 these sixteen, shrouded in their veils and mantles, marched out of their chapel and, saying good-by to their slaves, boarded a ship for Havana.

It will be remembered that Father Antonio Sedella had attempted during the time of Governor Miro to establish the Inquisition and that Miro had quickly sent him out of the colony and spared Louisiana the persecutions of that institution. Later Father Sedella returned to Louisiana under the name of Father Antoine and spent the rest of his life in New Orleans. He became one of the most beloved priests in Louisiana history, and when he died at the age of eighty-one in 1829, Protestants and Catholics alike mourned him.

The stern, Puritan-like Spanish Catholicism did not appeal to the French, and the Spanish constantly found fault with them. In 1792, Governor Carondelet criticized the religious practices of the French and of the French priests. He wrote that of all the Capuchins only three priests had "comported themselves with the general concept of good conduct." He pleaded for more non-French but French-speaking priests to be sent to Louisiana so that "our religion then will be loved, respected, and generally followed."

Time has, however, proven that the French Creoles are better Catholics than the Spaniards realized. The French Creoles possessed a quiet brand of faith, but it was strong and true.

Amusements. Despite their religious severity, the Spaniards were a fun-loving people, and they joined the other nationalities living in Louisiana in enjoying a full social life. They had a good time on Sunday afternoons and on feast days; and Christmas, New Year's, and the various Saints' Days were opportunities for celebrations. A *fiesta*, or party, was *made*, as the Spanish said, whenever possible. Everyone—French, Spanish, Acadian—was invited. On one occasion, after the feast was eaten, the Spaniards drank a toast "To Spain—Land of Queen Isabella, who made possible the discovery of the New World." The Frenchmen drank "To France—Land of Louis XIV, the Grand Monarch." The Acadians drank "To Acadia and Grand Pré—birthplace of the exiles." Then, all of them drank "To the Acadian Country,

the Golden Coast—the adopted homeland of all." And the dancing began.

Those were happy days, those days of Spanish Louisiana. Times
were good. The country was growing up, and providing opportunity for all.

Education. While a few of the wealthy Creole families educated
their sons in France or the United States and an even larger
number provided tutors to teach their children to read and write,
the majority had little interest in education. The Spanish government projected a public-school system in 1771 and sent Don
Manuel Andres Lopez de Armesto to New Orleans as Director.
Armesto thus has the distinction of being the first city-school
superintendent in the United States, but he accomplished little.
The people simply refused to send their children to public or
Spanish-language schools.

The Ursulines continued their educational work, largely for the
training of girls and young women. They disliked Spanish regulations, however, and opposed the receiving of "Spanish subjects
ignorant of French." By 1788 there were eight private schools or
academies in New Orleans with a total enrollment of about four
hundred pupils.

In 1803, Louisiana was still an educationally backward colony,
in which it was estimated that only a few hundred persons were
able to read and write well.

Medicine and Health. Spanish Louisiana was attacked by the
same diseases that attacked French Louisiana. Epidemics appeared
from time to time and there were the usual cases of smallpox,
mumps, and stomach disorders. The old home remedies continued
to be relied upon, for there were few doctors.

Organized medicine, however, appeared during the Spanish
period. By 1770, before a man could practice medicine he had to
show the records of his study as well as his books and instruments
and submit to an examination before the Spanish King's physician.
In addition he had to prove that he was of high moral character
and a good Catholic.

One of the most noted doctors of Spanish Louisiana was a

Scotsman, Dr. Robert Dow, who left a rather large number of records including medical bills. He was a genial, kindly man and it has been written that "no member of his profession ever acquired more popularity." The inventory of Dr. Joseph Dorquiny illustrates that physicians of the period dressed well, for he possessed numerous pairs of stockings, waistcoats, satin trousers, a "cravat buckle set with stones," and a silver-trimmed sword. By the end of the Spanish period there were practicing physicians living in most communities.

Culture. There had been little culture in colonial Louisiana prior to 1762; no printing, no literary or musical activities, no painting, no sculpture. The colonists were too busy clearing forest lands, draining swamps, and planting food crops to permit time for such things.

In 1763, Denis Braud was granted the right to set up the first printing press in Louisiana, and the same year he printed a proclamation for an English general who was stationed at Mobile. The proclamation carried the line "Published in Mobile." Shortly after this Braud began his Louisiana printing career, printing broadsides and handbills.

It is said that the first Louisiana newspaper, called *Le Courier du Vendredi* (*The Friday Courier*), was printed in New Orleans in 1785. This cannot be proved, however, for no copies exist today. During the 1790's a refugee from Santo Domingo named Louis Duclot arrived at New Orleans and in 1794 he began the publication of *Le Moniteur de la Louisiane* (*The Louisiana Monitor*). This was the first newspaper in Louisiana of which copies still exist. By 1797 the *Moniteur* had become the official paper of the government, and in it are found many of the official governmental documents of that time.

Louisiana literature began in 1777, when two short, unsigned poems were published. One of them congratulated Galvez on recovering from an illness, and the other heaped a great deal of plain flattery upon him. Two years later, in 1779, Julien Poydras, who was later to become a wealthy merchant, published a long epic poem on Galvez' capture of the English fort at Baton Rouge. Amateur theatricals gradually increased during the Spanish period.

The first record of a music teacher in Louisiana was during the late 1780's or early 1790's, when a New Orleans lady began to give lessons on the harp. Governor Carondelet's daughters were among her pupils. Organized musicales and music organizations had to await the American period.

Society. Society flourished in Louisiana after the period of the American Revolution, for the country settled down to peaceful pursuits and its wealth grew rapidly. Dress became fashionable and was copied after the styles of Paris or Madrid. Balls and dances were frequent.

The letters of the Spanish officials, written with quaint, formal phrases, reveal both their friendship with many of the citizens of the colony and something too of society in general. Carlos de Grand Pré, then the Commandant of the Natchez District, once wrote to Governor Miro: "Permit me to place myself at the feet of your wife, to whom I offer my respect and obedience, and to whom my wife offers her affectionate expressions of love and friendship, as well as to Your Lordship. I hope to have the honor of seeing her soon in the company of Your Lordship, whose life I pray the All-Powerful to lengthen the many years I desire. . . . I kiss Your Lordship's hands."

So life was lived during the Spanish regime. By 1800 the little colony of 1762 was a flourishing, almost-grown-up colony where life was much the same as it was all over the New World at that time.

PART FOUR

EARLY YEARS OF THE AMERICAN REGIME

14. THE PURCHASE OF LOUISIANA

Importance of Louisiana to the United States. During the American Revolution, Richard Henry Lee of Virginia wrote to Samuel Adams of Massachusetts a letter in which he said that the young republic must always have a strong navy for its protection. Two things, he thought, were necessary to make the navy strong—the development of fisheries and the control of the Mississippi River. In a similar letter to Henry Laurens of South Carolina, he wrote: "These, sir, are the strong legs on which North America can alone walk securely in Independence." From this time on many American statesmen dreamed of the day when the land west of the Mississippi would belong to the United States.

After the Revolutionary War, settlers began to push west of the Appalachian Mountains and settle in what are now the states of Kentucky, Tennessee, and Ohio. By 1790 there were in this region more than 100,000 settlers, who needed to reach world markets with their surplus pork, wheat, corn, and other products. The easiest way to reach these markets was to send the goods down the Mississippi to New Orleans and there transfer them to ocean-going ships.

In 1795, Thomas Pinckney, the United States Minister to Great Britain, signed a treaty with Spain in which the Spanish agreed to give the Americans the right to transport goods down the Mississippi River to New Orleans and there to deposit them until they could be loaded onto ocean-going ships. The treaty was to be in effect for three years and might be renewed. The Pinckney Treaty also secured for the United States undisputed title to all lands north of the thirty-first parallel and east of the Mississippi River.

129

The Mississippi River trade prospered during the next three years. After 1798, however, the western settlers had many difficulties with the Spanish over the river trade and the right of deposit at New Orleans. They complained to President John Adams and at times angrily talked of organizing an army and capturing New Orleans and Louisiana.

Spain Cedes Louisiana Back to France. In spite of Louisiana's prosperity during the late 1790's, the colony was costing the Spanish government over $300,000 a year. This was a serious problem, for Spain at this time was not a wealthy country.

France had been making plans to rebuild her colonial empire since 1798, and early in 1800, Napoleon Bonaparte began to put pressure upon Spain to trade Louisiana and Florida to France. He argued that France could better protect these colonies against the Americans and the English than could Spain. However, while Louisiana had not been acquired by Spain until 1762, Florida had been originally settled by the Spanish, and they would not consider giving it up. Louisiana was a different matter, about which one of the Spanish officials wrote that "it costs us more than it is worth." Louisiana under the French would serve as a strong barrier for Spanish Texas against the English and Americans.

The power of Spain had been declining for a number of years. If Spain had held her former strength, she would never have given up the Mississippi Valley. A Spanish writer explained the situation by saying that if Spain refused to give Louisiana back to France, France might declare war against her; and while Spain and France were fighting, the United States would be free to capture Louisiana. In either case, Louisiana would be lost to Spain.

At this time Napoleon was making plans for a new French Empire which would include Louisiana and the Caribbean island of Santo Domingo. France began to negotiate with Spain, and on October 1, 1800, Louisiana was returned to France by the secret Treaty of San Ildefonso. The treaty was not made public until about two years later.

Some Louisianians were very happy. For over twenty years they had been making appeals to France to take Louisiana back again. In 1793, for example, they had sent a petition to Paris bearing 150 signatures. Now their prayers had been granted. Excitedly they sang the "Marseillaise" and the "Ça Ira" at the cafes and coffeehouses in New Orleans.

The French Commissioner Arrives in Louisiana. On March 26, 1803, Pierre Clement de Laussat, a French colonial official, landed at New Orleans to make arrangements for the official transfer of Louisiana back to France. He was conducted to the government house where he was received by the Spanish Governor. The Louisianians celebrated with a large reception in his honor.

Laussat announced that he had been ordered to make preparations for the arrival of General Claude Victor, who had been appointed the new French Governor. When General Victor arrived France would take official possession of Louisiana. The Spanish Governor declared that everything was ready for turning the colony back to France.

A short time later over a hundred Louisianians presented to Laussat an address in which they thanked the French government for taking Louisiana back again. They said that they had been citizens of Spain for over forty years but that during all this time they had remained loyal sons of France. They were happy in having lived long enough to become French citizens again.

The great majority of the French Louisianians, however, showed little enthusiasm over becoming Frenchmen again. The Spanish government had been more efficient and more honest than the government under France had been, and Spanish silver money was much more stable than the French paper money. The merchants, planters, and farmers feared new French commercial regulations. Louisiana had never really prospered under France; it had prospered greatly under Spain.

The United States Plans to Acquire Louisiana. The Louisianians did not know that at this time negotiations were going on between the United States and France for the American purchase of Louisiana.

The United States government had heard that France was

about to regain Louisiana. In 1801, Rufus King wrote to President Thomas Jefferson from London that he feared that "Spain is ceding Louisiana to France, an inauspicious circumstance to us."

The American government did not want France to secure possession of Louisiana. France and Great Britain were now at peace, but everyone realized that they would soon be at war again. The English might then capture Louisiana, and the United States did not want Louisiana to become a British possession.

American newspapers began to argue that since New Orleans and the Mississippi River were very important to the people of the west, the United States should organize an expedition to capture New Orleans. President Jefferson wrote to Robert Livingston, the American Minister to France, in 1802, that the cession of Louisiana to France "works most sorely on the United States." He also wrote that "every eye in the United States is now fixed on the affairs of Louisiana. Perhaps nothing since the revolutionary war has produced more uneasy sensations through the body of the nation."

Jefferson believed that if France secured Louisiana, she would soon afterwards capture the Floridas from Spain. Canada already bounded the United States on the north. If Louisiana and Florida became French the American nation would be hemmed in on the west, the north, and the south.

The United States Tries to Buy Louisiana. Robert Livingston was an old man, deaf, and not considered a good diplomat, even though he was the American Minister to France. He had secured the appointment because he was a member of one of New York's old wealthy families and was a good friend of President Jefferson. Jefferson ordered Livingston to talk to the French officials about the possibility of the United States buying Louisiana.

Livingston wrote back that Napoleon was the dictator of France. "There is no people, no legislature, no counsellors. One man is everything. He seldom asks advice, and never hears it unasked. His ministers are mere clerks, and his legislature and counsellors are parade officers." Livingston promised to do the best he could.

In January, 1803, Jefferson appointed young James Monroe as a special representative of the United States to help Livingston in trying to buy Louisiana. It took Monroe three months to reach Paris. Meanwhile, the negotiations between Livingston and the French officials moved forward with incredible swiftness.

The Purchase of Louisiana. During the early months of 1803, Napoleon realized that he would have difficulty in protecting Louisiana from the English, with whom France was about to go to war. It was rumored that the English were already making plans to send a large fleet to capture the colony just as soon as the war started. Napoleon finally decided to sell Louisiana to the Americans. He said: "I already consider the colony as entirely lost." He sent for François Barbé-Marbois, his Minister of the Treasury, ordering him to begin negotiations with Livingston.

Many Frenchmen did not want to relinquish Louisiana, for they had hoped that France would rebuild her old colonial empire. One day Joseph and Lucien Bonaparte, two of Napoleon's brothers, visited him. Napoleon was taking a bath. They followed him into the bathroom, where they argued with him not to sell Louisiana, but Napoleon became angry and hurled his snuffbox at them.

Barbé-Marbois and Livingston began their negotiations, at first making rapid progress, for the rumors of the English fleet were indeed true. "They have twenty ships of war in the Gulf of Mexico," said Napoleon. "I have not a moment to lose in putting it [Louisiana] out of their reach." However, Barbé-Marbois was a shrewd diplomat and he argued over the selling price. On April 12, Livingston lost patience and wrote Jefferson: "Only force can give us New Orleans. We must employ force. Let us first get possession of the country, and negotiate afterwards."

Monroe arrived in Paris that night, and he, Livingston, and the French officials spent most of the next day working on a purchase treaty. Late in the afternoon the basic problems were settled, but it took three weeks to work out all the details. The Louisiana Purchase Treaty was officially dated April 30, 1803.

When Napoleon was informed that the work had been completed he said: "This accession of territory affirms forever the power of the United States, and I have just given England a maritime rival that sooner or later will lay low her pride." His prophecy came true during the War of 1812.

Department of Commerce and Industry

Livingston, Monroe, and the French officials signing the Louisiana Purchase Treaty

The Americans were well satisfied with their bargain. After they had signed the agreements, Livingston said: "We have lived long, but this is the noblest work of our whole lives. . . . From this day the United States will take their place among the powers of the first rank. . . . The instruments which we have just signed will cause no tears to be shed; they prepare ages of happiness for innumerable generations of human creatures."

Who was responsible for the purchase of Louisiana? Credit should be given to President Jefferson, Secretary of State James Madison, Minister Livingston, and Monroe, but Livingston earned most of the credit for the negotiations. He had proven to be a discreet and zealous diplomat, and one of the French ministers said that he was the most persistent negotiator he had ever met. The man really responsible for the Louisiana Purchase, however, was Napoleon, for his decision to sell had made it possible.

The news of the purchase of Louisiana reached the United States on July 3, 1803. It was a good Fourth of July present for the young Republic.

The Cost of Louisiana. The United States agreed to pay France 60,000,000 francs, or about $11,250,000, for Louisiana. In addition, the United States promised to pay the claims which certain of her citizens held against France, these claims to be limited to 20,000,000 francs.

The United States did not have the $15,000,000 needed to pay for Louisiana in its treasury, for its total annual income at this time was only about $10,000,000. Jefferson and the other officials, therefore, arranged to borrow the money from an English banking firm and from a Dutch banking firm, the rate of interest being fixed at 6 per cent. One-third of the principal was to be paid in 1819 and the remainder the two following years. Including the interest, the total cost of Louisiana was nearly $27,000,000.

France in Possession of Louisiana. It will be remembered that Laussat had already come to Louisiana to take possession for France. Although it had soon become known in Louisiana that the colony had been purchased by the United States, Laussat decided that France should take possession of Louisiana, even if it would be for only a short period.

The summer of 1803 passed and fall came. The sugar-grinding season started. Finally Laussat and the Spanish officials agreed that France should take formal possession of Louisiana on November 30.

At noon on this day the Spanish Governor took his place on a platform in the council room of the Cabildo at New Orleans. The legal documents were read and signed, and the keys of the city and of the forts were handed to Laussat on a silver platter. Then the officials went to the balcony and watched the Spanish flag being hauled down and the flag of France take its place.

Laussat immediately destroyed all traces of the Spanish government. He abolished the *Cabildo* and removed all the Spanish officials from their offices. He restored the laws of France and appointed Louisiana French Creoles to all the offices throughout the colony.

On December 1 Laussat gave a great fete "in honor of the French flag." A banquet was served to some seventy-five French, Spanish and American guests. Toasts were drunk to France, to Spain and to the United States. A final toast was drunk to the ladies present. Then the dinner guests went into the ballroom where over two hundred people waited for the dancing to begin.

During the next twenty days banquet followed banquet and ball followed ball. One of the banquets is supposed to have lasted for about twelve hours and during it more than twenty different kinds of gumbo were served.

The United States Takes Possession of Louisiana. President Jefferson selected General James Wilkinson and Governor William C. C. Claiborne of Mississippi Territory to take possession of Louisiana for the United States. General Wilkinson spent several weeks gathering a small military force at Fort Adams, in the southwestern corner of Mississippi. The American troops finally arrived outside New Orleans on December 17, and after several conferences with Laussat, December 20 was fixed as the date for the transfer of Louisiana to the United States.

The American troops marched into the city to what is now

From Fortier, *A History of Louisiana*

The United States takes possession of Louisiana

Jackson Square and stood fronting the Cabildo, where the ceremony was conducted with great pomp and military display.

Laussat later wrote a description of the scene: "The beautiful women and fashionable men of the city adorned all the balconies of the square. The Spanish officers were distinguishable in the crowd by their plumes. . . . The eleven galleries of the city hall were filled with beauties." The various formalities and the signing of documents took place in the council room of the Cabildo, after which the officials stepped onto the balcony and watched the French tricolor slowly lowered. The striped and starred American banner rose in its place. The audience was silent and nothing was heard but the deep rolling of drums. When the American flag reached the top of the flagpole the crowds broke forth with wild cheers, while the cannons roared and the rifles cracked out in salute.

That afternoon Laussat gave a large reception and the same evening he was host at a dinner for 450 guests. Four toasts were proposed. The first was in Madeira wine and was drunk to the United States. The second was in Malaga and Canary wine and was to Spain. The third was in pink and white champagne and was to France. The last toast was to the "eternal happiness of Louisiana." That night there was a grand ball which lasted until about nine o'clock the following morning.

Late that night William C. C. Claiborne wrote to James Madison: "The Standard of my Country was this day unfurled here amidst the reiterated acclamations of thousands. And if I may judge by professions and appearance, the Government of the United States is received with joy and gratitude by the People."

Attitude of the French Creoles Toward the Purchase. Many of the French Creoles had shown little enthusiasm when their colony was returned to France; some of them showed even less enthusiasm when they heard that Louisiana had been sold by France to the United States. Americans were strangers to them. They spoke another language and had different social and political customs. It would be many years before the American form of democratic government and American ways of life would become really appreciated by them.

French and Spanish Officials Remain in Louisiana. Laussat remained only about four months after the United States took possession of Louisiana. During this period he was occupied in listing and selling the property which belonged to France. Finally, on April 21, 1804, he sailed from New Orleans.

Some of the Spanish officials remained in Louisiana, among them former Governor Casa Calvo. Governor Claiborne feared that they planned to stir up dissensions among the people in the western part of Louisiana and finally ordered them to leave. In February, 1806, Claiborne sent Casa Calvo a passport with "best wishes for the health and happiness of the nobleman whose presence has become so unacceptable." Casa Calvo sailed from New Orleans, so it was said, "full of wrath and indignation."

15. FROM TERRITORY TO STATE

Louisiana in 1803. The purchase of Louisiana almost doubled the land area of the United States. At that time the young nation totaled a little over 900,000 square miles. The purchase added another 875,000 square miles of territory, an area which included the entire western side of the Mississippi Valley and the Isle of Orleans. It was larger than the combined countries of Great Britain, Germany, Italy, Portugal, and Spain and was seven times the size of Great Britain and Ireland.

It was one of the richest areas in the entire world, with agricultural and ranching lands, large tracts of timberland, and stores of minerals, oil, and natural gas. While many of these natural resources were not known at that time, everyone realized the value of Louisiana. Laussat had written back to France that the Americans "would have given $50,000,000 rather than not possess it." He prophesied that within a few years much of the area would be in a state of cultivation and that New Orleans would have grown into a port with a population of from 30,000 to 50,000.

At that time the population of the area of present-day Louisiana was only about 50,000. New Orleans, the largest city, totaled some 10,000 people, of whom nearly half were free Negroes or slaves. The rest of the Louisiana Purchase territory had comparatively few inhabitants, and most of these people lived along the Mississippi, Missouri, or other rivers.

New Orleans then did not suggest the great city of our own day. The city extended only a short distance above and below what is now the Vieux Carré section, which had a combination earth and wooden-palisade wall around it. There were five forts, one at each corner and one in the center of the side opposite the river. The walls and the forts, however, had not been kept in repair and were in bad condition. The rusty guns were mounted on dilapidated wooden carriages and the sentinels stood guard at hingeless gates. During the winter of 1803–1804, when the season was exceptionally

The Louisiana Purchase   PBL

cold and firewood scarce and expensive, the poorer citizens almost demolished the wooden portions of the fortifications.

The drainage ditches on either side of the streets had partially filled up with dirt and rubbish and the little bridges across them were in bad condition. The streets were unpaved and were littered with trash and garbage, and the air reeked with foul odors. The wooden buildings and the wooden doors and window shutters of the brick houses and stores were generally unpainted. Despite its appearance, however, New Orleans compared favorably with most Latin-American, French, or Spanish towns of its size at this time.

There were only a few business houses. These included four

or five general stores, a trio of Scottish banks, one German business firm, and eight or ten commission houses which had been opened by Americans from New York, Philadelphia, and Baltimore. However, the people of New Orleans enjoyed many luxuries, despite the fact that they lived in a small city. The shops carried quantities of Malaga, Bordeaux, and Madeira wines, olive oil, liqueurs, and such items as brandied fruits, anchovies, raisins, cheese, sausages, prunes, and almonds. Various types of expensive clothing materials could be purchased, as could home furnishings, jewelry, and other personal accessories. The women wore silks for balls and similar social occasions and brightly colored calicoes and muslins for everyday wear. The men wore the heavy clothing of Europe, with their "heads sunk in high collars, arms and hands lost in long sleeves." Their chins were buried in triple cravats and their legs were encased in high boots. Just as in Spanish or French colonial days, the children were dressed like their parents.

There were only a few other towns in Louisiana proper, and these were very small. Among them were Natchitoches, Opelousas, Baton Rouge, St. Martinville, and Monroe. Most people lived in what is now the southeastern one-fourth of the state, where there were farms and plantations. Only hunters, trappers, and a few pioneer farmers lived in the other sections.

The people of Louisiana were of many nationalities. As well as the French and Spanish Creoles, there were Germans who lived along the Mississippi above and below New Orleans. The Acadians lived along Bayous Lafourche, Teche, Vermilion, and in other scattered places. *Islenos* from the Canary Islands made a living from fishing and trapping in south Louisiana, from east of the mouth of the Mississippi to Bayou Teche. Americans were concentrated in New Orleans and in the vicinity of Opelousas. French refugees from the West Indies had been given grants in northeast Louisiana and along Bayou Teche. Many farmers, planters, and city dwellers owned Negro slaves, and a large number of Free Negroes lived in the towns, especially in New Orleans.

The French and Spanish Creoles looked with disfavor upon these other peoples. They were Catholics, while the majority of the Americans and British were Protestants. The Creoles spoke French, while the Americans and British spoke English, and the

Creole folkways and habits of living were quite different. They were very proud, enjoyed their leisure time, were carefree and easygoing. Governor Claiborne wrote that the planters were wealthy and had "luxurious and expensive" tastes. He also wrote that many of the Creoles were "deplorably uninformed" because the Spanish and French governments had not encouraged public education. The Americans and British were much more democratic, more aggressive in economic matters, and had a bustling enthusiasm.

A few years after this time, when young Alexander Porter planned to move to Louisiana to practice law, he met General Andrew Jackson. The General advised him: "And remember, Alick, you are going to a new country. . . . You will find a different people from those you have grown among, and you must study their natures, and accommodate yourself to them." Not all Americans who came to Louisiana during those early years had this good advice, and many of them were convinced of the backwardness and stupidity of the native Louisianians.

William C. C. Claiborne. William C. C. Claiborne had been one of the two commissioners who took possession of Louisiana for the United States. From December 20, 1803, until March 26, 1804, he was in charge of the civil affairs of the colony while General James Wilkinson was in command of the army.

During this period President Jefferson gave much thought to whom he should appoint as first Governor when Louisiana was made into a territory. He seriously considered the Marquis de Lafayette, the French nobleman who had so greatly aided the United States during the Revolution. Lafayette, however, was not able to accept the position, so Claiborne was named the first Governor of Louisiana.

Claiborne faced many problems. The French and Spanish Louisianians were not acquainted with democratic government and had to be educated to its principles. The old French and Spanish customs must be changed slowly, however, for people do not change their political habits quickly. Many Creoles did not like the Americans, their ideas of government, or their customs. About this time, for example, a small earthquake interrupted one of the New Orleans balls. An old Creole gentleman remarked sarcastically, as he glanced at the Americans present: "It was not in Spanish times or the French that the amusements of the ladies were interfered with."

However, Claiborne was able to write to Jefferson that the people were doing their best to understand the Americans and that the various problems could be solved.

Government of Territorial Louisiana. From March 26, 1804, until March 2, 1805, Louisiana was an "unorganized" territory of the United States. It was called the Territory of Orleans. The rest of the Louisiana Purchase was called the District of Louisiana.

Claiborne was appointed Governor by the President for a three-year term. He commanded the militia, granted pardons, and appointed all local officials. The President appointed a Secretary of the Territory for a four-year term, and he also appointed a thirteen-member Legislative Council, a federal District Judge, and three judges of the Superior Court.

On March 2, 1805, Louisiana was made into an "organized" territory. Under this new form of government a Legislature was added, which was composed of a Legislative Council of five members appointed by the President and a twenty-five-member lower house elected by the people. This form of government lasted until Louisiana became a state in 1812.

Claiborne was Governor during the entire period.

Local Government. At the first meeting of the Legislative Council in 1804, Louisiana had been divided into twelve counties. They were Acadia, Atakapas, Concordia, German Coast, Iberville, Lafourche, Natchitoches, Opelousas, Orleans, Ouachita, Pointe Coupee, and Rapides. In 1806 the territorial Legislature also divided the Territory of Orleans into nineteen parishes. These first parishes were Ascension, Assumption, Atakapas, Avoyelles, Baton Rouge, Concordia, Iberville, Lafourche Interior, Natchitoches, Orleans, Ouachita, Plaquemines, Pointe Coupee, Rapides, St. Bernard, St. Charles, St. James, St. John the Baptist, and St. Landry. The term "parishes" was used because it was the old Spanish custom. Both counties and parishes were in existence in Louisiana local government until 1845, when the counties

went out of existence. All the other states have counties instead
of parishes.

The parishes had several local officials such as judges, sheriffs,
coroners, clerks, treasurers, and justices of the peace. They had
Police Juries, which were called by this name because they had
twelve members as do ordinary juries. At first the Police Juries
only advised the parish judges, but in 1811 they became the govern-

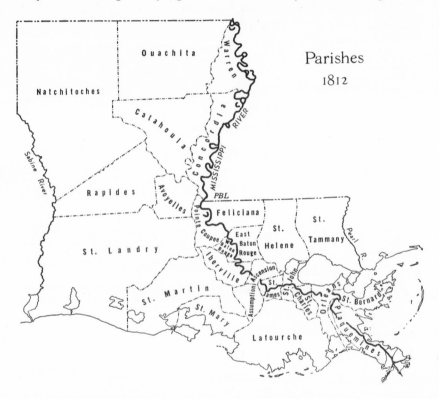

Parishes
1812

ing bodies of the parishes and the members were elected by the
people.

The parish officials handled most local governmental problems.
They collected taxes and spent the monies collected, built roads
and levees, and kept peace and order. As time passed the people
of territorial Louisiana, who had never before had a part in their
local government, began to learn how to govern themselves. Louisiana would soon be ready for statehood.

Territorial Law. Claiborne kept in force most of the old Spanish laws which were not in conflict with those of the United States. In 1805 the territorial Legislature passed a law which defined various crimes, but a code of criminal law was never passed. A code of civil law was adopted in 1808.

All laws of territorial Louisiana were written in both French and English, and all the business of the courts was conducted in these two languages. The membership of the juries had to be divided among those who spoke French and those who spoke English.

Problems of Governor Claiborne. Claiborne was only twenty-eight years of age when he became Governor, but he had sound and mature judgment. In his first speech to the people of Louisiana he promised that he would promote their general welfare and work for the good of the Territory.

The western part of Louisiana caused Claiborne much anxiety. The western boundary of the Louisiana Purchase had not been definitely fixed, and the Spanish in Texas considered the boundary to be somewhere east of the Sabine River. This territory east of the Sabine was sometimes called the Sabine Strip. The Spanish kept an army in eastern Texas and held their Louisiana settlements, which were only a few miles west of Natchitoches. The largest of these posts, Los Adaes, was the tip of the wedge which they thrust into Louisiana. Sometimes their army patrols came to the very outskirts of Natchitoches.

The Sabine Strip became a kind of "No Man's Land," and to it went large numbers of lawless people. The region became unsafe for traders on their way to Texas or on the return trips to Louisiana, robberies and even murders being frequent.

It was not long before the United States established a military post at Natchitoches to patrol the area and to keep the Spanish from further penetrating into Louisiana.

The Indians who still lived in northern and western Louisiana constituted another problem for Claiborne. In 1805 the United States appointed Dr. John Sibley as the Indian agent. He had settled in Natchitoches two years before and had become well acquainted with the Indians of that area. Dr. Sibley held many conferences with the various chiefs, helped them in their trading operations, and prevented white men from taking unfair advantage of them.

At various times before 1812 several Americans planned expeditions to invade Texas and take it from the Spanish. This was against American law, so it was Claiborne's duty to prevent such expeditions from being organized. Only a few of them succeeded in crossing the Sabine River and none of them was successful in capturing Texas.

Many of the land titles which had been granted by the French and Spanish were not clearly written or did not give exact boundaries. This was a serious problem both for the native Louisianians and the Americans who were coming into Louisiana.

In 1806 and 1807 it was rumored in Louisiana that Aaron Burr, a former Vice-President of the United States, was conspiring to start a revolution in the western part of the country. Some people said that General James Wilkinson, who commanded the United States army in Louisiana, was another of the conspirators. For some months everyone in Louisiana was much excited about this plot, but finally Burr was captured near Natchez, Mississippi. He was tried for treason, but acquitted.

Keeping order in Louisiana was another problem. In 1806 a police force, called the *garde de ville,* or city guard, was organized for the City of New Orleans. The men were armed with short spears and heavy swords when they patrolled the streets. The only really serious trouble which Claiborne faced, however, was a slave revolt in 1811 in St. John the Baptist Parish. The plot was discovered, a battle was fought with the slaves, who were defeated, and over a dozen of them were beheaded.

The West Florida Rebellion of 1810. What is now the Florida Parishes was not then a part of Louisiana. This region still belonged to Spain, but the people, who were mostly Americans and English, wanted a more democratic government. In 1810 they revolted against Spain, captured the Spanish fort at Baton Rouge, and organized a republic. The Republic of West Florida existed for only a few weeks, as the Florida Parishes were soon occupied by the United States.

Economic Life. When the people of the United States learned that Louisiana would be admitted into the Union when it had sufficient population and when the Creoles had learned the ways of democratic government, many of them moved to Louisiana. Soon Louisiana agriculture, business, trade, and commerce were booming. New Orleans and the other towns began to grow and new towns, such as Donaldsonville, were organized.

The Mississippi River was soon filled with boats of all descriptions carrying goods down to the people of Louisiana or carrying Louisiana's products upstream. The first river steamboat arrived in New Orleans in 1812, beginning the age of the great Mississippi steamboats. Foreign trade also increased, for the United States did not impose the restrictions which had been imposed by the French and Spanish.

The improved economic conditions created a need for banks, so the Bank of Louisiana was organized in 1805, and the Bank of Orleans and the Planters' Bank in 1811.

New roads became necessary. Although these roads were only narrow dirt trails winding through the swamps and forests, filled with holes and tree stumps, they greatly aided the people in traveling and in hauling their products. One of these roads ran from Madisonville, opposite New Orleans on Lake Pontchartrain, to Natchez. Two roads ran to Texas. One of these, sometimes called the Texas Road, went west from Vidalia through Alexandria and Natchitoches. The other, called the Nolan Road, went westward from Alexandria. Other shorter roads followed the rivers and streams or cut across the country to various towns and villages.

Mail service was irregular, at first being carried by men on horseback and later by stagecoaches. Advertisements in the newspapers or handbills usually announced the departure of the mail. In 1808, for example, it was announced: "An express will leave this office for Natchitoches (via Lafourche) on Thursday next, the 16th inst. at 8 o'clock A.M. The citizens are requested to have their letters in the Post-Office on Wednesday next at Sun set, at which time the mail will close. Post Office, New Orleans, March 7, 1808." By the end of the territorial period mail routes had been established throughout Louisiana.

Growth of Culture. Just before the United States took possession of Louisiana, President Jefferson sent a description of Louisiana to Congress. In it he said: "There are no colleges, and but one public school, which is in New Orleans." He proceeded to say that there were only a few private schools, where the pupils were taught only in the Spanish language. He said that not more than half the people could read and write and that not more than two hundred could do it well. But he explained that the Louisianians were "endowed with a natural genius" and that they had "an uncommon facility of learning whatever they undertake."

The Louisiana Creoles, however, did not favor public education. Most of them were Catholic and they preferred schools operated by their church. They did not agree with the American ideal of the separation of Church and State, so public education made little progress during the territorial period.

Governor Claiborne believed in public education, for he saw that the private schools had not educated a large enough percentage of the people. He said that there should be "a school in every neighborhood" and that it should be supported by public tax money. In 1805 an act was approved which provided for a system of secondary schools, and the next year a parish school system was authorized. In 1811 money was appropriated to each of the parishes for the purpose of organizing a public school, but by 1812 only three schools were in operation. Many years passed before public education became a reality in Louisiana.

The College of Orleans was authorized in 1805 and began operation a short time later. It was not really a college, as there were few courses of college grade. Boys were enrolled at the age of seven as "boarders" or as "day scholars." The historian Charles Gayarré has given a fascinating account of his education at the college and some good descriptions of the people there. Bruno was the Negro servant who at six o'clock every morning handed to each boy his breakfast of a cup of coffee and a piece of dry bread. Vincent, the doorkeeper, had a crooked neck and a doleful face. Marengo, the cook, was ugly and ferocious in appearance.

The first newspaper of which there are copies still in existence, *Le Moniteur de la Louisiane,* had been established during the late years of the Spanish period. The second newspaper was *Le Télé-*

graphe, founded in 1803. *La Lanterne Magique (The Magic Lantern)* began publication in 1808 but lasted hardly a year. Printed in both French and English, it criticized the newly established American government. The first English-language newspaper was the *Louisiana Gazette,* which began publication in 1804 and had for its motto "American Commerce and Freedom."

Amateur theatrical performances had been given in Louisiana during the Spanish period, but it was not long after the arrival of the Americans that theatrical societies and several small theaters were established. Plays and various other forms of entertainment were presented infrequently, many of them for charitable purposes. In 1812, for example, the *Louisiana Gazette* announced the presentation of a play titled *The Weathercock.* Box seats cost $1.50, while seats in the pit and the gallery were $1.00. The doors opened at 5 P.M. with the "curtains positively to rise at 6 o'clock."

Social Life. Social life continued much as it had during the French and Spanish colonial periods, for the Creoles loved social gatherings and entertainments of all kinds. They particularly loved their balls and for a short period believed that the Americans would stop them. But Governor Claiborne announced that the balls would continue and so the Creoles were happy. There were some problems, however, for the Americans wanted American music, while the Creoles wanted French or Spanish music. It soon became the custom for the musicians to alternate "Hail Columbia" with Creole songs, and after each number the Americans would yell, "Hurrah for the United States," while the Creoles would yell, "Vive la République."

Louisiana Admitted as a State. Before Louisiana was purchased, President Jefferson had written to a friend telling of his plans for Louisiana. "Our policy will be, to form New Orleans, and the country on both sides of it on the Gulf of Mexico, into a state." This became the official American policy toward Louisiana.

In February, 1811, President Madison signed a bill which gave the Louisianians the authority to hold a convention to draw up a state constitution. The election for membership in this convention was held and the convention met in November at Tremonlet's

Coffee House in New Orleans to draft the constitution. The new state constitution was approved by Congress on April 18, 1812.

Many of the newly arrived Americans in Louisiana hoped that the new state would be named after Thomas Jefferson. But Louis de Blanc de St. Denis, a member of the convention from Atakapas, said that if this were done he would "arm himself with a barrel of powder and blow up the convention." Nothing further was said about the matter.

William C. C. Claiborne was elected Governor and Louisiana was admitted into the United States as the eighteenth state on April 30, 1812, the ninth anniversary of the Louisiana Purchase.

16. LOUISIANA AND THE WAR OF 1812

The War of 1812. Thirty-two days after Louisiana was admitted into the Union as a state, President James Madison recommended that the Congress of the United States declare war against Great Britain. Congress debated the question for a little over two weeks; then, on June 18, the act declaring war was passed and signed by the President.

England had not treated the young Republic as an equal nation after the American Revolution. Her ships stopped American merchantmen on the high seas and took American sailors from them. She kept military posts on American soil near the Great Lakes, blockaded American ports, and urged the Indians to make war upon the western settlers. She hindered American trade with France and other European countries. On the other hand, many Americans, who were called War Hawks and who were interested in the development of western lands and in securing Canada for the United States, wanted a war with England.

At this time the United States was not prepared to fight a war. The country had only a small army. The people were not unified, for many citizens of New England and New York opposed the war. The national treasury did not have enough money to furnish the necessary funds.

The war on land went against the United States. General Isaac

Hull surrendered Detroit, and the garrison at Fort Dearborn (Chicago) was massacred when it tried to evacuate the fort. An attempt to invade Canada near Niagara Falls failed, as did the attempt to capture Montreal. In 1814 the British invaded the Chesapeake Bay region and captured Washington, D. C., where they burned the capitol, the White House, and many other buildings.

It was a far different story on the sea. The American navy was young and its ships small, but the ships were fast and the seamen could fire their cannon with deadly accuracy. During the early months of the war the navy won many victories and captured many British ships.

Louisiana and the War. Soon after the declaration of war, Governor Claiborne reorganized the Louisiana state militia. He traveled over the state getting better acquainted with the Creoles and urging their loyalty to the United States. It was not long before the people of Louisiana began to strengthen the militia companies for the defense of their state.

The British blockaded the mouth of the Mississippi River with two warships, which prevented merchant vessels from entering or leaving the port of New Orleans.

Encouraged by the Spanish and British, some of the Southern Indians took the warpath. General Andrew Jackson of Tennessee marched south with a small army to punish them and later occupied Mobile.

British agents attempted to secure the co-operation of the privateers who lived at Barataria. They proposed that Jean Laffite and his men join the British, but Laffite refused and sent their messages to Governor Claiborne. The British sent a military force to Pensacola and later attacked Jackson at Mobile. They landed marines and attacked Fort Bowyer from the rear while their fleet bombarded it from the bay, but the attack failed, and the British lost over 230 men while Jackson lost less than 10. A short time later Jackson captured Pensacola.

British Plan to Attack New Orleans. New Orleans was the key to the entire Mississippi Valley, and if the British could capture the city they would gain control of the entire area. Vast quantities of products of all kinds, particularly cotton, sugar, and tobacco, would be taken. Furthermore, the British might then move northward up the Mississippi and occupy Mississippi Territory and the states of Kentucky and Tennessee. They might even add the territories further up the river to the British Empire. It was a prize worth taking, and the British anticipated little opposition from the Americans and none from the French and Spanish Creoles of Louisiana, who were not expected to fight.

In August, 1814, Colonel Edward Nicolls, the Commander of His Britannic Majesty's forces in the Floridas, issued a proclamation to the "NATIVES OF LOUISIANA." He offered to "liberate" the soil of Louisiana from the "faithless, imbecile government" of the United States. He would stop this "unjust and unnatural" war which Britain was fighting against "those brawlers for liberty." But most Louisianians did not believe Colonel Nicolls, and continued with preparations to defend their state.

The British Expedition. During the late summer and early fall of 1814 the British concentrated a large fleet and a strong army at the island of Jamaica in the West Indies. This fleet of over fifty ships was commanded by Vice-Admiral Sir Alexander Cochrane, while the army of about ten thousand soldiers was led by General Sir Edward Pakenham. The expedition sailed from Jamaica in November, 1814, and the British were very confident of victory. A short time later in London, Lord Castlereagh wrote: "I expect at this moment that . . . we are in possession of New Orleans . . . and that the Americans are now little better than prisoners in their own country."

The British fleet first sailed to Pensacola. One of the Americans there immediately warned Master Commandant Daniel Patterson, who commanded a small American fleet then lying in Lake Borgne, that the British had arrived. He wrote that the object of the British was to capture New Orleans and that they had a strong fleet and a large and well-equipped army.

General Jackson started for New Orleans late in November with only a few men, moving along the Gulf Coast in order that he might "have a view of the points at which the enemy might effect a landing." He arrived at New Orleans on December 1.

Difficulty of Defending New Orleans. The American troops were widely scattered, some were in Alabama, some were in Mississippi, and a small detachment was stationed at Baton Rouge. A strong division of Tennessee militia was on the march and was expected to arrive at New Orleans about December 20. Another group of Kentucky militia would arrive about January 1. Meantime, the British fleet and army were sailing toward New Orleans.

Few preparations had been made for the defense of New Orleans. The Legislature had done very little and its members were quarreling among themselves. Some of the French Creoles had shown little enthusiasm and were distrustful of Jackson. They did not want to join the state militia, swore that they were Frenchmen not Americans, and claimed the protection of the French Consul at New Orleans. There were only small stores of weapons, powder, bullets, and the other supplies of war.

Jackson and Claiborne Work Together. General Jackson immediately went to work. At this time he was in his late forties, tall, lean, and straight of figure. His face was wrinkled and seamed; heavy brows shaded his bright eyes; his iron-gray hair bristled over his head. Although he was exhausted by exposure and suffering from malaria, his face revealed his restless energy, his strong sense of purpose, and his stern patriotic devotion. He dressed in a small leather cap, a short blue coat, well-worn pants, and frayed, high boots. At first glance he was not imposing to the well-dressed, debonair Creoles, but they soon found out that he was a man of iron.

Jackson inspected Fort St. Philip below New Orleans and the shores of Lake Pontchartrain and Chef Menteur. He rapidly trained the militia units which Governor Claiborne had mobilized, fortified the banks of the Mississippi just below New Orleans, and erected an artillery battery at the Rigolets and another at the mouth of Bayou St. John. Gangs of slaves built earthworks near the city. Jackson and Claiborne accepted the services of the Baratarians and pledged assistance in securing pardons for their past offenses against the government. Henry Miller Shreve, who had come down from Pennsylvania with the steamboat *Enterprize,* began to bring supplies to New Orleans from points up the Mississippi.

From Fortier, *A History of Louisiana*

General Andrew Jackson

Governor Claiborne and General Jackson did their work well. The majority of the people enthusiastically began to support the preparations for the defense of the state. The militia units drilled with grim purpose. One aged Louisiana mother wrote to the Governor: "My four sons are at the front with Andrew Jackson. I regret having no others to offer my country; I am bent under the load of years, but, if my services in caring for the wounded should be thought useful, command me, and in spite of age and distance I shall hasten to New Orleans." Louisianians soon felt more confident that their state could be defended.

But General Jackson was in a dilemma. Which approach to New Orleans would the British use? Would they approach from Barataria? Would they come up the Mississippi? Would they move by way of the Rigolets and Chef Menteur and then over high ground to the city? It was not long before Jackson knew the answer.

The Battle of Lake Borgne. On December 10 the British fleet sighted North Chandeleur Island, rounded the northern tip, and anchored in the channel between Cat and Ship islands. Here it was discovered by Lieutenant Thomas Ap Catesby Jones, who commanded six small American gunboats with 182 men. Three days later, the British ships sailed into Lake Borgne. The little American fleet stood fast, awaiting them.

The American ships were small and could sail in shallow water, where the large British ships could not follow them. The British therefore sent a squadron of small sloops of war with nearly twelve hundred men against Lieutenant Jones and his little fleet.

The American schooner *Sea Horse* was set on fire and blown up, and the rest of the ships withdrew further westward. Then the wind died and all the vessels became becalmed.

On December 14, 1814, the Battle of Lake Borgne was fought. It began about eleven o'clock in the morning. The British transferred their sailors and marines to boats and barges rowed by oarsmen, which were more maneuverable than the American ships. The American ship *Alligator* was taken; the other vessels fought on, but after a desperate fight they, too, were captured. The British lost about one hundred and seventy-five killed and wounded while the Americans lost six killed and thirty-five wounded.

The Battle of Lake Borgne gave the British control of Lake Borgne but it also delayed their advance upon New Orleans. This gave time for reinforcements to arrive there and for General Jackson to complete his plans for the defense of the city.

The Night Battle of December 23. After the Battle of Lake Borgne the British reorganized their fleet and army at Pea Island, near the mouth of Pearl River. On December 22 about sixteen hundred men, commanded by Colonel William Thornton, rowed across Lake Borgne in barges and the next morning landed at the mouth of Bayou Bienvenu. Thornton sent a detachment up bayous Bienvenu and Laurier about five miles to the mouth of Bayou

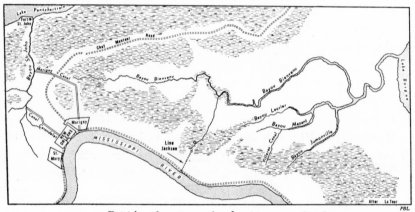

British   Invasion   of   Louisiana   1814-1815

Mazant, and then up this bayou about two miles to the Villeré Canal. The British followed the canal to the Villeré plantation, but Major Gabriel Villeré escaped to New Orleans to warn General Jackson that the British had landed.

The British raised the Union Jack from the treetops at the Villeré plantation, while their bands played "God Save the King." They distributed proclamations throughout the area, giving reasons why the people should withdraw their allegiance to the United States and join the British.

Jackson immediately ordered the American forces in New Orleans to gather at Fort St. Charles and then to march down the river about six miles to a place which had been selected by Major Arsene Latour.

As the Cathedral clock struck three, the American troops poured along the streets of the Vieux Carré singing "Yankee Doodle," the "Marseillaise," and other songs. Women and children crowded the balconies waving their hands while the old men stood on the banquettes waving their hats.

The troops rapidly assembled: the Bayou Sara Mounted Riflemen, Beale's Rifles in their blue hunting shirts, the free colored troops. The five companies of the Bataillon d'Orléans, which had been stationed at the old Spanish fort out on Lake Pontchartrain, came panting in, after a run of six and a half miles. Major Thomas Hinds's daredevil Mississippi Dragoons followed. After them rode Colonel John Coffee and his Tennessee-Cavalry "dirty shirts," clad in their home-dyed, copper-colored pants, woolen hunting shirts, and coonskin caps, and wearing long knives and tomahawks stuck in their belts. A band of about a hundred Choctaw Indians in their war paint came next, and the regular troops followed. Jackson swung his hat and the army marched off at the double-quick down the river.

The Americans soon reached the place selected by Latour. It was a narrow strip of solid ground about 1,500 yards wide between the Mississippi and the swamp. Across it was an abandoned drainage canal which marked the boundary of the Chalmette and Rodriguez plantations. The soldiers immediately began to throw up a breastwork on the New Orleans side of the canal.

Jackson decided to attack the British, who lay about two miles farther on, that night, saying, "By the Eternal, they shall not sleep on our soil!"

The Americans struck the British outposts at eight o'clock and in a furious attack drove them back. The British became confused and gathered in small groups, where the Americans attacked them with gun-butts, knives, and even fists. At four o'clock the next morning Jackson withdrew to his line of breastworks.

The British lost over 250, killed, wounded and missing, while the American loss was slightly over 200. Jackson had saved New Orleans from immediate capture by the British, but the danger was not yet past, for the enemy was still landing troops.

Jean Laffite, from an old drawing

The Grand Reconnaissance. For five days the British did not attack. Meanwhile, both armies celebrated Christmas and the British soldiers rejoiced at the arrival of their commander, General Sir Edward Pakenham. He would lead them to victory against the Americans, who were lying so smugly behind their earthworks.

On the morning of December 28, Pakenham ordered his troops forward to feel out the American defenses and if possible to pierce their line and move on toward New Orleans. The British advanced in solid columns, supported by their artillery. The Americans had fewer cannon than the enemy, but they had been strengthened only a few hours earlier by the arrival of "Capitaine" Dominique You, Oncle Beluche, and the rest of Jean Laffite's Baratarians. The Baratarians were excellent artillerists.

The British attack failed due to the accurate fire of the American riflemen and artillerists. One of the Englishmen wrote that "the Americans are excellent marksmen as well with artillery as with rifles," and that after the battle the English soldiers felt "both shame and indignation."

Pakenham decided to strengthen his batteries of artillery with naval guns from the fleet before attacking the Americans again.

The Artillery Battle of New Year's Day. The morning of New Year's Day was foggy and, believing that the British would not attack, the Creoles asked to have a grand review of the army. Jackson consented, and the bands began to play and the Americans to parade up and down across the open field. Then the fog lifted and a blast from twenty-four British heavy cannon broke over the line. All was confusion as the Americans ran back to their breastworks to man their fifteen guns.

A British battery centered its fire against Dominique You and the Baratarians who were manning one battery. You was wounded in the arm by a cannon shot, but he had the arm bandaged, and then yelled, "I will pay them for that!" Soon one of his guns knocked to pieces the carriage of the gun which had wounded him. The fighting had begun about eight o'clock in the morning. It lasted until about one in the afternoon, when the British artillerists abandoned their guns. One of their junior officers wrote: "Never was any failure more remarkable. . . . The sun, as if ashamed to shine upon our disgrace, was slow of making its appearance. . . . Our batteries were all silenced. The American works, on the other hand, remained as little injured as ever, and we were completely foiled."

The Battle of New Orleans. For a week the British landed and moved up reinforcements from their fleet, while Jackson strengthened the American earthworks, and two thousand Kentuckians arrived to reinforce the American army. Three regiments of the

Louisiana Militia were stationed just north of New Orleans to guard against a flanking movement by the British. General David Morgan was ordered to cross the Mississippi with about 850 men and nine cannon to protect that side of the river.

So far the British attacks had failed. The American soldiers had defeated them in the battles of December 23 and December 28, and the American artillery had won an important victory in the battle of January 1. Pakenham had about 5,300 men to attack

From Dimitry, *History and Geography of Louisiana*

The Battle of New Orleans

Jackson's line, over 1,200 to cross the river to attack Morgan, and about 1,200 men to hold in reserve. Jackson had about 3,000 men on his line of earthworks, with about 1,000 in reserve. Morgan had about 850 men on the other side of the Mississippi. Pakenham had less than a dozen cannon in fireable condition, while Jackson now had twelve guns behind his line and nine with Morgan across the river which could help cover the area near the river in front of Jackson.

After some hesitation Pakenham finally decided to attack Jackson and Morgan at the same time. The main attack would, of course, be against Jackson. One British division would attack Jackson along the river, while the main attack would be against the left side of Jackson's line. Pakenham foresaw the risk of making a frontal attack upon the American line, but Admiral Cochrane said, sarcastically: "If the army shrinks from the task, I will fetch the sailors and marines from the fleet, and with them storm the American lines and march to the city. The soldiers can then bring up the baggage."

The citizens of New Orleans were fearful during that Saturday night of January 7, 1815. The morning of January 8 broke with a heavy fog, and about six o'clock the British columns moved forward in solid ranks. The American batteries opened fire. On the British came, advancing to within 150 yards of the American line, then 100 yards. At this point the American riflemen opened fire, not firing in volleys, but each man firing when he had reloaded his gun. The advancing British soldiers fell by the hundreds. Only a few ever reached the American breastworks. General Sir Samuel Gibbs was mortally wounded; General John Keane was severely wounded; General Pakenham was killed. General John Lambert finally stopped the fight—slightly more than an hour after it had started.

As one American historian has described this moment: "From the field everywhere shattered and depleted regiments were now retreating in disorder. The proud British army was vanquished; its bugles silenced; its colors trampled in the earth; its guns unable to reply." The blood-soaked Chalmette Plain was covered with dead and wounded British soldiers.

The British lost over two thousand killed, wounded, and missing. The Americans had only seventy-one casualties, of whom only six were killed.

As soon as victory was assured, the Americans broke into cheers while Jackson rode along the line and congratulated his men. The New Orleans and Plauche bands, which had played throughout the battle, continued their playing of martial music. In New Orleans the church bells rang while the people ran and danced in the streets. The celebrations continued for some days. One jubilant American officer, writing to a friend, ended his account of the battle with a brief statement that the body of General Pakenham was put into a hogshead of rum and "sent home to England in good spirits."

After the Battle. As soon as the fighting had stopped at the Battle of New Orleans, Jackson ordered some of his troops forward to assist in burying the dead and caring for the wounded. About four hundred of the wounded were not in condition to be moved far, so they were brought to New Orleans where special hospitals had been prepared for them.

The day following the Battle of New Orleans, the British fleet sailed up the Mississippi and began a nine-day bombardment of Fort St. Philip, but that attack failed also.

January 23 was declared a day of prayer and thanksgiving and impressive ceremonies were held at the Cathedral. That night there was a grand ball. One European visitor described General Jackson and his wife: "To see these two figures, the general a long, haggard man, with limbs like a skeleton, and *Madame la Générale,* a short fat dumpling, bobbing opposite each other . . . was very remarkable."

On February 13, Admiral Cochrane wrote Jackson that he had received the news of the Treaty of Ghent, which ended the war with Great Britain. Nine days later, this news was confirmed.

But it was not until March 17 that the British fleet sailed away from the shores of Louisiana.

PART V

ANTE BELLUM LOUISIANA

17. A HALF CENTURY OF LOUISIANA GOVERNMENT (1812–1861)

The First Constitution. The convention had drafted a constitution for the soon-to-be state of Louisiana in the fall of 1811. It was approved the following April, and on April 30, 1812, Louisiana was admitted to statehood in the American Union.

The first constitution was modeled generally after the Kentucky constitution of 1799, which at that time was considered one of the most democratic.

The Governor was to be elected by the Legislature every four years from the two highest popular-vote candidates. He was required to be thirty-five years of age, a citizen of the United States, a resident of Louisiana for six years, and to own at least $5,000 worth of property. No minister of any religious group was eligible for the office. The Governor had authority to appoint the Secretary of State and the Attorney General with the consent of the Senate, and the State Treasurer with the consent of both legislative houses. He was required to tour the state once every two years to inform himself of "the general condition of the country."

The two-house legislature was called the General Assembly. Members of the Senate were elected for a four-year term, while those of the House of Representatives were elected for only two years. Senators must have property valued at $1,000 while Representatives were required to own only $500 worth of property.

The judiciary power was vested in a Supreme Court, having from three to five judges who were appointed by the Governor and confirmed by the Senate. The court was to hold its sessions at New Orleans and Opelousas.

163

Claiborne the First Governor. Although Claiborne had served as territorial Governor, his election to the first state governorship was not expected. He had been unpopular with the Creoles, and the period of his territorial governorship had been filled with dissatisfaction and controversy. Jacques Villeré, the favorite of the Creoles, was nominated, and it was thought he would win, but when the votes were counted it was found that enough Creoles had voted for Claiborne to secure his election. The good work which he had performed during his nine years as territorial Governor had earned their confidence.

No Governor had to solve more problems, face more opposition, make more important decisions, or meet more threatening dangers than did Governor Claiborne. He was distrusted by many of the Creoles, some of whom refused to serve in the Legislature. The Indians of northwest Louisiana caused trouble, and it was difficult to collect national, state, and local taxes. The pirates and privateers of Barataria openly smuggled all kinds of goods into the state, and after the declaration of war, the British blockaded the mouth of the Mississippi. Many Creoles would not support the state militia, and numbers of the newly arrived Americans refused to join the various units if it required leaving Louisiana. The New Orleans militia units would not be mustered into the service of the United States.

One of the most important of Claiborne's tasks was that of educating the Creoles in self-government, in which they had had comparatively little experience during the territorial period. Many of them did not care for politics, but they learned rapidly and by 1816 were becoming accustomed to taking part in state government.

Claiborne tackled these problems with justice and common sense, while meeting the crisis of the British invasion with calm assurance. In his last message to the people as Governor he paid tribute to their "generous character," realizing that he had won the affection of both Creole and American. In 1816 he was elected United States Senator, but he died the following year. Jacques Villeré called him "one of our best patriots, . . . distinguished for his virtues and talents." Louisianians generally praised his qualities of leadership and acclaimed him one of the most important leaders "in what was then the great Southwest."

National Party Politics in Louisiana. Louisianians were not much interested in national politics during the first years of statehood. While the majority of them were Jeffersonian Republicans rather than Federalists, they were not well enough acquainted with national party leaders to become excited during presidential campaigns.

After 1820, Louisiana generally supported Henry Clay or Andrew Jackson. Clay advocated a protective tariff which helped the sugar industry, while Jackson was very popular because of his victory at New Orleans.

After 1830, Louisianians became much more interested in national politics, and though the majority of them favored the Democratic Party in national elections, the Whigs won numerous local and a few state elections. Occasionally the Governor would be a member of one party while the majority of the members of the state Legislature would belong to the other. After the death of the Whig Party in the early 1850's the American, or "Know-Nothing," Party became strong for a time, but most of the elections continued to be won by the Democrats.

While most presidential elections were comparatively quiet, a few caused much excitement. During the election of 1844, for example, young Robert Patrick of Clinton recalled that "there were barbecues, public speeches made by the leaders, torch light processions, glee clubs, and all that sort of thing." During General Zachary Taylor's campaign in 1848 the people sang: "Old Zack, he's on the track, and we're at his back."

During the period several outstanding political leaders were elected to Congress to represent Louisiana. Alexander Porter, Edward Livingston, Pierre Soulé, John Slidell, and Judah P. Benjamin served ably in the Senate and were statesmen of national importance.

Governors and State Politics. Until the election of 1834 the most important issue in state elections for Governor was whether the candidate was "Creole" or "American." During this early period the Americans elected William C. C. Claiborne, Thomas Bolling Robertson, and Henry Johnson, while the Creoles elected Jacques Villeré, Pierre Derbigny, and A. B. Roman.

From *Harper's Magazine*

General Zachary Taylor at his home in Baton Rouge

After 1834 party politics became more important. The Whig Party elected governors in 1834 and 1838, when Edward D. White and A. B. Roman won the elections, but after this all the governors were Democrats: Alexandre Mouton, Isaac Johnson, Joseph Walker, Paul O. Hebert, Robert C. Wickliffe, and Thomas O.

Moore. Some of them, however, were elected by close majorities. Throughout the period many Americans believed that the Creoles were "constitutionally opposed to development and progress." The Creoles generally were conservative and, in turn, considered the Americans to be somewhat radical in their political ideas.

The great majority of the officeholders and legislators were either Creole or American, but there were also a few Italians and Englishmen plus, as one man wrote, "here and there a Scotchman, with his boat-shaped head and hard common sense."

Campaigns for state offices were usually hard fought, the candidates attracting much attention as they traveled about the state. Frequently they wrote stories or songs about their rivals. During the election of 1849, for example, the opponent of Joseph Walker sang a song about him to the tune of "Old Uncle Ned," the chorus of which ran:

> Take off the saddle from his back,
> Pull down the fodder from his rack;
> There is no more run in poor old Joe—
> Turn him out to grass and let him go.

Sometimes the legislators wrote poetry about each other. Bernard Marigny was very good at this, and one day he wrote a poem against several members, one of whom came back with the following:

> When you are sleeping with the dead,
> The spars we've had I'll not forget;
> A warmer heart, or weaker head,
> On earth, I'll own, I never met.

Marigny had had enough, and coming to this legislator's desk, he said: "Suppose you write no more poetry. I shall stop." And the two men remained friends.

Occasionally legislators quarreled, and challenged each other to duel. One of these challenges ended humorously. During the legislative session of 1817 the hot-tempered Bernard Marigny, became angry at the remarks of James Humble, by trade a black-smith, and challenged him. Humble was a giant nearly seven feet in height, while Marigny was a short, thin man. Humble did not want to fight—"I know nothing of this duelling business." His friends argued that no gentleman could refuse a challenge. "But

I'm not a gentleman," Humble insisted, "I'm only a blacksmith." Finally Humble gave in but insisted on his own terms: "The duel shall take place in Lake Pontchartrain in six feet of water, sledge-hammers to be used as weapons." Marigny's friends laughingly told him that he would have to fight standing on a box, but Marigny declared that it was impossible to fight a man with such a sense of humor.

Major Political Issues. During the early years of statehood governors Claiborne and Villeré were kept busy with many different types of problems. Taxation, the Choctaw and Caddo Indians, smuggling along the Gulf Coast, financial distress caused by the War of 1812, and relations between the Americans and Creoles all demanded their attention. It took hard work to get the government of the state running on a sound basis.

After 1820 the major political issues centered round more common matters of state government and the passage of legislation for economic and cultural betterment.

Louisiana's first civil code had been enacted during the territorial period and generally it followed the principles of French and Spanish law. A new civil code was compiled in 1825, and a code of criminal law adopted in 1828.

Throughout the period laws were passed regulating banks and banking and the construction and maintenance of roads, bridges, ferries, and levees. Late in the period, laws were needed for controlling railroads and telegraph lines, which were just beginning to be built. Education required much legislation, as also did the protection of the public health from epidemics and ordinary diseases.

The legislators had considerable trouble with the problem of language, for some of them spoke only English and others spoke only French. Interpreters were constantly needed and the laws of the state had to be published in both languages.

Moving of the State Capital. The first state capital was located at New Orleans, which had been the seat of the territorial government, but in 1825, after considerable debate, the legislature voted to move the capital to Donaldsonville. There had been much agitation for some years previously to move it from New Orleans, which, according to one newspaper correspondent, was a "city so justly compared to a modern Sodom" and a bad influence upon the legislators.

The Legislature voted $30,000 to build the new "statehouse," fifteen feet wide by one hundred feet long, at Donaldsonville, and here the Legislature met in 1830. But the legislators were "thoroughly disgusted" with the "unsightly and badly constructed" capitol and with its accommodations and, "under the shallow pre-

Baton Rouge Chamber of Commerce

The Old State Capitol at Baton Rouge

text that the roof was leaky, abandoned the place for good and all." The capital was moved back to New Orleans.

However, the agitation to move the capital away from New Orleans continued. In 1846 an act was passed moving it to Baton Rouge and $100,000 was appropriated for a statehouse. James H. Dakin, a noted New Orleans architect, drew the plans and became the contractor. The building was completed by 1850 and the seat of government officially moved when Governor Joseph Walker was inaugurated. The capital remained at Baton Rouge until it was moved to Opelousas during the Civil War.

The Constitutions of 1845 and 1852. The Constitution of 1812 remained in effect for thirty-three years, but by the early 1840's the people realized that the old document was out of date. Furthermore, the spirit of democracy was growing, and its conservative provisions regarding the privileges of the landowner class and the long terms of office caused many political leaders to advocate the adoption of a new constitution. The constitutional convention met in two sessions, one at Jackson during the late summer of 1844, and the other at New Orleans early the next year.

The spirit of the new constitution is well illustrated by a comparison of the two preambles. That of 1812 began "We the representatives of the people," while that of 1845 began "We the people of Louisiana." The property qualifications for voting or holding office were abolished, and general elections had to be "completed in one day" in contrast to the old custom of taking several days for an election. The Governor lost many of his appointive powers, and the office of Lieutenant Governor was created. Parish coroners and sheriffs were to be elected by the people. The office of a State Superintendent of Public Education was created, and the legislature was directed to "establish free public schools throughout the State."

However, the Constitution of 1845 did not satisfy all the citizens, many of whom believed that it should have been even more democratic. A new constitutional convention met at Baton Rouge in July, 1852, and drafted a new document.

Most of the features of the Constitution of 1845 were retained, but several new liberalizing clauses were added. Most of the state officials were made elective, state aid for public improvements was authorized, and the Governor's powers were reduced.

Louisiana and International Problems. During the ante bellum period there were many international problems in which Louisiana was involved. These included piracy on the lower Mississippi and the Gulf of Mexico, filibustering expeditions against various Spanish colonies and Latin-American countries, the western boundary dispute, the Texas War for Independence, and the war with Mexico.

After the War of 1812 some of the Baratarians continued to capture and rob ships in the Gulf of Mexico, and from time to time pirates captured river boats along the lower Mississippi. By the middle of the 1820's, with the aid of the United States government, they were finally driven from Louisiana.

Throughout the period many expeditions were organized in Louisiana to assist the Latin-American people in winning their independence from Spain or to fight in rebellions against existing governments. These were called filibustering expeditions. Prior to the War of 1812, the headquarters of these movements had been Turpin's Coffee House on Marigny Street in New Orleans. Later they plotted at Maspero's Exchange on Chartres Street. By the 1830's, they were meeting at Banks' Arcade on Magazine Street where they recruited soldiers for their expeditions. Dr. James Long led expeditions to Texas in 1819 and 1821, but each was defeated. General Narciso Lopez led a small body of men to Cuba in 1851, but the group was soon scattered. The leaders were captured and shot, and Lopez was garroted. In 1855, William Walker invaded Nicaragua and caused himself to be elected president, but was later defeated, captured, and finally shot.

The Louisiana Purchase Treaty of 1803 had not definitely fixed the western boundary of Louisiana. The Americans claimed eastern Texas and the Spanish claimed the western part of Louisiana. During the territorial period and the early years of statehood the area just east of the Sabine River was inhabited by large numbers of adventurers and fugitives from justice. The Sabine Strip, as this region was called, became noted for its "robberies, murders, and other crimes of an infamous and astounding character." The Florida Purchase Treaty of 1819 finally fixed the boundary at the Sabine River, and in 1823 the United States built Fort Jesup, a few miles northeast of present-day Many. The army soon brought law and order to the Sabine Strip, and Fort Jesup remained an important military post until the late 1840's.

After the Texas War for Independence began in 1835 the New Orleans *Bee* headlined an article: "AMERICANS TO THE RESCUE!" Hundreds of Louisianians joined military companies to fight for Texas or gave money and supplies. Banks' Arcade and the Rising Sun Tavern on Old Levee Street were the headquarters of those who wished to aid the Lone Star Republic. After the war had been won Louisianians recited:

On San Jacinto's bloody field
Our drums and trumpets loudly pealed
And bade a haughty tyrant yield
To Texas Chivalry.

Ten years later the Mexican War began. Soon six regiments of some six thousand volunteers had been equipped by the state and were on their way to join General Zachary Taylor in southern Texas, but these troops had enlisted for only three months and they were soon recalled by the federal government. This action made many Louisianians angry, and it was characterized by the *Picayune* as "the supercilious insolence of an incompetent Secretary of War." Later many citizens organized or joined military units and fought in Mexico. One newspaper editor simply closed his printing shop and put the following sign on the door: "I voted for Texas. I have gone to help do the fighting."

Parish, City, and Town Governmental Problems. During this period the parish, city, and town officials faced many of the ordinary problems of local government. The parish judge was the chief executive officer of the parish and he had civil, criminal, and police jurisdiction. The Police Jury was the parish legislative body and also had some executive functions. The cities and towns had a mayor, a recorder, a council of aldermen, a clerk, a treasurer and other minor officials. The city court and justices of the peace handled small crimes. In 1836 New Orleans was divided into three municipalities, but in 1852 they were consolidated into one city again.

Taxes were low during this period. The total tax levy for West Feliciana Parish in 1850, for example, was only $7,000, and five years later the parish spent only a little over $11,000, which included the burial of paupers, the care of the poor, and the expenses of the new courthouse.

Some of the parish and town regulations seem out of place today or at least a bit odd. In 1828 no one was allowed to have more than three dogs in Marksville. In 1843 anyone in Sabine Parish who was "aggrieved" by a wild or ungovernable horse, cow, or hog, could make a complaint to the nearest justice of the peace. Three years later the Police Jury declared a bounty of two dollars for every wolf killed. In 1848 the Methodist and Baptist churches were rented for use as a courthouse and as a jury room. In 1851 in West Feliciana Parish it became unlawful to race horses on the public roads. In 1852 the Avoyelles Parish Police Jury prohibited citizens from leaving "dead animals in the bayou in front of one's residence more than 24 hours."

During those years, however, the people of Louisiana believed that the government which governed least was the best government. The Legislature, the Police Juries, and the city councils passed only those laws and regulations which they believed necessary to the well-being and happiness of the citizens.

18. ECONOMIC LIFE DURING THE ANTE BELLUM PERIOD

Growth of Population. Louisiana's population grew steadily and rapidly during the years between 1812 and 1860. After the War of 1812 a constant stream of settlers came from the older states of the South and many arrived from the Middle Atlantic and New England sections. Foreigners landed at New Orleans, some of whom settled permanently in the state. The Germans and Irish were the most important immigrant groups, but there were also smaller numbers of people from other countries. By 1850 approximately one-fourth of Louisiana's total population was foreign born. Thousands of Negro slaves were brought in from the older states and a few were smuggled from Africa or the West Indies. Sizable numbers of Free Negroes from other states came to Louisiana until 1840, but after this the number entering decreased to comparatively few.

In 1812, Louisiana's total population had been slightly over 80,000; in 1820 it totaled over 200,000; by 1840 it had grown to over 250,000; and by 1860 it had topped 700,000. Throughout the period to the 1850's the Negro population outnumbered the white, the number of slaves growing from nearly 40,000 in 1812 to over 330,000 in 1860. The number of Free Negroes increased from about 8,000 in 1812 to nearly 19,000 in 1860.

The majority of the Free-Negro group were mulattoes and they outnumbered the pure Negroes by about four to one. Most of them

lived in the southern part of the state, though there were many along
the Mississippi, the Red, and other rivers and bayous. The majority
of them were common laborers, but many were skilled in various
trades or were farmers and planters. A few were businessmen.

In 1860 nearly 21,000 Louisianians owned slaves, but over half
of this number possessed 5 slaves or less. Nearly 4,500 slaveowners had from 6 to 10 slaves and slightly over 2,600 owned
from 11 to 20 slaves. Almost 1,800 people owned from 21 to 50
slaves and slightly over 700 owned from 51 to 100 slaves. Only
274 people owned from 101 to 200 slaves and only 36 owned from
201 to 300. Six planters owned between 300 and 500 slaves and
four planters owned between 500 and 1,000 slaves. Although few
birth records were kept, the great majority of the slaves were
born in the United States. The others had been born in Africa
or the West Indies.

Louisiana Parishes
1860

Growth of Cities and Towns. The population of New Orleans grew steadily, and from a city of about 18,000 in 1812, it grew to over 100,000 in 1840, and to nearly 170,000 in 1860. There were obvious reasons for the growth of New Orleans. It was the largest trading and business center of the lower Mississippi Valley and was the most important seaport on the entire Gulf Coast. A cosmopolitan city inhabited by people of all nationalities, it was also a "modern" city for that time; for by the 1830's it had large hotels, city-water and gaslighting systems, and many paved streets and other improvements. It also had recreational facilities, for there were theaters where operas and plays were presented, and numerous cafes, restaurants, ballrooms, and other attractions.

Most of the major Louisiana towns were located on rivers or bayous which could be navigated by steamboats, and of the few towns not located on these streams, most were parish seats. Only Baton Rouge and Algiers, outside of Lafayette, Jefferson and Carrollton which were suburbs of New Orleans, had more than 5,000 population in 1860. The smaller towns included Shreveport with nearly 2,200; Plaquemine with over 1,600; Donaldsonville, Alexandria, and Homer with nearly 1,500; Thibodaux with nearly 1,400; and Minden with nearly 1,200. All of the other towns had less than 1,000 inhabitants.

New Orleans during the late ante bellum period, from an old print

Thus, it can be seen that in 1860 the great majority of Louisianians lived in the rural areas. These people were planters and farmers, lumbermen, herdsmen, fishermen, or hunters and trappers. Until about 1830 the great majority lived in southeast Louisiana, but after this time northern and western Louisiana began to fill up rapidly.

Agriculture. Most of the rural inhabitants of the state were farmers or planters, their holdings ranging from the small frontier-like farms with only a few acres of general food crops to large plantations which produced sugar cane, cotton, or tobacco. Most of the agricultural holdings were, however, small or large farms rather than plantations. The large plantations were located chiefly along the Mississippi or lower Red River and along the streams and bayous of southeast Louisiana.

Land values varied greatly. During the early 1850's hill lands near Natchitoches could be purchased for two dollars to six dollars an acre. Along the Red River the price of good cotton or sugar-cane land was between fifteen and thirty-five dollars an acre. Along the lower Mississippi River, Bayou Lafourche, and Bayou Teche, land prices were even higher.

Most of the ordinary farmers lived in plain, comfortable houses behind which were located barns, granaries, sheds, other outbuildings, and perhaps a slave cabin or two. They produced food crops, raised cattle, hogs, and poultry, and grew cotton or tobacco for money crops. They lived comfortable but work-filled lives. The pioneer farmers had only a few acres in cultivation, herded their livestock over the open or timbered land, lived in poor and sometimes ramshackle houses, produced few money crops, and lived hard lives.

In contrast, the planters were generally fair businessmen with ample capital, and lived in comfort and sometimes in luxury. The Tchoupitoulas Plantation, about twelve miles up the Mississippi from New Orleans, serves as a good example of the large plantation. The Soniat family had a large, two-story brick mansion, in front and on both sides of which were gardens of trees, plants, and flowers. On one side of the house was a *garçonnière* for visiting young men or travelers, and on the other side was the *pigeonnier* where doves and pigeons were raised. Behind was the kitchen, the storehouse, the slave hospital, stables, and other outbuildings. Farther to the rear was the sugarhouse and below it the overseer's house, beyond which were two long rows of brick slave cabins.

Only a man of considerable wealth could acquire, outfit, and stock a large plantation, particularly one which produced sugar. In 1830 it was reported that a 1,250-acre, 50-slave, sugar plantation in St. Martin Parish required about $90,000 capital.

Sugar production steadily increased throughout the period, for sugar-cane cultivation spread up the Mississippi north of the mouth of the Red River and up that river to the Natchitoches country. After 1830 "ribbon" cane, which was a very hardy variety, replaced the older "Creole" cane, steam-driven mills were introduced, and improvements in the manufacturing process were made. Sugar production grew from 75,000 hogsheads in 1833 to 449,000

From *Harper's Magazine*

A Louisiana sugar house

hogsheads in 1853, which was the largest amount produced before 1860.

Cotton was grown over the entire state, the least amounts being produced in the low country of south Louisiana. Until 1837 prices were high, and after a five-year depression, good prices returned and there was a constant expansion of the cotton-producing areas into north and northwest Louisiana.

Tobacco was raised in large amounts north of the Red River. Frequently planters raised both tobacco and cotton, with the two crops cultivated and harvested at alternating periods. "Perique" tobacco, a strong tobacco used for flavoring, was grown only in St. James Parish.

Corn was grown over the entire state for human as well as livestock consumption. Oats were grown in central and north Louisiana and rice in the southeastern section. Hay, truck crops, fruits, and berries were grown on most of the general farms.

Livestock raising was most important in southwest Louisiana. Here there were large ranches, very much like those of the west, where herdsmen watched over large numbers of horses, cattle, and hogs. Much of this country was open prairie, dotted here and there with patches of trees along the watercourses. One traveler who viewed it in 1816 wrote: "It is no extravagant declaration to call this one of the meadows of America." This area produced cattle, hides, tallow, beef and pork, and some cheese.

Most of the agriculturists of ante bellum Louisiana were plain "dirt" farmers, only a few of them being acquainted with "scientific" agricultural methods. But as time passed many of them subscribed to agricultural publications and organized local fairs. The Baton Rouge Agricultural Society was founded in 1827, while the Louisiana State Agricultural Society came into existence in 1833 and began to plan the establishment of a "model farm." After this farmers and planters began to buy more and better machinery, to rotate their crops in some sections, and generally to improve their methods of production. By 1860, Louisiana had one of the largest agricultural incomes in the Union.

Manufacturing. Manufacturing was of secondary interest to ante bellum Louisianians. Only about 7,500 persons were employed in manufacturing industries in 1840, whereas over 79,000 were employed in agriculture. No cotton or woolen manufacturing was reported in 1850 and only a little ten years later. By the end of the 1850's fewer than a dozen iron-casting establishments were reported, and these employed fewer than 500 persons. In 1850 the total value of all manufacturing, mining, and mechanical products was slightly over $7,000,000, and this sum had not materially increased by 1860.

There was a considerable amount of small-scale home manufacturing. During the early years, for example, most of the cottonseed was separated by hand, and this was still being done on the smaller farms in 1860. The cotton was then carded, thread spun, and the cloth made and dyed with certain plants or walnut hulls, after which the garments were sewn by hand. Other home industry included the making of hats, shoes, furniture, tools, and simple farm implements.

Banks and Banking. Louisianians needed strong banks for the financing of their agricultural and commercial economy. The planters and farmers needed long-term loans to purchase land and slaves and short-term loans to pay expenses during the few months prior to the sale of their crops. The merchants and other businessmen needed funds to finance their businesses adequately.

Louisiana banking from 1812 to 1860 may be roughly divided into four periods. The period from 1812 to the late 1820's was generally a period of sound banking. Then came a period which has been called an era of madness, for the banks overexpanded. The panic of 1837 broke, and in the last ten months of that year over 2,500 foreclosure suits were filed in Orleans Parish alone. Hundreds of farmers and planters lost their farms and plantations. Deposits in banks decreased from nearly $12,000,000 in 1836 to about $3,000,000 in 1841.

In 1842 and 1843 the state Legislature passed new banking laws which placed all financial houses under state control. Business began to revive and by 1860 Louisiana was again a very prosperous state, its citizens having nearly $20,000,000 on deposit in the banks. Experts agreed that Louisiana's banks were the safest in the country and one writer said that they were simply "overflowing with gold."

Transportation. The numerous waterways offered the easiest means of transportation to ante bellum Louisianians. During the early years of the period the rivers and bayous were filled with cargo pirogues, arks, broad horns, keelboats, and numerous other varieties of flatboats which were propelled by oars. The steamboat era began in 1812 when the *New Orleans* arrived in New Orleans from Pittsburgh, and although she soon sank from a boiler explosion earned $20,000 above her cost carrying passengers and goods to and from Natchez. By 1830 there were numerous steamboats on the Mississippi and the number of flatboats had begun to decline until in 1840 most of them had disappeared.

During the 1840's and 1850's large or small steamboats carried cargoes and passengers throughout the state. The larger boats became "floating palaces" with private staterooms, luxurious furnishings, and even gaslights. In the 1840's a British traveler, Sir Charles Lyell, thought the dinner on board the *Magnolia* "only too sumptuous." The meal began "with turtle soup, and two kinds of fish; then followed a variety of dishes, admirably cooked, and then a course of cocoa-nut pies, jellies, preserved bananas, oranges, grapes, and ice-creams, concluding with coffee."

But travel was not so pleasant on board some of the boats which coursed the smaller rivers and bayous. In 1840 one traveler complained that the Red River steamboat *Concord* "should be named Discord, for the firemen abused the mate, the cook fought the steward, the mosquitoes waged war on the passengers, and the passengers are not yet done cursing mate, firemen, steward, mosquitoes—in fine, the boat and all connected with her. A more miserable, dirty, slow moving, improvided, chicken thievish craft never walked the waters . . . it excites my spleen to think of her."

Louisiana's first railroads were built in the 1830's and connected New Orleans with its suburbs. The Pontchartrain Railroad was the first, followed by the Mexican Gulf Railroad, and the New Orleans and Carrollton Railroad. Then short railroads were built to shipping points along the Mississippi River, such as the West Feliciana Railroad from Woodville, Mississippi, to Bayou Sara, and the Clinton and Port Hudson Railroad. By 1860 there were nine railroads in the state with a total of 334 miles of track.

Only a few canals were dug for the numerous bayous and streams

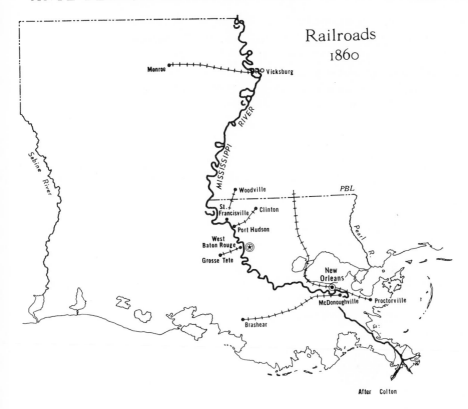

Railroads
1860

Monroe

Vicksburg

RED RIVER

MISSISSIPPI RIVER

Sabine River

Woodville

PBL

St. Francisville   Clinton

Port Hudson

West Baton Rouge

Grosse Tete

Pearl R.

New Orleans

McDonoughville   Proctorville

Brashear

After Colton

provided hundreds of miles of waterways. By 1860 the state had only four canals with a total of thirty-six miles.

Louisiana had no state highways during this period, for road construction was left to the parishes. Most of the poorly graded, dirt roads crookedly followed the line of least resistance around hills, trees, and other obstructions. There were a few "plank" roads, so-called because they were floored with heavy boards. Bridges were few in number and were found only across the smaller streams, the larger bayous and rivers being crossed by ferry.

Trade and Commerce. Most economic goods were carried by the various types of boats over the state's great water system. Hogsheads of sugar arrived at New Orleans from southern Louisiana plantations, tobacco from the northern sections and from St. James Parish, cotton from up the Red River or from the Mississippi above

Natchez. Cattle, sheep, hogs, hides, and other products came from the western and southwestern sections. Manufactured goods, sundries and staples which the people needed were shipped to all points of the state.

The Mississippi was the great highway of interstate commerce. Goods from the entire Middle West came down the river either for consumption in Louisiana, reshipment to other states, or export to foreign countries. Trading boats stopped at the landings with manufactured goods from the East. Boats from the Ohio River country sometimes flew the "Wabash" coat of arms, which was a "flag-staff with a mammoth Irish potato, a big ear of corn, a golden-hued apple, and a side of bacon pendant, and at the topmost peak a bottle of whiskey."

In 1858 one boat, the *Philadelphia,* arrived at New Orleans with 2,000 barrels of flour, 1,990 sacks of corn, 1,100 sheep, 1,000 chickens, 400 barrels of pork, 400 turkeys, 180 hogs, and several hundred bales of hemp and cotton.

After the Louisiana Purchase, President Jefferson wrote that New Orleans was destined to be a "mighty mart of the merchandise brought from more than a thousand rivers." His prophecy soon came true for the old "city walls were torn down, the forts de-

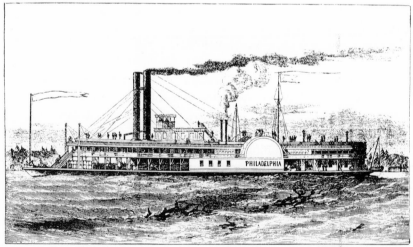

From Mackay, *Life and Liberty in America*

The Mississippi River Steamboat Philadelphia

molished, the moat was filled and made into boulevards: Canal, Rampart, and Esplanade."

New Orleans became a great commercial city. When a British traveler, Charles Mackay, came down the Mississippi in 1858, he wrote:

> On the seventh day morning we entered New Orleans,
> The joyous 'Crescent City'—a Queen among the Queens—
> And saw her pleasant harbor alive with tapering spars—
> With 'union-jacks' from England, and flaunting 'stripes and stars,'
> And all her swarming levee, for miles above the shore,
> Buzzing, humming, surging, with Trade's incessant roar;
> With negroes hoisting hogsheads, and casks of pork and oil,
> Or rolling bales of cotton, and singing at their toil. . . .

From New Orleans goods were shipped to the various coastal ports of the Gulf of Mexico and the Atlantic seaboard, to South and Central America, the islands of the Caribbean, and the countries of Europe. Before 1830 the Gulf and Atlantic ships sailed whenever they got a cargo, but after this date they began to sail on regular schedules.

Some were as palatial in their accommodations as the river steamboats. In 1837, Mrs. Mary Austin Holly went to Texas by Gulf steamer, and she wrote to a friend: "The Captain a gentleman —always at the head of his table—set out in the best style—silver forks, or what looks like silver—large & small, with ivory knives. White waiters, neat & orderly—French Cook . . . & Bedding the finest & whitest linen—water closets—& lady-like chamber maid, every thing nice."

Mail service was generally slow and irregular, but service gradually improved. Letters and newspapers were carried by boats, by stagecoaches, or by mail riders on horseback. Until 1848, when the envelope came into use, letters were simply folded and sealed with wax. The adhesive stamp made its appearance in 1847, and stamped envelopes became common after 1852. By 1855 it was possible to register letters.

Labor. Negro slaves furnished most of the plantation labor in ante bellum Louisiana. While there was some slave labor in the towns and cities, with the exception of house servants most of the workers were white. Many Free Negroes worked at skilled trades as carpenters, barbers, bricklayers, or blacksmiths.

Some of the Free Negroes owned slaves. In Iberville Parish, for example, the records reveal that Cyprien Ricard left sixteen slaves at his death in 1825, Antoine Dubuclet left twenty in 1828, George Deslonde left thirteen in 1836, and Claire Pollard left twenty-five in 1852.

On the whole, slaves were adequately housed, clothed, and fed. They worked from sunrise to sundown, as did white workers at this time, and on many plantations had Saturday afternoons off. Many of them were permitted to own property, and by working nights, Saturday afternoons, Sundays, and on holidays were able to accumulate a little property and sometimes to even purchase their freedom. The life of the slaves was not very different from that of the pioneer farmers in western and northwestern Louisiana, the small farmers who cultivated the poorer lands, or the common white laborers. Each of these groups worked long hours, receiving only a bare living in return for their labors.

Throughout the period many Germans and Irishmen and smaller numbers of other nationalities settled in Louisiana. They dug the canals and drainage ditches, built the railroads and did other kinds of unskilled work. Some of them became sugar engineers, carpenters, blacksmiths, cotton-ginners, maintenance men, or other skilled or semiskilled workers. Most of these laborers worked by the day, though some contracted by the week, month, or even by the entire year. All of them were poorly paid. In 1860 unskilled workers averaged slightly over one dollar per day without board, while skilled workers averaged a little over two dollars per day.

19. ANTE BELLUM SOCIAL AND CULTURAL LIFE

From Pioneer Cabins to Plantation Mansions. Louisiana's ante bellum houses ranged from the rude cabin of the pioneer to the palatial mansion of the rich planter or city businessman. In between these two extremes were the ordinary frame houses occupied by the great majority of the people.

The pioneer settler who moved to the northern and northwestern sections of the state during this period usually built a rude log cabin where he lived until he could afford a house of rough-sawed lumber. Generally of British ancestry, he laid the logs parallel to the ground, in contrast to the French colonial pioneer who had placed them vertically. The slab doors and windows were hung with leather straps. The cabin had an earthen floor and contained only crudely made beds, tables, chairs, and a chest or two. Cooking was done at the fireplace.

Farther south, the simple homes of the French and Spanish Creoles were little changed from those of the colonial period. The typical "Acadian" house, as it is sometimes called today, had a front porch or gallery and a high and steep roof enclosing attic bedrooms, the stairway to which was on the outside, at one end of the porch. The timbers and boards were hand-hewn, mortised, and wooden-pegged. Fireplaces were placed either outside or inside the building, which sometimes was whitewashed. The furniture was plain and simple. A picket fence, called a *barrière de pieux,* enclosed a small yard.

In contrast to these homes were plantation mansions, built according to French or English architectural styles and with kitchens set apart from the main building. A few of them were huge palaces. The plantation "Chatsworth" had fifty rooms and "Belle Grove" had seventy-five. While the majority were plainly furnished, some were filled with fine furnishings brought from Europe.

Their names suggest Creole sensibility and American energy. There were "Versailles," "Chateau de Clery," "Fontainebleau," and "Austerlitz"; "Ivanhoe," "Rob Roy," "Kenilworth," and "Nottaway"; "Old Hickory," "Uncle Sam," and "Rattle and Snap." One of them, at New Iberia, now considered one of the finest examples of plantation-home architecture in America, was called "The Shadows." Many of these are still standing and efforts are being made to preserve them.

Unusual features were sometimes found in these homes. In some in south Louisiana huge "Punkah" fans hung from the dining-room ceilings. After 1835 a few were equipped with gaslights. Shady Grove, which was completed in 1857, had a bathroom, while

Office of the Secretary of State

"The Shadows," New Iberia; built in 1830 by David Weeks

Walnut Grove had running from the dining room to the kitchen a miniature railroad which was used to bring in the piping-hot food.

Clothing. Until late in the period most of the clothing of the common people was homemade of cotton, wool, or a mixture of linen and wool called linsey-woolsy. The women wore simple dresses of homespun cloth, sunbonnets reinforced with split-cane ribs, and crudely made shoes. The men wore pants of cottonade cloth, sewed with alternating blue and white thread; shirts and jumpers; heavy shoes; and straw, split-cane, or reed hats. Children, as in the colonial period, were dressed like their parents.

Wealthy planters or townspeople followed Paris or London fashions and employed tailors, dressmakers, seamstresses, and milliners. They used imported materials and even in the 1850's seldom bought readymade garments. The men wore tight-fitting pants, waistcoats, high and pointed shoes, and high hats. The women were dressed in full skirts with hoops, tight bodices, fragile shoes, and well-trimmed hats. Their accessories included ribbons, parasols, and much jewelry. During the 1850's one writer described an old French gentleman. He wore a nankeen blouse, a loose-fitting frock coat, a yellow vest with bright buttons, gray trousers, light and fancy shoes, and gaiters. His hat "had a brim so narrow that two flies could not walk arm-in-arm around it," while the gray crown "rose upward into the air above him like a rusty stove-pipe."

Food. The climate and natural features of Louisiana gave the people a wider variety of food than most Americans. There were all types of meats and plentiful game and wild fowl. Fresh- and salt-water fish, oysters, shrimp, crabs, and turtles were obtainable for table use. Numerous varieties of vegetables, fruits, and berries were cultivated, as were corn, rice, and wheat. Common staples were brought from the northern states, while fancier goods were imported from Europe. Water came from cisterns or from the rivers and bayous and was purified with alum. Ice for cooling drinks and for ice cream was brought during the late winter from the north until the 1850's, when it began to be manufactured.

In north and northwestern Louisiana, dishes were generally plain and without much seasoning as they were in most of the United States. The common people ate various corn-meal breads, fried beef or pork, a few staple vegetables, and drank thin coffee. In south Louisiana everyone ate a wider variety of Spanish and French Creole dishes, quantities of fish and seafood, and drank thick, black coffee. One lady who visited south Louisiana in the 1830's wrote to a friend: "The oranges, the delicious wines and liquors, the coffee, the innumerable delicate dishes, you would be an epicure in spite of yourself."

In the larger towns and in New Orleans peddlers sold all kinds of edibles, and their picturesque chants advertised the specialties of each seller:

> *Cantal—ope—ah!*
> *Fresh and fine,*
> *Just offa de vine,*
> *Only a dime!*

Or,

> *Oyster Man! Oyster Man!*
> *Get your fresh oysters from the Oyster Man!*
> *Bring out your pitcher, bring out your can,*
> *Get your nice fresh oysters from the Oyster Man!*

Sometimes the peddler added a bit of humor to his chant:

> *Icecream, lemonade,*
> *Made with brown sugar and a rotten egg!*

Medicine and Social Welfare. Medicine made slow progress during those years, for there were few medical schools and most doctors had been trained by being apprenticed to older physicians. Few of them had received college medical training. While the larger towns and cities had enough doctors to care for the sick, there was a general deficiency in the rural areas, where the people depended upon home remedies and patent medicines to cure their ills.

Epidemics of yellow fever and cholera were a scourge to native Louisianians, and dealt even harder with those who had only recently arrived in the state. New Orleans was usually the hardest hit, but epidemics frequently covered the entire state. The epidemic diseases attacked quickly. One traveler on a steamboat saw a man "seized, dead within an hour, revived by being put in his coffin, dead again by noon, and finally cast overboard without a prayer."

The worst yellow-fever epidemic occurred in 1853. At one time in 1853 physicians reported that there were over 40,000 cases in the city. A writer has described New Orleans during one of these epidemics: "Funeral processions crowded every street. . . . The hum of trade was silent. The levee was a desert. The streets, wont to shine with fashion and beauty, were silent."

Many of the doctors were quacks. One of them advertised that he could cure "with the greatest ease" a long list of over twenty diseases by the use of "direct magnetism." There was much super-stition—"night air" was bad for the health, wearing boots made of yellow paper covered with tallow, snuff, and mustard would cure the fever, applying leeches to the nape of the neck would cure a headache.

The state made some efforts to protect the public health and to provide for unfortunates. A State Board of Health functioned briefly during the 1820's and was reorganized in the 1850's. The state give some assistance to the Howard Association, a New Orleans group which cared for the sick, and to various medical societies. Until the 1840's parish Police Juries cared for the deaf, dumb, blind, and insane, after which time the state provided insti-tutions for these unfortunates. Orphans were usually cared for by private or religious asylums.

Amusements and Sports. Louisianians enjoyed all forms of amusements and sports; there were celebrations and rallies, pro-cessions and barbecues, firework displays and holiday parades, balls, parties, and charivaris. The people attended circuses, animal shows, and performances of freaks, acrobats, and sleight-of-hand artists. They heard lectures on scientific and general subjects—hypnotism, animals and birds, spiritualism, ventriloquism, laughing gas, and many others. They played billiards, cards, chess, checkers, and other indoor games. Weddings and family anniversaries were gay occasions.

Dancing was enjoyed by all classes of society. In the rural sections dances were held at private homes, to which people came on horseback or in buggies, the girls carrying their party shoes in little bags. The well-to-do had more formal balls. The Negroes danced the calinda, the bamboula, the *carabine,* or the *pile chactas.* Masked balls were very popular, particularly in New Orleans.

By the end of the period the Mardi Gras season, from Twelfth Night to Shrove Tuesday, had developed into a time of fun and frivolity in south Louisiana and in New Orleans, culminating in maskings, parades, and balls on Mardi Gras day and night. The custom of celebrating Mardi Gras originated in southern Europe, was brought to Louisiana by the French, and later continued by the Spanish. During those colonial days, however, it was simple and only involved masking and walking along the streets on Shrove Tuesday. Masking was forbidden by the Spanish during the 1790's, was revived after the Louisiana Purchase, but was again forbidden by the Americans in 1806. Masked balls were permitted after 1823, and by 1827 masked marchers were thronging the streets of New Orleans and other towns.

The first formal Mardi Gras parade was held in 1838, and according to the New Orleans *Daily Picayune* featured "several carriages superbly ornamented—bands of music, horses richly caparisoned—personations of knights, cavaliers, heroes, demigods," and other figures, all mounted. The following year numerous balls were held during the weeks following Twelfth Night. The Mistick Krew of Comus was organized in 1857, using John Milton's *Paradise Lost* as the subject of its parade.

Sports were always popular, and many planters bred and raced horses. There were several important race tracks in the state by 1860, the St. Francisville track and the Metairie track at New Orleans probably being the most noted. Perhaps the most famous race was run at the Metairie track in 1854, when the Louisiana horse Lecompte was beaten by the out-of-state horse Lexington in a match race.

Both bull- and bearbaiting were popular during the early years, but by the 1820's had generally disappeared. Boxing, cockfighting, foot racing, boat racing, ring tournaments, hunting, and fishing were all popular sports throughout the period.

One of the most unusual sports was shooting at the *papegai*. A crude animal or bird was made of wood, and each man paid for the chance to shoot at it and win a prize.

Education. Elementary education may be divided into two periods during the ante bellum years. The first or so-called Period of Beneficiarism began in 1803 and ended in 1845. Public education was under the direction of the Secretary of State. During this period the state gave limited support to private, neighborhood, and religious schools, but state funds were intended to aid only these children whose parents could not afford to send them to other schools. Louisiana Catholics favored religious rather than public schools, and it was some years before Protestants and liberal Catholics could secure the establishment of a public school system. In 1817 there were fewer than 400 pupils enrolled in all the public elementary schools of Louisiana, but by 1840 the number had grown to over 5,000.

The Period of Public Education began with the Constitution of 1845, which created the office of State Superintendent. Alexander Dimitry, who has been called the "Father of Louisiana Elementary Education," held this office from 1847 to 1851, during which period he organized and put into operation a state-wide public-school system. By 1860 there were several hundred elementary schools in the state.

In rural areas schoolhouses were built of logs with holes left for windows. They had earthen floors, and seats made of split logs with wooden pegs for legs. Sometimes schools were conducted in the small Protestant churches of the Florida Parishes or the northern and western sections, being named after either creeks or Biblical characters. The school term usually varied from six weeks to two months.

Throughout the period, however, the majority of the schools were operated and taught by private schoolmasters who advertised their schools in the newspapers. In one advertisement, it was announced that classes would be held from five to nine o'clock in the morning and from four to seven in the afternoon. The owner teacher of the school guaranteed to teach the elements of reading, writing and arithmetic in two to three months. He would correct the "most vicious hand-writing" in six to eight lessons, unless the student was "unprovided with intelligence."

Secondary education was handled by academies, most of which were short-lived. They accepted boarding and day students, the great majority taught boys rather than girls, and very few of them accepted both sexes. By 1860 there were over 150 of these academies scattered over Louisiana with a total of nearly 450 teachers and nearly 12,000 students.

Few of the colleges were of modern college grade, and most

of them would compare favorably with the better high schools of the present time. They were generally for men only and offered few scientific or professional courses.

The colleges may be divided into three groups. The first group was supported by the state and included the College of Orleans (1805–26), the College of Louisiana (1825–45) at Jackson, and the University of Louisiana which was founded in 1845 at New Orleans. The second group received limited state support, the most important of them being the College of Franklin (1831–45) at Opelousas and the College of Jefferson, which was organized in 1831 at Convent. The third group consisted of those colleges operated by the various religious denominations. The most important of these were: College of St. Charles, Catholic, founded in 1837 at Grand Couteau; the Centenary College of Louisiana, Methodist, founded in 1845 at Jackson; the College of the Immaculate Conception, Catholic, founded in 1847 at New Orleans; and Mount Lebanon University, Baptist, founded in 1852 at Mount Lebanon in north Louisiana. By 1860 there were fifteen colleges in Louisiana, with nearly 100 teachers and over 1,500 students.

The Constitution of 1845 provided for the establishment of a state university, and the institution was chartered ten years later. The Louisiana State Seminary of Learning and Military Academy, the present-day Louisiana State University, was opened at Pineville in January, 1860.

College life differed greatly from that of today. Historian Charles Gayarré, recalling his student days at the College of Orleans, wrote: "Students were required to rise very early, in the winter season before day; then had breakfast, which consisted of a half loaf of dry bread. . . . From half past 7 until 12 students were engaged with their books and recitations; an hour was then given for dinner, which was a more generous meal than breakfast, and for recess. From 1 o'clock until about 7 they were back again at books. Then came supper, and the evening was devoted to recreation. On Sundays they went to church at 8 o'clock."

Religion. When the state was admitted into the Union in 1812 the great majority of Louisianians were Catholics. In general the Catholics occupied south Louisiana, while the Protestants were more numerous in the northern and western sections of the state. From 1801 to 1815 the Louisiana Catholic Church was without a bishop and was administered by a Vicar-General, under Bishop John Carroll of Baltimore. Bishop William Dubourg was consecrated in 1815 and was succeeded by Bishops Leo de Neckere and Antoine Blanc, who served until 1850, when Father Blanc became Archbishop of Louisiana.

Baptists, Methodists, and Episcopalians migrated to Louisiana in large numbers during the territorial period, and by 1812 their churches were well established. Presbyterians, Lutherans, Disciples of Christ, Unitarians, and Universalists followed, and in communities where there were not enough members of any one denomination, the people joined together and organized "Union" or "Community" churches. Among the most noted Protestant ministers of the ante bellum period were Dr. Benjamin M. Palmer, Dr. Theodore Clapp, and Bishop Leonidas Polk.

Louisiana boasted 572 churches in 1860; the Methodists had 199, the Baptists 161, the Catholics 99, the Presbyterians 42, and the Episcopalians 33. The Catholic churches were larger and more costly than the Protestant ones and were valued at nearly $1,750,-000. The Methodist churches ranked second with a valuation of about $337,000.

Journalism. Many newspapers and a few magazines were published in ante bellum Louisiana. During the period, New Orleans had over fifty newspapers and well over one hundred were printed in the smaller cities and towns. The newspapers tended to be short-lived, were weeklies rather than dailies, and usually received some financial help from public printing or from political groups. They all copied news items from each other and from the newspapers of other states and foreign countries.

During the early years local political and general news received little space, but after the 1830's news of a local nature began to receive increasingly more consideration. Most of the news space was devoted to state news, agricultural material, communications from other papers, and tales and poetry copied from English or American magazines. Medical, legal, and local advertisements frequently occupied more than half of the total space. Most newspapers were printed on cheap paper in folios of four pages, and subscriptions ranged from $1.50 to $2.00 a year. Many southern Louisiana newspapers were published in both French and English, and in New Orleans several were published in Spanish and German.

The leading newspapers of New Orleans were the *Picayune, Delta, Crescent, Bee, Courier, True Delta, True American, Daily Topic,* and *Bulletin.* Other notable newspapers were the Baton Rouge *Advocate,* the Alexandria *Red River Republican* and the *Red River Whig,* the Opelousas *Courier,* the Vidalia *Concordia Intelligencer,* the Shreveport *Caddo Gazette,* and the Franklin *Planter's Banner.*

The most noted editors included George W. Kendall of the *Picayune,* John Gibson of the *True American,* and Alexander C. Bullitt of the *Bee.* Many of the smaller city and town editors were influential leaders in their communities.

A majority of the periodicals were published in New Orleans. *DeBow's Review* was filled with economic and agricultural information, the *Southern Quarterly Review* contained articles, fiction and poetry, and *La Propagateur Catholique* (*The Catholic Propagator*) printed articles of a religious nature. With the appearance in 1843 of *L'Album Littéraire* came the first recorded literary magazine published by Free Negroes. It presented stories, articles, poems, and folklore.

The library movement had started during the territorial period when the New Orleans Library Society was founded. By 1860 the state could boast over fifty libraries containing a total of over 100,000 volumes. The most noted of these libraries were the State Library, and the B. F. French Library and the Fisk Free Library, both of which were also in New Orleans. Many towns had small subscription libraries. Some of the plantation families, such as the Butlers of "The Cottage" in West Feliciana Parish, had extensive collections of books, maps, and magazines. In New Orleans, booksellers sold volumes in English, French, Spanish, and other languages, while in smaller towns the general stores usually had a few books for sale.

The Theater, Music, and Literature. Although plays had been presented in Louisiana during the Spanish colonial period, it was not until after 1803 that theaters were built in New Orleans. In 1808 was built the St. Philip Theater, where plays were presented in both French and English. The Orleans Theater was completed in 1809, burned in 1813, and was rebuilt later, following another fire. Theatrical performances began about 6:30 P.M., lasting until nearly midnight, and the program would frequently include an opera, a serious drama, a farce or comedy, with several song, dance, and skit specialties in between. Throughout the period New Orleans was one of the leading theatrical towns in the United States.

Many of the smaller towns had theaters, one of the earliest of which was at St. Francisville, having been built sometime prior to 1812. By 1850 many towns had a theater and a theatrical group which presented the plays, sometimes importing professional actors of national reputation.

The prominent theatrical managers of New Orleans included Noah Ludlow, James H. Caldwell, Sol Smith, and John Davis. These men brought noted actors to New Orleans and to the larger cities of the state. Among them were Junius Brutus Booth and his son Edwin Booth, Charlotte Cushman, Lola Montez, Charles Keane and his wife Ellen Tree, Charles Macready, Fanny Ellsler, and many others. P. T. Barnum, who later became such a noted showman, had little success in Louisiana during his early years. After playing in New Orleans for a week in 1838, the company went to the Atakapas country. As Barnum later described the venture: "At Opelousas we exchanged the steamer for sugar and molasses; our company was disbanded, and I started for home."

New Orleans was the first American city permanently to establish opera. Beginning in 1808 it had a series of noted opera houses, ending in 1859 with the building of the New Orleans Opera House, affectionately called the "French Opera." New York did not open its first opera house until the 1830's, and many noted operas had their first American presentations in New Orleans. The opera was important socially as well as musically, and many planters and their families, together with their servants, went to New Orleans and remained for the entire opera season.

Concerts were also very popular, and Louisianians heard Jenny Lind, Anna Bishop, Madame Ablamowicz, and many other vocal and instrumental artists.

The most noted native composer of the period was Louis Gott-schalk. After completing piano studies in Paris, he toured Europe as a concert artist before returning to the United States. His most noted compositions were "La Bamboula," "Cradle Song," "Creole Eyes," and "Danse Nègre."

Negroes were blessed with natural musical talent and played instruments, danced, or sang at every opportunity. Many of their orchestras were made up of primitive instruments. One such band had only three musicians, with a group of singers; one tapped a cowhide-covered barrel with his hands, another beat upon the sides of a barrel with sticks, and a third scraped a stick over the teeth of a large jawbone. This percussion section was the forerunner of modern jazz music. But the educated Free Negroes of ante bellum New Orleans made music history in 1838 by organizing one of the first symphony orchestras in the United States.

As late as 1850 most of the literature of Louisiana was written in French, though English was making rapid progress. History was popular, as was poetry and drama. The two most important historians were François Xavier Martin and Charles Gayarré. Probably the best poetry was written by Free Negroes. Selections of this Free-Negro poetry were collected and published by Armand Lanusse in 1845 in *Les Cenelles* (The Hawthorns), the first anthology of Negro poetry in America.

20. THE ELECTION OF 1860 AND THE SECESSION OF LOUISIANA

Background. Twenty years before the election of 1860, New Orleans businessman Paul Tulane visited France with his father. They viewed the economic desolation of Bordeaux, whose trade had been ruined by the abolition of slavery in the French West Indies. Tulane's father told him that slavery in the United States would one day be destroyed "and New Orleans will be ruined," not realizing that within two decades his prophecy would come true. The election of 1860 led to the secession of the southern states and civil war, and the following seventeen years were the most tragic in all Louisiana history.

The slavery issue had long troubled the United States. During the colonial period the people of the North had held slaves, but slave labor was not profitable there and the northern states had gradually abolished the institution. By 1820 they had begun to agitate for the abolition of slavery in the South, and by the 1830's this movement had politically divided the country.

It was hoped that the Compromise of 1850 would settle the problem, but during the 1850's a series of events further excited the people of both the North and South. *Uncle Tom's Cabin,* an antislavery book, appeared in 1852 and by mid-1853 had sold over a million copies in the North. The Republican Party was organized in 1854, principally to oppose the extension of slavery in the territories. Shortly afterwards came a bloody struggle between northern and southern settlers for the control of Kansas. The Dred Scott Decision of the United States Supreme Court irritated the North in 1857, and two years later John Brown's Raid on Harper's Ferry, Virginia, inflamed the South.

In his last message to the Legislature in January, 1860, Governor Wickliffe recommended that Louisiana stand with the other southern states in protecting "our Constitutional rights." A week later, on January 23, Thomas O. Moore, the new Governor, spoke of the loyalty of Louisiana to the Union but insisted that every state "must be permitted to determine her own social institutions." It was his hope that harmony and peace would "be restored to our people without a sacrifice of interest or loss of honor."

The Election of 1860. The Democrats were the strongest political group in Louisiana. The old Whig Party was dead, and its former members could not join Abraham Lincoln and the Republicans, who were opposed to slavery. The Democratic Party split at the national convention, and the Louisiana delegates walked out with the other southerners, formed a southern wing of the party, and nominated John C. Breckinridge of Kentucky for president. Many Louisianians, however, were not satisfied with Breckinridge and instead supported John Bell, who was the candidate of a new party called the Constitutional Union Party. Only a small number of Louisianians supported Stephen A. Douglas of Illinois, the candidate of the northern wing of the Democratic Party.

The presidential campaign of 1860 was a lively one in Louisiana. There were meetings, barbecues, newspaper editorials, parades, fireworks, the firing of cannon, banners, music, and flags. Clubs were organized, the "Young Bell Ringers," the "Young Men's Douglas Clubs," the "Minute Men of '60," and numerous others. Lincoln was described as "the dirtiest and meanest Abolitionist alive," Bell was a "quaint, homely, sleepy old gentleman," and Douglas an "Abolition traitor" who wanted to rule or ruin the South. At a Breckinridge rally in New Orleans "20,000 voices uprose in earnest plaudits in approval of his manly sentiments."

Judah P. Benjamin spoke for most Louisianians when he said: "I have no stomach for a fight in which I am to have the choice between the man who denies me all my rights, openly and fairly, [Lincoln], and a man who admits my rights but intends to filch them, [Douglas]."

On election day, Louisiana gave Breckinridge 22,681 votes, Bell 20,204 votes, and Douglas 7,625. It is not recorded that Lincoln received a single vote. The Breckinridge majorities were principally in the central and northern sections, while Bell and Douglas received their majorities in the plantation sections of the southeast and in the industrial and commercial center of New Orleans.

Lincoln had, however, been elected President. As his course of action was not clear, public opinion was sharply divided in Louisiana, some hoping for a compromise solution to the critical problems. One group believed that the South should wait until after Lincoln's inauguration and see what he would do before taking any action; another argued that the time for the secession of the southern states had arrived; yet another group counseled a convention of all the southern states. A few people proclaimed that "we are doomed if we proclaim not our political independence."

Governor Moore called a special session of the Legislature, to meet on December 10, 1860, whose deliberations were marked by general harmony. The Governor recommended an election of members to a convention which would "determine the relations of Louisiana to the Federal government," for the problem rose "high above ordinary political considerations. It involves our present honor and our future existence as a free and independent people." A bill was passed calling for an election on January 7 of delegates to a state convention to meet on January 23 at Baton Rouge.

Most Louisianians approved of Governor Moore's action. The New Orleans *Weekly Delta* stated that "Governor Moore is not what may be called a 'fast man' in politics; but if he is slower than some others, he is just as sure to come right in the end."

Public Opinion During Early Winter of 1860–61. The winter of 1860–61 in New Orleans promised to be gayer than usual. The crops had been good and prices were satisfactory. The hotels were filled with planters and businessmen and their families from all sections of the state; the opera house and the theaters were crowded and excitement was in the air. Everyone talked politics, on the street, at public places, even at church. On November 29 Bishop B. M. Palmer preached a two-hour sermon using a text taken from Psalms 94:20: "Shall the throne of iniquity have fellowship with thee, which frameth mischief by a law?" He argued that the South should stand against the North, even to the extent of war, and that the South had a trust to defend, perhaps with the sword. "Not till the last man has fallen behind the last rampart, shall it drop from our hands; and then only in surrender to the God who gave it." Within a few days over thirty thousand copies of the sermon had been printed and sold. Many people no longer spoke of co-operation with the North. Instead, they talked of secession, *and then* co-operation with the United States.

But public opinion throughout the state was divided. One citizen challenged Palmer in the *True Delta:* "You would destroy the constitution and the union—this glorious and peerless fabric which has so long and so safely sheltered us, and what, sir, would you rear in its stead?" At a mass meeting at Franklin it was resolved to oppose the "unconditional secession of Louisiana," while those attending a St. James Parish meeting believed that the northern states should be expelled from the Union. At a New Orleans meeting "The Southern Marseillaise" was sung: "Sons of the South, awake to glory!"

Most newspapers favored secession, though some argued that the movement should not be hurried. Of the important newspapers the New Orleans *True Delta* and the Baton Rouge *Weekly Gazette and Comet* led the fight against secession. *La Propagateur Catholique* counseled moderation. The *Constitutional,* of Alexandria, joked about secession: "If Louisiana secedes from the Union . . . we shall be compelled to advocate the secession of the parish of Rapides from the State. . . . We have a large territory and a numerous population and are perfectly able to take care of ourselves."

Perhaps one New Orleans newspaper best summed up the public's attitude when it stated: "We are secessionists because we honestly believe that it is the only possible way in which we can enjoy the rights and privileges which the Union, as originally designed, was intended to bestow upon all the States, according to the just measure of perfect equality."

As the election of January 7 approached, the people divided into two groups. The "Immediate Secessionists" believed that Louisiana should secede at once, while the "Co-operationists" thought that Louisiana should co-operate with the other southern states, and wait and see what Lincoln would do when he became President.

The Secession Convention. In the election of January 7, 1861, twenty-nine parishes were for secession, while nineteen parishes were for co-operation with the Federal government. To the Convention went eighty secessionists, forty-four co-operationists, and six men who were undecided.

The Convention met at Baton Rouge on January 23. Former Governor Mouton was elected president of the meeting and a committee of fifteen members was selected to report on the matter of secession.

Governor Moore reported that during the week after the election he had seized Forts Jackson and St. Philip below New Orleans, the United States Arsenal at Baton Rouge, a Federal revenue cutter, and some other government property.

On January 24, Chairman John Perkins, Jr. presented the report of the committee. The report was in the form of an ordinance, "An Ordinance to dissolve the union between the State of Louisiana and other States, united with her under the compact entitled 'The Constitution of the United States of America.' " The next day the Convention heard speeches of commissioners to Louisiana from

Alabama and South Carolina asking for the co-operation of Louisiana in the forming of a Southern Confederacy. A communication from Louisiana's United States Senators John Slidell and Judah P. Benjamin asking for secession was also read.

Several members of the Convention opposed the Ordinance of Secession when it came up for debate, led by James G. Talliaferro from Catahoula Parish. Joseph A. Rozier of Orleans Parish and James O. Fuqua of East Baton Rouge Parish offered substitute ordinances, which were voted down. A motion to submit the matter to the people likewise failed.

The arguments were completed on January 26. The Ordinance of Secession was adopted by a vote of 113 to 17. When the vote was announced Mouton proclaimed: "I now declare the connection between the State of Louisiana, and the Federal Union dissolved; and that she is a free, sovereign and independent Power." Then Governor Moore, preceded by the Pelican Flag of Louisiana, entered the room and took his position on the platform. The Reverend W. E. N. Linfeld offered a prayer and Father Darius Hubert blessed the flag.

Later, when the Ordinance of Secession was signed, eight of the seventeen members who had voted against it signed the document. Thus the Ordinance received 121 votes to 9.

Public Reaction to the Ordinance of Secession. Most of the newspapers received the news with enthusiasm. The *Picayune* said: "The deed has been done. . . . The Union is dead; . . . To the lone star of the State we transfer the duty, affection and allegiance we owed to the congregation of light which spangled the banner of the old Confederacy. . . . The South says to every child of hers, 'Son, give me all your heart.'" The *Crescent* reported that "with a calm dignity and firm purpose, Louisiana resumes her delegated powers, and escapes from a Union in which she could no longer remain with honor to herself or to her sister States of the South." The *Crescent* further stated that secession had been accomplished "with no unseemly haste, nor with any exhibition of unnatural passion."

Some of the newspapers, however, took an opposite position or counseled moderation. The *True Delta,* for example, flatly stated that "everything in this city appears to be in rapid progress towards a war establishment." At the same time, the editor reported that everyone "looks dubious and bewildered not knowing what to expect or what may happen."

Other newspapers expressed sincere regret at leaving the Union. The Shreveport *South-Western* stated with emotion: "We this day, as orderly citizens, lower the 'stars and stripes' from our masthead! It is with heart-felt emotions, better imagined than portrayed, that we fold the saucy looking 'star spangled banner' that we have always loved, and place the precious memento under our pillow."

Most people were enthusiastic. In New Orleans guns thundered at the foot of Canal Street, state flags were flung to the breeze, and at night public buildings and private homes were brilliantly lighted. The *Picayune* reported that "every one seemed to breathe more freely, every one's heart beat with a more rapid and pleasurable pulsation." Everywhere the people were ready to "defend the sovereignty of Louisiana, come what might, and in the face of every obstacle."

Mayor John T. Monroe of New Orleans ordered "all citizens to illuminate their residences, or places of business" on the night of February 6 in honor of the secession of the state. The *Bee* reported that Canal, Royal, and St. Charles streets were filled with people. The Pelican and Boston clubs on Canal Street and Kittredge's store and the Pickwick Club on St. Charles Street were particularly well lighted. The militia units paraded, fireworks were shot off, and speeches were made, the marching formations of the militia companies adding much to the popular demonstration in honor of Louisiana's new independence.

One young soldier, however, soon wrote in his diary: "If I only had the fanatics of the North and the fire eaters of the South in equal numbers in a pen together, I'd make 'dog eat dog.' I'd make Rome howl for once."

The Republic of Louisiana. For almost two months, from January 26 until March 21 when it joined the Confederate States of America, Louisiana was an independent nation. Governor Moore acted as president, the Legislature acted as congress, and the state courts served in the place of Federal courts.

For nearly three weeks the old state flag was the national flag of Louisiana. Then on February 11 the Convention adopted a new flag. It had thirteen stripes, six of white, four of blue, and three of red. In the upper left-hand corner was a red field with a five-pointed yellow star. The flag represented the thirteen stripes of the original Union, the tricolor of France, and the red and yellow colors of Spain. The first flag was made by H. Cassidy, a tent- and sailmaker of New Orleans, and it flew over the New Orleans City Hall until the city was captured in April, 1862.

By the middle of February, Governor Moore had appropriated all the property of the United States in Louisiana. Forts Pike and Macomb had been occupied by the state militia; the United States Mint and Custom House in New Orleans had been secured, along with over $600,000 which was in the Mint.

The state Legislature and the Secession Convention continued to meet, the Legislature passing laws and the Convention adopting ordinances which had the same effect as laws.

The work of the Convention was the more important, but it performed functions which should have been handled by the Legislature. It met in New Orleans for two sessions after the Baton Rouge meeting. It named delegates to the Convention of the Southern States at Montgomery, Alabama; it transferred the powers of the national government to the government of the state and handled problems of finance, court, and postal affairs; it opened the Mississippi River to all friendly nations. Finally, on March 21 it ratified the Constitution of the Confederate States of America, which had been organized at the Montgomery meeting of the southern states, and transferred funds to the new national government of the South.

Meanwhile, the Legislature invited the people of southern Indiana and Illinois to join the Confederacy as a state. It appropriated $1,500,000 for the defense of Louisiana, provided for the organization of military units, and outfitted warships at the Algiers shipyard.

The Legislature and the Convention adjourned on March 26. During those two months Louisiana had been successively a state of the American Union, an independent nation, and a member of the Confederate States of America.

The people of the state generally supported the action of the two bodies. The *Daily True Delta,* however, blasted the work of the Convention. "The Lyceum hall wigwam, jocosely called a state convention, ingloriously fizzled out yesterday. By the usual appliances of the rag-and-lampblack aristocracy, they succeeded in getting all they required of the wigwam convention." It predicted a dreadful and bloody future for Louisiana.

Louisiana Mobilizes for War. During these months Louisiana was busy mobilizing her military strength. The Governor appointed a Military Board and by February 14 the board had issued weapons to nearly 1,800 eager young members of volunteer companies. These volunteers took an oath to "bear true allegiance to the state of Louisiana, and serve it honestly and faithfully . . . and obey the orders of the governor and such officers as may be appointed over me."

The organization of military companies continued over the entire state. A British traveler wrote that Confederate flags were flying everywhere, military companies were constantly parading, and that New Orleans looked like a military camp. The "Louisiana Marseillaise" was sung everywhere. New Orleans Irishmen implored New Orleans Spaniards to join the colors: "For the love of the Virgin and your own soul's sake, Fernandey, get up and cum along wid us to fight the Yankees." Most of the cadets at the State Seminary at Pineville marched off to enlist in the army. "Get ready for the fight," urged the *Daily Crescent,* "and meet it to the death when it comes."

The War Begins. On April 12, 1861, the Confederate batteries at Charleston, South Carolina, opened fire on Fort Sumter, which was on an island in the bay. The fort surrendered and on April 15, President Lincoln called for 75,000 volunteers to force the South back into the Union. Four days later the first of these troops passed through Baltimore and in a fight with the citizens killed and wounded a number of them. The next morning the *Daily Crescent* screamed with the headline, "NORTHERN TROOPS MOVING SOUTHWARD."

The next night young Maryland-born James R. Randall, an

English and Latin teacher at Poydras College in Pointe Coupee Parish, seized his pen and wrote the words to one of the most noted songs of the Confederacy:

> *The despot's heel is on thy shore, Maryland!*
> *His torch is at thy temple door, Maryland!*
>
> .   .   .   .   .   .
>
> *Thou wilt not yield the vandal toll;*
> *Thou wilt not crook to his control;*
> *Better the fire upon thee roll,*
> *Better the shot, the blade, the bowl,*
> *Than crucifixion of the soul.*
>   *Maryland! My Maryland!*

In New Orleans, young Kate Stone wrote in her diary: "A nation fighting for its own homes and liberty cannot be overwhelmed. Our Cause is just and must prevail."

Donelson Caffery later said in a speech in the United States Senate: "I was a quiet, peaceful citizen, pursuing my calling as a sugar planter in my native state. Suddenly the tocsin of war was sounded throughout the length and breadth of the land. I revered the Union and I honored its flag. But when my state called me to arms, I had to answer the call of the state of my nativity and the state of my love."

The conventions and the campaigns and the speechmaking were over. It was time for the work of war.

PART SIX

CIVIL WAR AND MILITARY OCCUPATION

21. LOUISIANA AND THE WAR FOR SOUTHERN INDEPENDENCE

Explanation. Many names have been given to the war which was fought between the United States of America and the Confederate States of America from the spring of 1861 to the late spring of 1865. When the official records of the war were published by the United States government some years after the war had ended it was called the "War of the Rebellion." Southerners have generally named it "The War Between the States." A New England historian, Edward Channing, titled it "The War for Southern Independence" and this title, in the writer's opinion, is the best and the most accurate. Most people today simply call it "The Civil War," for this is a short and handy title.

1861. This was the year of preparation. Military supplies of all types were assembled in Louisiana government warehouses. Small industrial plants were established for making those goods which normally were imported from outside the state. Boats were sent along the rivers and bayous to collect scrap iron to be sent to iron foundries in New Orleans for manufacturing war supplies. Uniforms, hats, shoes, tents, and other goods were produced. The planting of food crops was encouraged. It was a year of feverish activity.

Governor Moore called for volunteers, and the towns and villages were soon witnessing drills and parades. One visitor to New Orleans wrote that "the streets are full of Turcos, Zouaves, Chasseurs; walls are covered with placards of volunteer companies." The Louisiana soldiers gave picturesque names to their companies

—the Knights of the Border, the Catahoula Guerrillas, the Caddo Lake Boys, the Mounted Wild Cats, the Yankee Pelters, and of course the Louisiana Tigers. Over sixty thousand troops were enlisted in the state during the war and about one-third of this number during the first nine months of 1861. Many of the companies, however, marched off to war without adequate supplies or proper equipment.

The government fitted out gunboats for river-patrol work and strengthened the defenses of Fort Jackson and Fort St. Philip below New Orleans. The Legislature, meeting in November, passed several emergency laws; the state spent over $1,500,000 during the year on military equipment and supplies; and by December New Orleans boasted that "Chalmette's glories will be repeated," should the enemy attack the city.

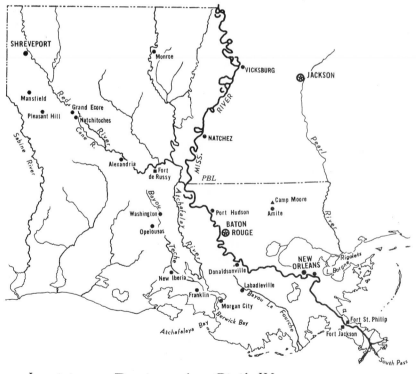

Louisiana During the Civil War   After King and Ficklen

1862. Governor Moore was fearful of an attack on New Orleans, and early in 1862 he made plans for improving the city defenses. Under General Mansfield Lovell entrenchments were built, additional cannon were mounted, and adjacent bayous were obstructed. Rafts held together by heavy chains were strung across the Mississippi between Forts Jackson and St. Philip.

In mid-April the attacking Federal fleet commanded by Flag Officer David G. Farragut appeared off the mouth of the Mississippi, accompanied by a large military force under the command of General Benjamin F. Butler. The bombardment of the forts began on April 18, and early on the morning of April 24 the fleet succeeded in running past them. As General Lovell had only about three thousand militia troops, he ordered them to withdraw from New Orleans to Camp Moore, just north of Amite.

One Confederate soldier described the scene in New Orleans on the night of April 24: "It was in the wildest confusion. Anxious men and women thronged the streets. . . . The burning of cotton in various parts of the city added a grim feature to the scene."

New Orleans was officially occupied on April 28, and on May 1 General Butler took formal possession of the city.

Not long after the fall of New Orleans, the Federal fleet moved up the river, took possession of Baton Rouge, and on May 28 a military force arrived at the capital. In early August a Confederate army attacked Baton Rouge but failed to capture the city, which, however, was evacuated by the Federals late in the same month. Butler had previously ordered that the town be burned, but at the last moment he relented and countermanded the order. A Federal officer wrote, however, "This place has been nearly completely sacked by the soldiery. . . . Even officer's tents are filled with furniture from deserted houses."

In October a strong Federal force commanded by General Godfrey Weitzel marched down Bayou Lafourche and defeated the Confederates at Labadieville. Weitzel then continued on to the Bayou Teche country to attack General Alfred Mouton, son of former Governor Mouton, near Franklin. In the middle of December General Nathaniel P. Banks superseded General Butler in command of the Federal army in Louisiana, and on December 17 reoccupied Baton Rouge, which he called "the first rebel position on the river."

The year 1862 was a fateful one for Louisiana. New Orleans was captured; Baton Rouge was twice captured, the partial burning of the capitol destroying many of the state's records. Southeast

From *Leslie's Illustrated History of the Civil War*

The burning of the Capitol at Baton Rouge

Louisiana was ravaged and sacked by Federal troops, as were parts of the northeast section of the state. By the end of the year the Federal gunboats were in complete possession of the lower Mississippi River.

1863. Early in 1863, General U. S. Grant invaded northeast Louisiana as a part of his movement against Vicksburg, and although there was little fighting in this area, much property was destroyed. In March a Federal detachment occupied a considerable portion of the Florida Parishes but was forced to return to New Orleans a short time later.

The following month General Banks advanced up Bayou Teche, captured Opelousas, and in early May occupied Alexandria, Confederate opposition coming from two small armies commanded by General Mouton and General Richard Taylor, the son of former President Zachary Taylor. Though this campaign was of little military importance, during the course of it the Federal army destroyed or carried off considerable property from the countryside. Banks reported that he had confiscated over 20,000 horses, mules and cattle, over 5,000 bales of cotton and "many hogsheads of sugar." One northern soldier wrote that "the army is doing nothing else but gathering cotton." Later in May, Banks crossed the Mississippi at Bayou Sara, moving south to lay seige to Port Hudson, and within a few weeks the Confederates had recaptured Alexandria, Opelousas, and the towns along the Teche.

Port Hudson was defended by slightly over 5,000 Confederate troops, while the attacking Federal army totaled about 13,000. The siege lasted forty-five days, including twenty-one days of hard

From *Harper's Pictorial History of the Civil War*

Confederates repulsing an assault at Port Hudson

fighting. The Confederates ran out of food supplies, and one soldier reported that a boiled rat was a "better dish than he had expected." On July 4, Vicksburg surrendered to General Grant and five days later Port Hudson fell. All the Confederate forts along the Mississippi had now been captured and President Lincoln could say that "the Father of Waters rolls unvexed to the sea."

After the fall of Port Hudson there was little heavy fighting in Louisiana.

1864. Federal military plans called for the complete occupation of Louisiana in 1864. This was to be accomplished by sending a large military and naval expedition up the Red River to capture Shreveport, after which the Federal army would be able to invade Texas. At the same time the central Louisiana area would yield large amounts of cotton, livestock, and other supplies.

In early March, Admiral David Porter of the United States Navy assembled a strong fleet of gunboats at the mouth of the Red River, where he was quietly joined by an army of about 10,000 men which had come down the Mississippi from the vicinity of Vicksburg. As this combined force began to move up the Red River, about 20,000 Federals moved northward from Franklin. Fort De Russy, about thirty miles below Alexandria, was captured on March 14, and two days later Alexandria fell.

The united Federal armies, under General Nathaniel P. Banks, then moved up the south bank of the Red River, followed by the river fleet. The Confederate army of under 9,000 men, commanded by General Richard Taylor, retreated, fighting rear-guard actions to slow up the enemy. It retreated through Natchitoches but stopped about three miles southeast of Mansfield, where the bloody Battle of Mansfield was fought on April 8. It was a costly Confederate victory, for General Mouton was killed. General Taylor reported that "the charge made by Mouton across the open was magnificent" and that "seven standard-bearers fell one after another with the flag of the Crescent Regiment." The defeated Federals retreated about twenty miles that night to Pleasant Hill. The next afternoon there was another battle, which was won by neither side, although the Federal army immediately afterwards retreated towards Alexandria.

From *Harper's Pictorial History of the Civil War*

*Confederates attacking Federal Red River fleet during the retreat of
General Banks after his defeat at Mansfield*

The retreating Federal army left such destruction in its wake
that the area became known as "the burnt district." As one
Louisiana woman described it: "Houses, gins, mills, barns, and
fences were burned; negroes all carried off; horses, cattle, hogs,
every living thing, driven away or killed." Before the Union troops

retreated from Alexandria they set fire to the city, despite the orders of General Banks. Other Federal officers were not so considerate, and one general was reported to have said, "Boys, this *looks like war!*" The angry Confederates closed in on the Federal army below Alexandria, and the Federal retreat became a rout until the protection of the powerful Mississippi River gunboats was secured.

1865. There were no important battles or campaigns in Louisiana during 1865. The Federal armies controlled the whole of the southeastern part of the state and the Confederate forces were not strong enough to attack them.

By the beginning of 1865 the entire South was exhausted and even the army of General Robert E. Lee in Virginia could not be supplied. There was no hope in Louisiana. People became dispirited; soldiers began to desert and go home, one soldier reporting that from six to twelve of his comrades were deserting every night. The war was almost over.

General Lee surrendered at Appomattox, Virginia, on April 9 and General Joseph E. Johnston in North Carolina a few days later. On May 17 Major David F. Boyd wrote from Alexandria: "All is confusion and demoralization here, nothing like order or discipline remains. . . . We must look the matter square in the face and shape our actions (personally and officially) accordingly."

On May 26, General Simon B. Buckner, acting for General Kirby Smith who had gone to Houston, surrendered the Confederate armies west of the Mississippi. General Smith signed the official documents on June 2.

The fighting had ended. The South had lost its war for independence.

Billy Yanks and Johnny Rebs. Both Federal and southern soldiers generally accepted army life without much complaint. The northern soldier, being much better equipped, complained less than his southern opponent about clothing, food, and other supplies. As the war progressed, the Confederate supply system gradually failed and her soldiers had to acquire clothing as best they could and to learn to eat practically anything.

Northern soldiers complained about Louisiana rains, snakes, lice, and particularly mosquitoes. One soldier wrote: "I don't suppose there is a spot on earth where there are so many snakes to the acre as right here." From Port Hudson, another soldier complained: "Every hollow became a puddle before the fellows sleeping in it could get out. . . . We are soaking wet before we know. . . . We stand around and growl for awhile and then settle down and are soon asleep again." Body lice did not cause too much trouble for "we just boil our clothes and that's the end of them. Their feeding time is when we are still for awhile, but at the first move they all let go and grab fast to our clothing." All the soldiers hated mosquitoes: "If I had a brigade of men as determined as these Brashear City mosquitoes, I believe I could sweep the Rebellion off its feet in a month's time."

The citizen soldiers of both sides adapted themselves to war and the constant threat of death as best they could. One Confederate wrote that "some of the boys seemed a little frightened under their first fire; as to myself, . . . I did not feel brave at all." A northerner scrawled in his diary that the cannon balls "keep coming, and we dodge less and less. If they keep at it long enough I suppose we shall get used to it, as we have to a great many other things." Another Yank complained that "the Rebs seem to be getting madder all the time," while a third grumbled, "those cusses jest shot my pipe square out of my trousers' pocket. Look at that hole, now! . . . I wish I was in Massachusetts."

Northern and southern soldiers believed strongly in the cause for which they fought. Young Robert Patrick thus expressed his feelings at the grave of a dead enemy: "You were not satisfied to remain at home, and let us alone; you must come to the South to murder our citizens, burn our houses, desolate our homes and lay waste to our country. . . . You for one have met your just reward, which is a grant of land from the Confederates, of three feet by six, in an obscure spot, where your friends, if you have any, will never be able to find your body, for there is nothing to mark the spot except a small hillock of red clay, which a few hard rains will wash away and it will disappear forever."

Most soldiers, North and South, fought bravely, accepted hardships, remained loyal, and were a credit to their armies. There were exceptions, however. One Louisiana soldier revealed his true character in letters to his wife. Lazy and cowardly, he somehow managed to avoid fighting and continually complained and griped about everything. Finally he was able, through political influence, to secure a soft military job at Opelousas, where he was stationed during the last year of the war. He spent several days during the first week of April, 1865, near St. Martinville, fishing, visiting, and enjoying fresh strawberries and cream. Hearing of Lee's surrender, he wrote his wife bitterly: "Gen'l Lee has sold the Confederacy." Later he boasted of his "military record" and rose to a political position of importance in the state. This soldier's war record, however, was the exception rather than the rule in both armies.

Government During the War. Thomas O. Moore served as Governor until January 25, 1864, when he was succeeded by Henry Watkins Allen. Both governors were conscientious men who did the best they could for a war-torn state.

As the Federal armies advanced, the state capital had to be moved. It was at Baton Rouge when the war began, but with the occupation of that city in May, 1862, it was moved to Opelousas, the executive offices being located in the old Lacombe Hotel. Here it remained until January, 1863, when it was moved again, this time to Shreveport. Here the Parish Courthouse was used as a capitol, while the Governor's office was in an old frame building on the north side of Texas Street.

The state government faced many wartime problems. The Legislature passed laws, which, because of the presence of the Federal army, were impossible to enforce. The raising of armies and the furnishing of supplies were problems of outstanding importance. Supply depots were established, and numerous small factories were built, including packing houses, cotton-cloth factories, and medical laboratories. The raising of war funds and the collection of taxes was difficult. Many governmental and legal records were captured or destroyed.

Local Police Juries and town officials also had many responsibilities. They paid bounties to men who enlisted, equipped the soldiers, furnished relief to needy families, repaired roads, bridges, and ferries, and tried to maintain order in the towns and parishes.

Not all Louisianians were loyal to the state. Outlaws hid in the hills and swamps, while bands of armed men called "Jay-Hawkers" evaded military service, plundered the countryside, burned houses and other buildings, and killed civilians. Patrols, Home Guards, and Rangers were organized to defend the people of Louisiana who lived within the Confederate lines. In Rapides Parish, for example, two of the most noted companies of Rangers were led by David C. Paul and James A. McWaters.

Louisiana state and local government began to disintegrate during the spring of 1865. Governor Allen did what he could to keep the processes of government in action, but to no avail; soldiers and civilians broke into warehouses and carried off supplies; law enforcement ceased. Finally, Governor Allen issued his last message to the people of Louisiana. He advised them to accept defeat, to refrain from acts of violence, to go to work and rebuild the state. He said: "If possible forget the past. Look forward to the future. Act with candor and discretion, and you will live to bless him who in parting gives you this last advice."

Many of the Confederate officials, both civil and military, left Louisiana for foreign countries, where they remained until it was safe for them to return home. They accepted the loss of brothers and sons, financial ruin, and exile. It was written of Governor Allen that "he never whined, nor sought sympathy, nor bored people with his misfortunes." The majority of Louisianians were like him.

Life in the Federal Occupied Areas. Many sections of the state were occupied by Federal armies during the war, some of these areas being occupied continuously, while others were held for short periods only. Generally speaking, the southeastern section of the state was occupied after the fall of New Orleans in April, 1862.

General Butler took formal possession of New Orleans on May 1, 1862. He was a former Massachusetts Democratic political leader, a stout man, with a fair complexion and bright but squinting eyes. He was generally popular with his soldiers, largely because they enjoyed making fun of his high-pitched voice and his somewhat grotesque actions. One of them wrote that he "tumbles all

to pieces with distress. His body jerks forward; his elbows flap up
and down like wings; he seems to trot several feet ahead of his
horse; he arrives at the scene of confusion with a face of anguish."

One of General Butler's first acts was to order the execution of
forty-one-year-old William B. Mumford, who had pulled down an
American flag flying from the United States Mint two days before
the formal occupation of the city. To the people of the South,
Mumford was a hero and a martyr, and Butler was his murderer.

Butler issued strict orders regulating the actions of the people
of the city, and when the women refused to obey the regulations
or to act with discretion toward the Union soldiers, he issued his
infamous Order No. 28 against them. Southerners believed that
this order gave the Federal troops permission to insult the women
of New Orleans. There was severe criticism from southern and
foreign leaders alike. Butler appealed to the Negroes to enlist in
the Union armies and recruited four regiments; by the end of the
war over 24,000 Louisiana Negroes had enlisted. Only in Kentucky and Tennessee were there comparable Negro enlistments.
He ordered the people of New Orleans to take an oath of allegiance
or register as "enemies of the United States."

These acts inflamed the people of New Orleans, all of Louisiana,
and the entire South, and made Butler the most hated man in all
Louisiana history.

But Butler did much for which the people of New Orleans should
have thanked him. He fixed prices so that profiteers could not
operate, installed a system of public works which cleaned up the
city, and gave free food and clothing to the destitute. He closed
the gambling houses and stopped the sale of intoxicating liquors.
Finally, he brought teachers from the North and reorganized the
school system.

But on September 24, 1862, Butler ordered the Confiscation
Law to be put into effect. This law stated that the property of
all citizens who had not registered their allegiance to the United
States was to be subject to confiscation. By late October nearly
seventy thousand persons had registered, and those who had not
done so suffered greatly. While the common soldiers were held in
tight rein, Butler's officers began to acquire property of all types
under the guise of confiscation. In all probability Butler himself

did not acquire property in this manner, but his brother, A. J. Butler, was reputed to have made a fortune for the family by various forms of unlawful practice. The word "Butlerize," meaning "to steal," came into common use.

General Butler was replaced in December, 1862, by General Nathaniel P. Banks. One New Orleanian reported Butler's departure from the city: "There was not one hurrah, not one sympathizing cry went up for him from the vast crowd which went to see him off—a silent rebuke. I wonder if he felt it!"

General Banks eased regulations but the confiscation of property in areas occupied by the Federal armies continued until the end of the war. Most Louisianians, in New Orleans and throughout the rest of the state, never became reconciled to Federal occupation. On one occasion someone remarked to General Banks that New Orleans was a Union city. Banks replied: "A Union city? I could carry every Union man in it on a hand-car."

Life of the People During Wartime. Life was difficult for the people at home during the war. The state and local governments were unstable and often powerless to enforce the laws; sugar, cotton, and other crops could not be sold; banks did not have money to lend and merchants could not afford to give credit; ordinary manufactured goods could not be found. Many Negroes refused to work or ran away from plantations and farms, so that crop production fell off, and some families left the state and went to Texas in order to make a living. Much of the labor had to be performed by women and children, since the men were in the army.

Nearly all goods sold for high prices, which many people could not afford, and Confederate money consistently depreciated in value. By 1864 butter sold for $5.00 per pound; eggs, $5.00 a dozen; and beans, $2.50 a quart. Watermelons were sometimes priced as high as $5.00 each, but from Alexandria in August, 1864, one soldier wrote that melons were plentiful "and in consequence I was never melon-cholly."

People used many substitutes. Old-fashioned home remedies took the place of ordinary medicines, cloth was woven at home and then hand-sewn into clothing, socks were knitted, straw hats were woven, and shoes were made from odd bits of leather and cloth, and sometimes soled with paper and wood. He lived well who could secure or afford the bare necessities of life.

Much property was destroyed wherever the armies moved. The Federal forces systematically looted the countryside, thus preventing supplies from being sent to the Confederate soldiers and compelling them to live off the country through which they marched. Many Federal officers deliberately ordered the burning of property. Years afterward, General James Tuttle admitted that he had been a "house-burner" and that he was the "General Tuttle whose troops, on the march from Milliken's Bend to Grand Gulf, burned so many fine houses on Lake St. Joseph." The slaves of more than one plantation had a "perfect jubilee." A neighbor wrote to Governor Moore, regarding his plantation, that every morning he could "see the beeves being driven up from the woods to the quarters," and that the contents of the plantation house were distributed among the slaves.

Most people accepted hardship and loss of property without complaint, but there were exceptions. One man said that he was brave, that he could stand to be shot at as well as any man, but that *gentlemen* could not endure camp life for they could not eat pork and beans. In his opinion Virginians and Mississippians were not gentlemen and ought to do the fighting. Thereafter his New Orleans neighbors treated him with contempt.

Louisianians were proud of their steadfastness during the war. They were proud of the fathers, brothers, and sons who served in the armies, and long afterwards boasted of them. Years later when a Louisianian was asked something concerning General Robert E. Lee, he might stop and look puzzled for a moment. Then he might reply, "Lee?—ah, yes, I now recall hearing General Beauregard (or it might be General Taylor or some other Louisiana soldier) speaking well of Lee!"

Both North and South deplored the war and each side was glad when it ended. Perhaps northern General E. R. S. Canby, who succeeded General Banks in Louisiana in 1864, summed it up best. "I tell you what it is, Betty," he said to his wife, "this war of brothers has been one of the most terrible things in history. Politicians made it, soldiers fought and deplored it, but it is something to have the Stars and Stripes—the flag of Washington and Jefferson —floating and inviolate over an undivided Union."

22. THE PERIOD OF MILITARY OCCUPATION: 1862–1877

Explanation. This period falls into two separate divisions. The first was the war period, which began in April, 1862, when New Orleans fell, and lasted until the surrender of General Kirby Smith in June, 1865. New Orleans was held by the Federal army until the end of the war, while other sections of the state were occupied and controlled by Federal military forces for periods of varying length. The second period began with the end of the war and lasted until the spring of 1877, when President Rutherford B. Hayes withdrew the United States army units from Louisiana.

In American history the era from 1865 to 1877 is generally called "The Reconstruction Period." This name, however, is hardly apt. "Reconstruction" means "rebuilding," and there was little of that done by the Federal government in the South during those years. More accurately, it was a period of military occupation, for troops remained in the South for several years after the war had ended. They stayed in Louisiana from June, 1865, to April, 1877. During these years the army commanders directed or controlled Louisiana's political, economic, and social life.

General Summary of the Period. The soldiers of Louisiana returned home in 1865 to a war-ravaged state. They faced four major problems: the restoration of state and local self-government, the rebuilding of agriculture, the development of industry to supply basic home needs, and the definition of the place in society of the newly freed Negro. Louisianians would have liked to be left alone to solve their own problems in their own way, but this, of course, was not to be.

Many northerners wanted revenge on the South. One northern historian has written that "Northern revenge in the guise of the preservation of the dearly won Union was worse for the South

Roy J. Bailey

"Belle Grove," near White Castle

than the war." Another has described the "outrages, and humilia-
tions worse than outrage, of the period of so-called reconstruction
but actual servile domination." The wife of General George A.
Custer, who was stationed at Alexandria for a time, wished that
"Abraham Lincoln could have been spared to bring his justice and
gentle humanity" to the solution of the problems.

Probably the most vital problem was presented by the relation-
ship between former white master and former Negro slave. The
whites, unaccustomed to the new situation, still treated the Negroes
as slaves, while the Negroes, inflated with their new situation,
wanted political power, complete equality, and freedom from work.
It would have taken wise national statesmen to have solved the
problem, but there were few wise statesmen in the Federal government.

It was a period of almost constant disorder in Louisiana. The
soldiers of the occupying army insulted and humiliated the people;
Negroes aimlessly roamed the land, stealing and committing other
crimes; radical white and colored political leaders systematically
looted the state.

Loyal Louisianians had to operate outside the law to preserve
order. The Ku Klux Klan, the Knights of the White Camellia, and
other secret organizations did much good until they came under the
control of revengeful leaders and had to be disbanded. Radical
leaders organized the Union League to oppose these organizations,
and as a result there were race riots in several sections of the
state, particularly in 1866 and in 1874.

Many United States army officers stationed in various towns
sincerely attempted to prevent disorder. They counseled moderation, urged the ex-slaves to return to farms and plantations, and
tried to prevent lawlessness. General Custer said that all persons
would be treated as friends and that everyone should try to act
the part of a statesman and patriot.

Three groups of Radicals generally controlled the state government during the period. Carpetbaggers were persons from outside
Louisiana who had packed their belongings in a carpetbag and
come to the state to win political power and make personal gains;
scalawags were Louisianians who joined the Radicals for reasons
of personal profit. The newly freed Negroes formed the third
group.

Several Negroes rose to positions of political importance and
one became Governor for a short period. Of these men P. B. S.
Pinchback, Oscar J. Dunn, C. C. Antoine, Francis Dumas, Antoine
Dubuclet, and P. G. Deslonde were the most prominent. Hundreds
of Negroes became minor state officials or were given offices in

parish or town governments. Many of these were school-board members, justices of the peace, legislators, and other officials who could not read or write or at best could barely sign their names. A Louisiana Negro historian has written that while the Negroes were "illiterate and unprepared for such a transformation in the majority of cases," here and there were men "whose background and training" fitted them for office.

The Negro Radicals, however, should not be too seriously blamed for the part they played during this tragic period. The majority of them were only a short time removed from slavery, had little if any education and no experience in politics or government, and were used as tools by unscrupulous white men. The New York *World* admitted that a "White Man's Party" had been forced upon Louisiana through the organization of a "Black Man's Party," which Radical white leaders had used to rule the state.

The Governorships of Shepley and Hahn. President Lincoln believed that a state could not lawfully leave the Union. As soon as New Orleans was occupied plans were made to establish a civil government and General George F. Shepley was appointed Military Governor of the state on June 11, 1862. He was, however, under the authority of General Benjamin F. Butler.

Shepley restored partial civil government in those areas which were under Federal control. He ordered a congressional election to be held in December in the first and second districts, and Michael Hahn and Benjamin F. Flanders, both of whom were citizens of the state, were elected. They were finally admitted to their seats in the House of Representatives, serving until March, 1863. No other Louisiana Representatives or Senators were admitted to Congress until after the end of the war.

Two political parties were organized, the Conservative Party and the Free State Party, which was favored by the national government. In August, 1863, Lincoln asked General Shepley to aid the citizens of the southeast portion of the state, which was controlled by the Federal armies, in the reorganization of their government. An election was held in February, 1864, and Michael Hahn was elected Federal Governor of that section of Louisiana. Hahn was a Bavarian who had been reared in Louisiana and had taken the oath of allegiance to the United States after the surrender of New Orleans.

Federal Governor Hahn was inaugurated in March, 1864. A few days later an election was held for members to a constitutional convention which met in New Orleans in early April. The Constitution of 1864 abolished slavery, permitted limited Negro suffrage, broadened the powers of the Legislature, and extended public education. Otherwise there were few fundamental changes from the Constitution of 1852. Federal Governor Hahn resigned in March, 1865, after his election to the United States Senate.

Generally, the governorships of Shepley and Hahn were marked by good government and a sincere desire to help the people of Louisiana.

During this period, of course, Thomas O. Moore and Henry Watkins Allen were the governors of Confederate Louisiana. The regular election had been held in November, 1863, and Allen had been elected Governor, taking office in January, 1864. Until the end of the war, therefore, Louisiana had two state governments, the Confederate government and the government supported by the Federal army in the occupied areas.

Governors Wells, Flanders, and Baker. Lieutenant Governor J. Madison Wells of Rapides Parish became Federal Governor of the occupied section of the state upon the resignation of Governor Hahn. The war ended soon after, and the paroled Confederate soldiers, many of whom recovered their citizenship by taking President Andrew Johnson's amnesty oath, returned home. The civil government of Louisiana was recognized, and at the November election Wells was elected for a regular term. It was not long, however, before he was accused of exceeding his authority as Governor and thereby lost the respect of many white citizens. On June 3, 1867, General Philip Sheridan, the army commander in Louisiana, removed him from office, probably because he had not followed closely enough the radical congressional legislation which had been passed in March, 1867.

Benjamin F. Flanders was appointed to succeed Governor Wells, but resigned after serving only about six months. In January, 1868, General Winfield S. Hancock, who had succeeded General Philip

Sheridan, appointed Joshua Baker as Governor. The Constitution of 1868 was ratified in March and went into effect immediately. This constitution was the first such Louisiana document to contain a formal bill of rights. For the most part it was a radical constitution, chiefly designed to give to the Negro the political and civil rights which he had been denied by the Constitution of 1864.

A state election was held at the same time that the Constitution of 1868 was ratified, and Henry Clay Warmoth was elected Governor, with Negro Oscar Dunn as Lieutenant Governor. Warmoth was to take office on July 13, 1868, but on June 27, General U. S. Grant removed Governor Baker and appointed Warmoth to serve until he was inaugurated for his regular term.

Henry Clay Warmoth as Governor. The worst evils of the entire period began with the administration of Governor Warmoth. Louisiana historian Alcée Fortier stated that Warmoth "may have had good intentions . . . but his administration proved to be as disastrous to Louisiana as the scourge of the epidemic and the torrents of the Mississippi." Factional politics plagued the state, each faction stealing as much money as possible. The Governor secured the passage of the Metropolitan Police Bill which organized a police force for Orleans, Jefferson, and St. Bernard parishes under his personal control, and he became practically a dictator through his control of the Legislature and through his police powers. He secured the election of a Legislature in which nearly 50 per cent of the House of Representatives and nearly 20 per cent of the Senate were Negroes; this Legislature ratified the Fourteenth Amendment to the Constitution of the United States giving the Negroes citizenship, and the Fifteenth Amendment to the same giving them the right to vote.

These actions brought a storm of protest. The Ku Klux Klan spread fear and terror among the Negroes, while the Knights of the White Camellia frightened scalawags and carpetbaggers and broke up Radical Negro-white political meetings. The Radicals organized the Union League, and it was not long before Louisiana was practically in a state of civil war, with race riots and other disorders in many sections of the state.

In the election of 1872, William Pitt Kellogg was the candidate of the Radical faction, while the Democrats and Liberal Republicans supported John McEnery. Although the election returns proved the election of McEnery, the Radical Returning Board declared that all the Radical candidates had been elected. However, Warmoth and his faction quarreled, and on December 9, 1872, he was impeached by the House of Representatives and suspended from office. He was succeeded by P. B. S. Pinchback, a Negro who had been elected President of the Senate after the death of Lieutenant Governor Dunn.

Little occurred of importance during the brief one-month governorship of Pinchback. Warmoth denied the legality of the Legislature's action in impeaching him and refused to appear to answer the impeachment charges. Thus matters remained until the inauguration of Kellogg on January 14, 1873.

The Governorship of William Pitt Kellogg. If Warmoth's governorship had been stormy, Kellogg's days in office were tempestuous. It was a period of constant lawlessness and political turmoil.

There were bloody riots in Colfax, New Orleans, Coushatta, and other cities; the Negroes of St. Martin Parish plotted to "kill the inhabitants and to set fire to the residences and plantations." The people refused to pay taxes and organized the People's League for resisting their collection. Kellogg added to the Governor's power by persuading the Legislature to organize the Metropolitan Police into a Metropolitan Brigade on a state-wide basis, subject to the call of the Governor. About this time the White League was organized in Opelousas to oppose the Radical white and Negro domination of the state. A unit of the Brigade was soon sent to St. Martinville where Alcibiade De Blanc, a former Justice of the State Supreme Court, organized a unit of the White League and defeated the Brigade.

Reaction set in, and Negroes in several sections of the state deserted the Radicals and joined the Liberal Democrats and Republicans. Radical officials were forced to resign in some parishes. Songs were composed and jingles written ridiculing the Governor, one of which read:

> *The other day in a swampy bog,*
> *A serpent bit William Pitt Kellogg.*

Who was poisoned, do you say?
The snake; it died that very day.

President U. S. Grant realized that the military occupation of Louisiana must end or a new Civil War would begin, but he left the decision to withdraw the troops to his successor.

The Election of 1876. The campaign of 1876 began with the organization of political clubs throughout the state. The Radicals organized the Packard Guard, the Councils of Freedom, the Antoine Defenders, or the Invincibles. The Liberal groups, in turn, organized the Nicholls-Wiltz Club, the Tilden-Hendricks Club, the Conservative Colored Club, and numerous others. The Radicals nominated Stephen B. Packard for Governor, while the Liberals nominated Francis T. Nicholls, a Louisiana war hero.

The campaign was a bitter one and was the final fight for the restoration of Home Rule. Both the Republican presidential candidate, Rutherford B. Hayes, and the Democratic candidate for the presidency, Samuel J. Tilden, were known to be well-disposed towards the South. The New Orleans *Republican*, a Radical newspaper, threatened Negroes who had joined the Liberals:

He that from the polls shall stay,
May live to vote some other day.

The Liberals came back in their newspapers with such jingles as:

Then come, boys, come,
Make haste to crowd the polls,
The tide of reform,
It rises and it rolls.
The thieves and the rogues
Will have to hunt their holes.

The Radical Returning Board, which counted the election ballots, threw out thousands of Liberal votes and declared Packard elected. On inauguration day, January 8, 1877, the Liberals marched to St. Patrick's Hall in New Orleans and swore in Nicholls as Governor; at the same time Radicals inaugurated Packard at the State House.

The Nicholls Legislature immediately went to work. Departments of the state government and parish and city governments recognized his authority; he appointed a new Supreme Court which began holding sessions; taxes poured into his government's treasury. Packard's followers began to desert him. President Grant refused to permit the troops to interfere.

On March 24, Nicholls proclaimed that his state government was complete in all its branches, and a few days later President Hayes dispatched a commission to Louisiana to secure information regarding the election. On April 20, the President directed that the troops be removed from the State House as soon as possible. This took place on April 24, following which the Nicholls government took possession. The period of military occupation had ended. Home Rule had finally returned to Louisiana. The *Daily Picayune* exaltingly said that the day of the Radical had ended: "His sun has gone down in the gloom of an infamy which will never have a returning dawn in Louisiana."

Finances and Corruption During the Period. The total cost of this corrupt period will never be accurately determined, for much of the corruption was well covered and many of the most damaging records were deliberately destroyed. The state bonded debt rose to over $50,000,000, while taxes increased over 500 per cent. Parishes and towns alike suffered severely.

In 1861 the valuation of all property in Natchitoches Parish, for example, was slightly over $8,000,000. By 1869 it had dropped to under $3,000,000, and by 1873, to only about $1,275,000. In

Department of Archives, Louisiana State University

A twenty-five-cent paper bill issued by Pointe Coupee Parish in 1862

1861 the parish tax was one and two-thirds mills, which yielded approximately $13,500; by 1869 it was sixteen mills, which netted nearly $47,000; in 1873, it had risen to sixty-four mills, which produced slightly over $82,000. By 1874 property valued at $3,250 was taxed a total of $258.01. The same year the parish had a school fund of $15,000 to $20,000, yet had only one three-teacher Negro school operating. Raford Blunt, an illiterate Negro State Senator, was one of the teachers and was also a member of the Parish School Board.

Many of the Radicals made fortunes. A Federal investigating committee in 1873 reported the following figures regarding Governor Warmoth: "He has been governor four years, at an annual salary of $8,000, and he testified that he made far more than $100,000 the first year, and he is now estimated to be worth from $500,000 to $1,000,000." Others may not have done as well as the Governor, but there is little doubt that they did not fare badly.

23. EVERYDAY LIFE DURING THE PERIOD OF MILITARY OCCUPATION

Economic Conditions at the End of the War. Shortly after the end of the Civil War, aged Dr. Sol A. Smith of Alexandria wrote to General Kirby Smith that Louisiana was quiet and that the people were displaying great heroism and fortitude in accepting the destruction caused by the war. He said that Louisiana, like the other states of the South, "lies mangled, rent and palpitating in supreme agony of a ruined and trodden down people." His own plantation, which before the war had been valued at about $200,000, was now worth about $10,000 and had a $14,000 mortgage. Because of the Negro-labor situation, he did not believe that his plantation could be successfully operated and had decided to move to New Orleans and to practice medicine. Returning soldiers were working at all types of jobs to make a bare living.

Many other persons have described Louisiana during those summer days of 1865, and one of them, Stephen Powers, wrote that the saddest thing about the war was its ending. The victorious soldier of the North returned to his home, which had been untouched by the bloody conflict, to "ovations, to pensions, to a happy home." The southerner, on the other hand, returned "to humiliation, to unspeakable poverty and despair."

Another writer described the areas of destruction: the Mississippi River section, the Red River Valley south of Natchitoches, the whole of southeast Louisiana, and concluded that "the state had been quite well destroyed." The Shreveport *Times* described the water front along Red River, as "a barren waste, over which now and then could be seen probably a sleepy mule with an empty dray." Mark Twain wrote that the "whitewash is gone from the negro cabins now; and many, possibly most, of the big mansions, once so shining white, have worn out their paint and have a decayed, neglected look. It is the blight of the war."

A small number of the returning soldiers and civil leaders did not return immediately to their homes, believing that the government meant to prosecute them for their actions during the war. Some went to Mexico and Central America, others to Brazil, the West Indies, or to Europe. Former Governor Henry Watkins Allen wrote from Mexico that every boat was bringing families from every section of the South.

However, Louisianians faced the future with calm courage. One ex-soldier wrote that "we must build a new life, a new South, and not die in the memory of the old." He said that Louisiana was still "our country," and that Louisianians must "not pull apart and refuse our share of work." Armand Lanusse, who before the war had been a prominent Free-Negro writer, wrote to a friend that it was up to the young to rebuild the state's broken economic life.

Negroes During the Period. Before the war Louisiana Negroes were divided into two groups, the Free Negroes and the slaves. The majority of the Free Negroes were educated to some extent and possessed property, and many of those who lived in New Orleans were cultured and had traveled in the North and in Europe. The slaves, on the other hand, were uneducated and possessed little if any property.

During the occupation period many of the former Free Negroes enjoyed economic prosperity and political prestige. They organized businesses which were patronized by the occupying military forces and even established newspapers, such as the New Orleans *Louisianian,* the *National Republican,* and *La Tribune de la Nouvelle-Orleans.* The wealthiest and most cultured of the Free-Negro group frequently entertained Federal officers in their homes or at public places of amusement.

Of all the population groups, it was the former slave who suffered most during the period. At the end of the war wild rumors flooded the state that he would be given land, farm animals, and equipment, and even that the government would completely support him. Unscrupulous politicians promised him "riches, free markets, continual basking in the sun, places in the Legislative Halls, possession of white people's houses, and a great deal more." Misdemeanors and even criminal acts were generally protected during early months of freedom. Being uneducated, all of these things "went to his head."

After the first glorious days of freedom had passed, the rural Negroes realized that the government was not going to support them. A Federal officer advised: "Return to the plantations owned by your former masters. Those who once held you in slavery are not your enemies, they are your best friends. . . . The government will not give you any land or stock. . . . You can get nothing except by working for it."

Many of the rural Negroes had remained loyal to their masters during the war and afterwards worked for wages or a share of the crop. On Brokenburn Plantation in northeastern Louisiana, for example, one ex-slave was given land rent free, eventually becoming a successful farmer. Many of the former slaveowners had sympathetic feelings for their ex-slaves and aided them whenever possible. Governor Henry Watkins Allen wrote from Mexico to his former slave Vallery: "You must be temperate, and prudent, and industrious, and save your money. If I am ever a rich man again, I will help you. . . ." So upon the advice of Federal army officers and their former masters, many ex-slaves returned to the farms and plantations of Louisiana and contributed much to the economic rebuilding of the state.

Slow Economic Progress. Agriculture made slow progress during the period. Markets had been destroyed; lands had depreciated in value; livestock had been killed or driven off; implements and tools had been stolen or had worn out. Large areas had not been planted for some years and had grown up in brush, while many farmers and planters were bankrupt and could not secure working capital or credit. There were bad crop years, and insects and other pests attacked growing plants. In 1870 and 1872 there were serious floods. It was several decades before agricultural production equaled that of 1860.

Transportation facilities recovered slowly. During the war roads had been neglected, railroads had been worn out or abandoned, and steamboats had been destroyed by Federal gunboats. By 1870, however, some of the roads had been repaired, the railroads were partially in operation, and steamboats were again carrying products and goods along the rivers and bayous.

The banks suffered greatly during both the war and the period of occupation. In 1861, Louisiana had had thirteen banks representing a total capital of nearly $25,000,000. In 1865 there were only ten banks whose joint capital had dropped to slightly over $7,650,000. Ten years later only five banks were left, with a total investment of slightly over $3,700,000.

Prices for goods and supplies remained high throughout the period. The average Louisianian could afford few if any luxuries, and many could not afford all of the necessities of life. Home manufacturing of furniture, clothing, tools, and other items in general use was common throughout the country.

Little assistance was received from the Federal government in restoring the economic well-being of the state. The Radical state government political leaders did little, for their principal objective was to line their own pockets. Some assistance was given by Federal officers in the various towns and parishes, but their efforts were limited by governmental red tape and lack of funds.

Education. Public education had languished during the war but in 1865, State Superintendent Robert M. Lusher started a program of recovery which continued until 1868. In that year Lusher was ousted and a carpetbagger named T. W. Conway was placed in the position to enforce the educational provisions of the new Constitution of 1868.

Little was accomplished, for the Radical political leaders stole most of the funds which should have gone to education. The newspapers of that time labeled Conway as an "ignorant, drunken, incompetent politician," and he was finally succeeded by William G. Brown, a Negro. Shortly afterwards P. B. S. Pinchback was appointed Director of the New Orleans school system.

Education reports during the period, which made no distinction between Negroes and whites, reveal that only a small percentage of the children were actually enrolled in school. In 1870, for example, Conway reported that Plaquemines Parish had 4,000 educables with only 100 enrolled, while Livingston Parish had 2,000 educables with only 34 enrolled. Even New Orleans had only 19,000 students out of a total of 90,000 boys and girls under the age of twenty-one.

At the first Louisiana Teachers Convention, held in New Orleans in 1872, delegate W. Jasper Blackburn from Claiborne Parish threw the convention into an uproar when he made charges against the Radicals. He said that the public schools were "utterly worthless, serving no purpose whatever except to provide salaries for the higher-ups." Blackburn could have said much more. The state public-school fund in 1870 totaled over $500,000, but in New Orleans alone over $370,000 was expended on only 350 teachers. By 1871 the sale of public-school lands had yielded nearly $2,200,-000, most of which was stolen by politicians. Thefts by school boards, superintendents, and principals became common occurrences. In 1875 in Concordia Parish, the secretary of the school board was charged with the theft of $34,000.

Realizing the educational plight of the South, London businessman George Peabody, who had lived for a time in the United States, established a large fund to assist southern education. From 1867 to 1877 the white schools of Louisiana were kept alive mainly by this fund and by individual contributions. The Radicals protested but the directors of the Peabody Fund understood the situation and refused to give assistance to Negro education. But still many white children received little or no education during the period and in 1877, out of over 265,000 white children, only 54,390 were in school.

Several Negro colleges or universities were established, the most important of which were Straight University, New Orleans University, and Leland University. Despite private and state assistance, these institutions remained small, but they accomplished much in the way of Negro education.

Louisiana State Seminary of Learning and Military Academy, 1866, from an old drawing

After being open for a short period during the war, the Louisiana State Seminary of Learning and Military Academy was reopened in October, 1865, under the leadership of Major David F. Boyd and four instructors. The seminary building burned four years later, and the institution was moved to the School for the Deaf, Dumb, and Blind at Baton Rouge. The school consistently refused to admit Negroes and after 1872 barely remained alive because of the lack of state appropriations. It was reorganized in the fall of 1877 with the new name of Louisiana State University and Agricultural and Mechanical College.

Religion. Religious institutions languished because of the lack of money to pay ministers and repair churches and because of the poor conditions of travel. But there was much religious activity and Protestant ministers and Catholic priests tried to bring whites and Negroes closer together. They also performed heroic work for the relief of people of both races and all creeds. When Father Gergaud, for example, died of yellow fever in 1873, everyone in Monroe remembered how he had labored during the epidemic; and

From Biart, *My Rambles in the New World*

New Orleans during the period of military occupation

the entire population, regardless of their religious beliefs, attended the funeral.

Revivals or "protracted meetings" were popular among the Protestants, particularly in northern and western Louisiana, during the summer and early fall seasons. In New Orleans, Dr. B. M. Palmer preached with renewed vigor, thundering out his matchless eloquence to crowded congregations. Numerous Negro Catholics left the Church in south Louisiana after listening to the missionary preachings of Protestant ministers.

But the general moral life of the people was at a low ebb during the entire period. New Orleans was a "wide-open" city where all forms of vice existed, and conditions were almost as bad in other cities and towns over the entire state.

Social Life. During the years following 1865 all forms of amusement flourished in New Orleans, where corrupt politicians and practices made easy money available. In winter there were operas, plays, concerts, variety troupes, circuses, horse races, and balls. In summer the people enjoyed water sports, athletic events, and numerous other attractions. After 1869 roller-skating was introduced and the New Orleans Lawn Tennis Club, one of the first tennis clubs in the United States, was founded in 1876.

In the other sections of the state people provided their own amusements, for they had little money. There were "calico balls," "starvation parties," and dances where everyone dressed plainly and jointly furnished modest refreshments. There were church "socials," picnics, fishing and hunting parties, and amateur dramatics.

End of the Period. When the period of military occupation finally ended, the people of Louisiana had suffered the presence of troops and of Radical political control longer than had the people of any other state in the South. The memory of the corrupt government, the economic distress, and the many social problems gradually faded as Home Rule returned and economic, cultural, and social conditions improved.

Years later, an old lady expressed Louisiana's feelings. She said: "It is all over and done with, and let's have an end of it."

PART SEVEN

DAYS OF OLD LOUISIANA, 1877-1920

24. PROBLEMS OF GOVERNMENT

An Age of Political Conservatism. The period from 1877 to 1920 was one of political conservatism. Louisianians had witnessed too many excesses during the period of military occupation and Radical and Negro rule to take chances with liberal ideas or liberal legislation.

Although the Republican Party was active in political campaigns until 1900, it never seriously rivaled the Democratic Party, to which Louisiana, like other southern states, had developed a strong allegiance. This one-party system gave rise to factions within that party, and the political campaigns of the time were usually struggles between two or more Democratic factions. However, no single group was able to dominate state politics for very long at a time.

Louisiana was ordinarily divided for political purposes into three sections: North Louisiana, South Louisiana, and Orleans Parish. Until 1900, North and South Louisiana generally united against New Orleans to elect governors and to control legislatures. After the turn of the century groups from the two sections joined with New Orleans in order to win elections.

Both candidates and factions called themselves "conservatives" or "liberals," but it made little difference. "Safe" governors were the rule, governors who were in the broader sense conservative in their political beliefs. The result was that comparatively little political and legislative progress was made during this period.

Major Political Issues. Between 1877 and 1900 several major political issues caused the people concern and led to hard-fought campaigns. By 1900, however, when the majority of these issues had been settled, voters lost much of their former enthusiasm for politics.

The carpetbaggers, scalawags, and newly freed Negroes who had governed the state during the period of military occupation from 1865 to 1877, had committed many excesses, plunged the state deeply into debt, and caused governmental, economic, and social disorder. The most important single political issue, therefore, was the position of these three groups in state politics, the great majority of voters supporting candidates who promised opposition to them. The carpetbaggers and scalawags lost their offices first, and the last Negroes were elected to the state Legislature in 1896.

Another major problem for the government was the rebalancing of the powers of Governor and Legislature, as the Radical constitutions of 1864 and 1868 had given too much power to the Legislature. The constitutions of 1879 and 1898 attempted to restore the proper balance.

The question of state lotteries caused considerable political agitation. Lotteries had long been used in Louisiana by societies and by religious and educational institutions to raise money. The largest of the lotteries was organized as the Louisiana Lottery Company in 1868. It was not long, however, before antilottery societies were organized. The agitation against lotteries and particularly against the Louisiana Lottery Company continued until 1892, when the Legislature passed an antilottery bill. The company then moved to Honduras and continued to sell tickets in Louisiana until an act was passed in 1894 which prohibited the sale of tickets and ended the lottery business throughout the state.

Before the war, levees had been constructed by the various parishes, but there had been little levee building or repair work done since the beginning of the Civil War. In 1886 the Legislature created levee districts and the officials of these districts made plans to build large-scale systems of levees along the rivers and bayous of the state.

State Government. During the period from 1877 to 1920 nine men served as the state's chief executive. All of these governors were Democrats and all of them were conservative in their general political beliefs.

There was little dishonesty in government; the majority of political leaders were men of high purpose, many of whom were war veterans and very popular with the people. Francis T. Nicholls was probably the most beloved. He had lost a leg and an arm during the war and this gave opportunity for some interesting stories about him. Once, when he spoke on Bayou Lafourche, an old Confederate veteran, who was also minus an arm and a leg, came up to him and said: "Gineral, all what's left of me is going to vote for what's left of you."

Governor Nicholls, whose term was shortened by the Constitution of 1879, served until 1880, when he was succeeded by Louis A. Wiltz. Wiltz died the following year and was succeeded by the Lieutenant Governor, Samuel D. McEnery. McEnery was elected in his own right in 1884 and was followed by Nicholls, who served a second term. Murphy J. Foster served two consecutive terms, from 1892 until 1900, but many people did not approve of a Governor succeeding himself and they prohibited this practice in the Constitution of 1898.

After 1900 the governors were William W. Heard, Newton C. Blanchard, J. Y. Sanders, Luther E. Hall, and Ruffin G. Pleasant, and they completed the economic reconstruction of the state. As more money was available by that time, additional funds could be appropriated for education, roads, ferries, bridges, and other improvements.

New State Constitutions. The constitutions of 1864 and 1868, having been drafted by Radical governments, were generally unsatisfactory to the people of Louisiana. A constitutional convention, therefore, was called in 1879. The new constitution of that year was the first in Louisiana to ask for the guidance of Almighty God, "the author of all good government." It took away many of the former powers of the Legislature and gave them to the Governor. It was a long document of over 260 articles, and it served the state well until near the end of the century.

By 1896 the Negro vote was almost as large as the white vote, and many whites felt that if the Negroes won the next election there would be a return to Radical government. A constitutional convention was therefore called and the Constitution of 1898 was drafted restricting voters to three groups; those who were literate, property owners and their sons, and the voters of 1867 and their descendants. These restrictions cut the number of Negro voters about 95 per cent and white voters by nearly 24 per cent. The constitution also contained guarantees for honesty in elections, forbade the Governor and State Treasurer to succeed themselves, improved the court system, and gave additional powers to parish and local governments. It was even longer than the Constitution of 1879, having 326 articles.

By 1913 yet another constitution was needed. This one, which contained the same number of articles as that of 1898, completely revised the old constitution, and for some time the state government was in a state of confusion. On the whole, it was not a satisfactory document and was rewritten in 1921.

The Spanish-American War and World War I. The United States fought two wars during this period and Louisiana did her part in both conflicts. The old bitterness which followed the War for Southern Independence had almost disappeared, and Louisianians were loyal American citizens again.

In 1898 the United States declared war against Spain in order to help the Cubans win their war for independence. The First Louisiana Infantry Regiment and three batteries of Louisiana artillery did not leave the United States, but the Second Infantry Regiment served in Cuba for several months.

During World War I in 1917 and 1918, Louisiana responded with strong patriotism. Louisianians were eager to assist France, for many of them were the descendants of French Creoles. One lady, who lived in New Orleans, reported that the Crescent City "was thrown into a state of wild excitement." As the troops completed their training and departed, thousands of people assembled at railway stations, the bands playing the "Marseillaise" and patriotic American songs. At New Orleans, on one occasion, the French Consul General waved his hat and shouted: *"Adieu, mes enfants,"* "good-by, my children." But later there were many heartbroken families whose sons and husbands had died in France.

Thousands of men joined the military services, several military camps were established in the state, and various local organizations raised money and furnished needed war supplies. Louisianians bought more than $200,000,000 worth of Liberty Loan bonds. The Jennings Cavalry became a part of the noted Rainbow Division, the Loyola Medical Unit served on the Italian front, and many nurses were furnished by the Tulane Medical Unit. Marine Major General John A. LeJeune of Pointe Coupee Parish became one of the most famous leaders during the war and later became the commander of the Marine Corps.

Parish and Local Government. After the withdrawal of the troops in 1877, parish and local governments quickly reverted to control by the native whites. Of first importance was the repair of parish, city, and town buildings which had been allowed to fall into near ruin. Many records, particularly land records, had been destroyed during either the war or the period of Radical government and those that remained were in disorder. These records had to be organized to enable the various offices to function properly. Taxes had to be lowered although there were many jobs to be done, so local governments economized as much as possible.

Parishes, cities, and towns made slow but steady progress. In 1888, for example, the Concordia Parish Police Jury reported that the parish was out of debt. The president of the Police Jury congratulated the Jury: "The rate of taxation is now lower, the roads are in better condition, . . . and more cash is now in the treasury than at any time since the Civil War." By 1907, Concordia Parish had enough money to begin building new and more modern roads.

Some parishes relocated their parish seats as towns grew larger. Delta was the parish seat of Madison Parish until 1885, although by this time Tallulah was its largest town. After much argument and agitation, the records were suddenly moved to Tallulah one night in a boxcar, and the next morning Tallulah, "by right of possession," was declared by the Police Jury to be the new parish seat. A new courthouse was completed there two years later.

Some regulations made by Police Juries and local officials during this period sound a little out of place today. In 1878 the Donaldsonville *Chief* reported that "horse-racks are being placed in front of the Court-House." In 1887 the Donaldsonville town council adopted resolutions complaining loudly of the "reckless, furious and noisy manner in which plantation carts, etc.," were being driven through the streets. In 1895 the Police Jury of Ascension Parish adopted an ordinance "requiring three or four-mule carts and wagons to zig-zag on the public roads." They had only dirt roads at the time and deep ruts were cut by the wheels of the carts and wagons unless they zigzagged along the roads.

The Police Jury of Avoyelles Parish made many improvements between 1897 and 1918. In 1897, $300 was appropriated for a new well at Marksville, the well to have a windmill with a thirteen-foot wheel atop a forty-foot tower. The same summer a normal school for the teachers was held at the high school. Two years later a new stove was provided for the school at West Par-en-haut. In 1901 the Avoyelles Telephone Company was given the right to build lines from Bunkie to Marksville, Simmesport, Bordelonville, Plaucheville, Moreauville, and in-between points. About the same time loose hogs on the levees became troublesome, so hog killers were appointed.

In 1906 the parish voted $250 to defray expenses of fighting yellow fever and built a new six-foot-wide brick walk around the courthouse square. A new jail was constructed in 1908, and the same year a watering trough for horses was built in front of the courthouse square and spittoons were furnished to the offices and rooms of the courthouse.

In 1910 new regulations were passed regarding automobiles. The speed of cars was limited to fifteen miles per hour on straight roads, eight miles per hour on roads with curves, and only four miles an hour while crossing a bridge or passing a buggy, a rider of a horse, a wagon, or in front of a church. Automobiles, when signaled, must stop until a buggy or other horse-drawn vehicle had passed. An eight-inch square number had to be attached to the rear of every automobile, white on a black car and black on a white car, and each automobile had to be registered with the sheriff, who collected a license fee of $10.

In 1915 owners of dogs were required to purchase dog licenses. By 1918 automobiles were permitted to drive as fast as twenty miles an hour on country roads and twelve miles an hour in towns, but signals must be given when passing other vehicles and headlights must be equipped with "dimmers." Fines for violations of these regulations were set at $10 to $25.

Residents of Plaquemine received a real scare when it was discovered that the 1782 title to the original plantation on which the town was built was defective, but in 1897 the United States Congress passed a special act confirming all land titles in Plaquemine.

During the period the city of New Orleans was ill-paved, ill-policed, and spent little money on public improvements. Much of the time the city government was controlled by a ring of money-hungry politicians, and it was not until the time of World War I that the city began to emerge into a modern, up-to-date metropolis.

Law and Order. The disorder of the period of military occupation slowly subsided in all parts of the state except New Orleans after the restoration of Home Rule in 1877. In New Orleans, however, the change from Radical government brought little improvement despite the efforts of citizens' groups "to suppress crime, to compel the authorities to perform their duties, to watch the city government," and particularly to assist in securing the punishment of dishonest city officials.

Gangs of so-called "tuffs" or "knockers" roamed the city and openly violated the law. A jingle, written about them, closed:

> All over de town dey call me a tuff;
> And when I get roudy I paints de town red.
> I know all de cops; I stan' in wid de rough,
> Yer kin bet yer sweet life I'm er Nu'leens tuff.

After 1877 many Italians settled in New Orleans and some of them belonged to a secret society called the Mafia, whose members committed all kinds of crimes. In October, 1890, Chief of Police David C. Hennessey, who had begun to prosecute all classes of criminals, was shot to death by the Mafia. Nineteen Italians were arrested for the crime, and when a jury freed six and failed to convict the remainder, a mob formed, raided the city prison, and killed eleven of the men. The lynching caused international complications, three of the murdered men being Italian citizens, and the United States government finally paid nearly $25,000 to the families of the slain men. After this, the Mafia committed no other acts of violence in Louisiana.

There were few crimes of a serious nature in the rural sections or in the small towns of the state. In all probability the crime which received the most attention during this period was the murder of Narcisse Arrieux of Donaldsonville, for which crime four men were convicted and hanged. It was estimated that about four thousand people witnessed the executions, which at that time still took place in public.

From King, *The Southern States of North America*

Charity Hospital about 1880

Social Legislation. During the period, there was little legislation passed for the care of the blind, insane, deaf and dumb, or for the aged or poor who could not earn a living. The state maintained schools for the deaf, dumb, and blind, but the Legislature appropriated only small amounts of money with which to operate them. Most of these unfortunates were cared for by the various parish governments.

The insane were usually placed in jail if their families could not take care of them. Private citizens or religious organizations were paid to take care of other unfortunates. After 1880, poor farms were established by many parishes to care for those who could not support themselves.

Many of the sick people of the state were sent to Charity Hospital in New Orleans. The hospital had suffered much during the Civil War and afterward, but after 1880 conditions improved. Modern ambulances were purchased in 1884, electricity was installed in 1890, and new buildings were constructed between 1898 and 1910. By 1914 the total annual expenses of the hospital amounted to over $300,000, part of which was paid by the City of New Orleans and part by the state. That same year the hospital treated over 17,000 patients.

Leprosy, now usually called "Hansen's Disease," had existed in Louisiana since colonial times. During the Spanish period those suffering from the disease had been treated at a hospital built by Governor Miro on a ridge of land between the Mississippi River and Bayou St. John near New Orleans. Some years later the number of diseased declined and the hospital was abandoned. In 1892 the Legislature passed an act which provided a modern hospital, and two years later the Leprosarium was established at Carville. This hospital was taken over by the Federal government in 1921.

25. ECONOMIC PROGRESS

General Observations. Louisiana made slow but steady economic progress between 1877 and 1920. The major task was recovery of the ground which had been lost between 1860 and 1877, and in some economic fields this was not achieved until after the turn of the new century. A noted Louisiana educator recalled that in the 1880's "the people were all poor . . . nobody was rich . . . at the time in which my lot was cast—save in the heritage and the tradition of the curiosity to know, eagerness to learn, the desire for education, appreciation of culture, and aspiration towards better things." As the years passed, agriculture and industry recovered and the discovery and exploitation of new raw materials after 1900 speeded up economic progress and helped to develop industry in Louisiana.

Towns grew slowly, with the exception of New Orleans, which made rapid growth as a trade-distribution and commercial center. By 1912 it was written that "the swamp-land all around New Orleans is rapidly being reclaimed. Pretty, quaint little houses and bungalows, brilliantly painted, are being built, and the outskirts of the town offer a gay and exotic appearance. . . . The road to Lake Pontchartrain, where there is a club and a tea house and boats . . . for hire, is now lined with motors."

The cities and towns outside New Orleans had not yet awakened to the activity of the twentieth century and were just beginning to install such modern conveniences as city lighting and water systems, paved streets, and good drainage facilities. In 1890, Louisiana historian Alcée Fortier visited St. Martinville, describing it afterwards as a quaint "old Creole town" where there was not much activity in business, but "order and decency prevailed everywhere and the people were uniformly affable and polite." The town had but one hotel, which had a wide gallery and massive brick columns, where "everything is as in ante-bellum days; no register awaits the names of the guests, and the owner seems to have implicit confidence in the honesty of his boarders."

New towns were being established in the northern and western sections. Ruston, for example, was founded in 1884 when the Shreveport, Vicksburg and Pacific Rail Road pushed westward across the northern part of the state. The new town was named for R. E. Russ, who owned the land on which it was built. Prospective merchants drew lots for the locations for their establishments, and the first business was the "eating-house" of Joe Schwab, "who possessed a mockingbird that whistled popular tunes and a wife with a generous disposition but a quick temper." In 1887 two brothers named Duson founded Crowley and named it for a Southern Pacific Railroad employee named Patrick Crowley. Plans for the town were drawn, streets were laid out, drainage ditches were dug, and the first sale of lots totaled over $25,000. Crowley became the parish seat of newly formed Acadia Parish the same year, and the year following, a brick courthouse was completed. In 1890, Crowley had over 400 inhabitants and by 1900 the population exceeded 4,000.

Agriculture. During the late 1870's the editor of the Chicago *Tribune* visited Louisiana. He wrote that if Louisiana could be moved to Illinois "it would create a commotion that would throw the discovery of gold in California in the shade" and that the land would bring "three to five hundred dollars per acre." A few years later, at a state-wide fair in Shreveport, a speaker made a strong plea for exploiting the "wonderful resources" of the state. These men and others like them helped to awaken Louisianians to the economic opportunities to be found in agriculture.

It was not until after 1900 that agriculture and general agricultural production recovered the ground which had been lost during the period from 1860 to 1877. In 1860 the value of farm lands had been approximately $248,000,000; in 1890 their value was only $110,500,000. Farm equipment had declined from over $18,000,000 to about $7,000,000 and the value of livestock from $24,500,000 to $18,000,000.

The increasing use of scientific agricultural methods gained momentum as the years passed. The World's Industrial and Cotton Centennial Exposition, which was held in New Orleans in late 1884 and early 1885, greatly stimulated the farmers. The first agricultural experiment station was established at Kenner about the same time and others were soon in operation, all under the directorship of Dr. W. C. Stubbs. Demonstrations were given in the terracing of land to prevent washing away, in the use of new farm machinery, and in the treatment of animal and plant disease, but many farmers were slow in adopting the new discoveries and methods. One man refused to admit that farming could be taught by a "college professor," saying: "Why I've worn out two farms; you can't tell me how I ought to farm." Dr. Seaman A. Knapp came to Louisiana in 1885, and for nearly twenty years taught farmers how to provide their own laboratories, teach themselves new methods, and through this new knowledge to make more profits. When he died in 1911 at the age of seventy-seven, the entire nation paid tribute to his genius and to his achievements.

Up to about 1905 the home, blue-ribbon, or Noble varieties of sugar cane were most cultivated, but they became subject to various diseases and the D-74 and D-95 varieties were then introduced from Cuba. These varieties were soon attacked by root rot, the mosaic disease, and insect pests of several types. About 1920, D. W. Pipes, Jr., and Elliott Jones of Houma introduced POJ seed canes from Java. Still later other varieties were introduced from Florida and from India.

In 1914, 4-H clubs came into existence, and the next year witnessed the introduction of home-canning clubs and the organization of the Agricultural Extension Service by the State University. Agricultural meetings and conferences, where papers were read and discussions were held on various subjects of interest to farmers, increased in number.

Meanwhile, numerous agricultural journals and magazines were being established, over forty of them appearing during the period from 1877 to 1920. Most of them were published for only a few years, but they accomplished many services for the farmer. These publications included the Crowley *Louisiana Farmer and Rice Journal,* the Franklin *Planter's Home Journal,* the Morgan City *Rural Topics,* the New Orleans *Cotton Trade Journal,* the New Orleans *Louisiana Planter and Sugar Manufacturer,* and the Winnfield *Farmers' Union Banner.*

By 1920, Louisiana was abreast of the times and had taken its place in modern American agriculture.

Industry and the Exploitation of Natural Resources. After 1900 the state entered a new industrial era. Not only were additional natural resources of great commercial value discovered in many sections of the state, including natural gas, sulphur, oil and new beds of salt, but the older known resources, such as fur-bearing animals, fish and seafoods, and lumber, also entered a new period of development. Industries began settling in Louisiana because of the location of her raw materials and, in addition, because of the mild climate, abundant water resources, low-priced fuel, good labor supply, and new transportation facilities.

Oil was discovered in 1901 in two places, near Jennings and White Castle, but did not become really important until five years later, when it was also discovered near Shreveport. The commercial

Early oil field near Jennings

mining of sulphur began in Calcasieu Parish in 1895, and until 1914 this field produced about 75 per cent of the nation's supply. Meanwhile, other deposits had been discovered in southern Louisiana. Gas was found near Monroe in 1916 and soon the north Louisiana oil and gas fields were booming. Large-scale lumbering operations began in western Louisiana during the 1890's and in the Bogalusa area shortly after the turn of the century.

Spanish moss, another natural resource, began to be extensively used in the manufacture of mattresses and upholstered furniture. The national fur industry was supplied with Louisiana opossum, mink, skunk, raccoon, and muskrat pelts. The state's more than 7,000 square miles of tidewaters supplied abundant amounts of shrimp and oysters, and fresh-water and salt-water fisheries furnished many varieties of fish, as well as turtles, frogs, and craw-fish.

By 1920 the leading natural-resource industries were petroleum refining, lumbering, sugar refining, paper manufacturing, and rice cleaning and polishing. General manufacturing plants produced lumber products, boots and shoes, brick, cigars and cigarettes, barrels, soda, packaged foods, fertilizers, and hundreds of other products. While Louisiana was still a rural, agricultural state, she was rapidly developing a balanced economy.

Transportation. When the period began, water transportation was the most important method of travel and all of the larger Louisiana rivers and bayous were highways of trade and commerce. By the end of the century, railroads had been built throughout the state, and the smaller lines had been consolidated into the major systems. Roads were greatly improved during the years after 1900.

One Louisiana writer has said that "the most glorious days of steamboating were those between 1880 and 1898." Regularly scheduled river boats ran from New Orleans, Baton Rouge, Alexandria, and other Louisiana towns to Natchez, Vicksburg, Memphis, St. Louis, Louisville, Pittsburgh, and other upriver cities. Smaller and unscheduled boats threaded the smaller and shallower waterways of the state.

These river boats carried the farmer's products to market and brought him farm tools, supplies for his family, and the luxury goods which he desired. Some of the boats carried large numbers of passengers and many tons of freight. In 1897, for example, the *Natchez,* captained by Blanche Douglas who was the wife of noted steamboat captain T. P. Leathers, reached New Orleans with 500 passengers and 4,247 bales of cotton. Small trading boats that plied the lesser rivers and bayous carried a small tonnage of freight and only a few passengers.

Steamboats still had to meet the usual river problems of snags, shallow water, crevasses, boiler explosions, scarcity of wood for fuel at given points, and trouble with the roustabout crews. The larger ocean-going ships sometimes were unable to get over the bars at the mouth of the Mississippi, but this was remedied in 1879 when James B. Eads completed his jetty system which deepened the mouth of the river. The Red River had been cleared of its obstructions much earlier by Henry M. Shreve, but those of the smaller streams and bayous still caused steamboat captains considerable worry. Bayou Plaquemine had become unnavigable in the

1880's, but work to correct this was started in 1895, and the bayou was cleared and a new lock at Plaquemine completed in 1909. Boats could then pass from the Mississippi into Bayou Plaquemine and continue by way of Grand River to the Atchafalaya.

The larger steamboats had become "floating palaces" by the 1880's. Steam hoists replaced manpower, coal replaced wood for fuel, and electric lights took the place of kerosene lamps and wood torches. The cabins were fitted with elaborate furnishings, the dining-room chefs prepared banquets, and the passengers lived in complete comfort.

The old boat songs, however, were still sung and they amused many a passenger.

> *We'll give her a little more rosin,*
> *And open her blower wide,*
> *To show them the way to Natchez,*
> *Runnin' against the tide.*
> *Oh, a little more rosin,*
> *A little more pitch and pine!*
> *Throw in a can of glycerine*
> *And a barrel of turpentine.*

The verses of another song went this way:

> *Late in de fall de ribber mos' dry,*
> *Water lie low and de banks lie high,*
> *Bullfrog roll up his pants jes' so,*
> *An' he wade acrost from sho' to sho'.*
>
> *Water so shaller dat de eel can't swim*
> *'Dout kickin' up de dus' in de middle o' de stream;*
> *Sun shine hot, an' de catfish say,*
> *We'se gettin' right freckly-faced down our way!*

The old steamboat days came to an end shortly after 1900 when the railroad networks were completed. Boats began to decline in number on the Mississippi, Red, and other rivers, but men long remembered them for their whistles, each of which had an individual sound. Albert L. Grace wrote fondly of the "melodious" whistle of the *Edward J. Gay*, which was sunk in 1889. He wrote that the *Jesse K. Bell* had the "loudest whistle," and that the *Paris C. Brown* had "the freakiest of all river whistles; it was of the 'wild cat' variety, up and down, tending to startle one out of two nights'

The steamboat J. M. White

sleep." Another writer sadly admitted that "Stately steamboats with mellow whistles have no place in the modern hurly-burly of reeking gas fumes, nerve-shattering shrieks of freight locomotives and buzz-saw drones of airplane motors."

In 1861 there were only a little over 300 miles of railroad track in the entire state and the longest line was only 88 miles in length. The many miles of track abandoned during the War were reclaimed and a few new lines built between 1865 and 1877. The New Orleans, Mobile and Chattanooga Railroad reached Donaldsonville and began to run trains to New Orleans in 1871. The Donaldsonville *Chief* of October 14, proudly announced that the train arrived at noon each day and departed on its return trip at one o'clock and that city papers not six hours old could now be purchased. The trains had some disadvantages, however: "A man might find a lucrative business in traveling up and down the railroad and picking up the hats that blow from the heads of the

Railroads
1900

passengers. . . . We are of the opinion that there have been enough hats scattered along the road since it has been opened to fill a small size hat store."

Other railroads were organized or reorganized: the New Orleans, Opelousas and Great Western; the New Orleans and Pacific; the St. Louis, Avoyelles and Southwestern; the Vicksburg, Shreveport and Pacific, and several others. Baton Rouge was reached in 1881, and it was proclaimed that "trains will run through from New Orleans to Baton Rouge, and return every day." So many New Orleans people wished to visit the capital of the state that the railroad organized excursion trains. In 1883 the first through-train service was started between New Orleans and California. The Shreveport, Vicksburg and Pacific pushed westward to Shreveport in 1884.

There are some amusing and interesting anecdotes connected with railroad building. When the railroad came through the region of what is now Bunkie, it wanted a right of way across R. B. Marshall's land. His little daughter had a pet monkey but she pronounced the word "bunkie," so Marshall stipulated that the new railroad station must be called Bunkie. When Samuel H. Lockett first traveled from Tallulah to Delhi he protested to the public: "I wish to record as a warning to all travelers that that run of eighteen miles cost me nine dollars." Out in the western part of the state a stage driver called "Captain" Kelly heard that they were going to build a railroad to Texas. "I don't believe they will ever do it, because thar ain't any use in it. I can carry all the mail and all the passengers that ever will want to go between here and Shreveport. But if they do build their railroad I shall quit driving a stage, for I'll be durned if I'll go to Texas."

Most people still traveled to small towns and parish seats over ungraded dirt roads, which were dusty in both summer and winter when the weather was dry and filled with ruts and mudholes when it was wet. There was no system of state highways, individual parishes having to build and maintain the roads within their boundaries.

Chan Lee

An old oil field plank road

During the early years of the period, caravans of wagons traveled over the state, hauling goods into the country areas from the river towns. The wagoneers usually stopped at night at "wagon yards" where stalls and feed were provided for their horses, and the men slept either in their wagons or in near-by rooming houses. One of the last wagon yards in Louisiana was owned and operated by E. G. Calvery at West Monroe.

Louisiana's most unusual road during this period was the noted "Shed Road" of Bossier Parish. This road ran from the hills southward to within about two miles of Bossier City. The brownish-red soil of the Red River Valley was without bottom when it rained, so the planters and farmers tried to make a satisfactory "corduroy" road of logs laid crosswise but failed, for the mud would not hold the logs firmly in place. Finally Judge John W. Watkins of Minden secured a special charter from Congress to build an entirely different type of road; a nine-mile shed was constructed, with ditches on either side, and the road was built under the shed. A four-yoke ox team and wagon was charged a toll of $1.50; a four-mule team and wagon, $1.00; and a person afoot, five cents. The road was profitably operated for a number of years.

Distributing Everyday Commodities. Goods in everyday use were distributed to the people of Louisiana in several ways. In New Orleans and the larger towns were both general stores which sold all types of merchandise and stores which specialized in one particular commodity, such as shoes, men's or women's clothing, or hardware. In the smaller towns and villages the general store was usually the only one found. Though the stores in the large towns were much as they are today, the small-town general stores have largely disappeared. They carried everything that was needed by the farmers, planters, and townspeople—clothing, shoes, foodstuffs of all sorts, tools, farming machinery, harness, patent drugs, notions, saddles, hats, bolts of cloth, spices, and many other goods.

The floating store, or trading boat, was another distributive agent. The owner put his stock of goods on a boat and traveled along the rivers and bayous selling his goods to both townsfolk and farmers. The trading boat resembled an ordinary ferryboat, except that its large cabin was filled with groceries, dry goods, hardware, notions, and other goods. The boat was frequently operated by a man and his wife, the man running the engine while his wife acted as pilot. It would stop at small towns or at the wharves of planters, blow its whistle and then wait for customers. Sometimes the people had very little money, and the floating storekeeper would accept poultry, cured meat, vegetables, and other farm products in payment for his goods.

The peddler operated in much the same way, except that he carried his goods on his back or in a covered wagon or hack and camped by the roadside at night or stopped with customer friends. He traded for his food supplies, supplementing his meat supply by hunting or fishing. While the majority of peddlers carried general stocks, some of them specialized in a particular commodity. A few peddlers were gypsies, and they usually carried only cheap jewelry, trinkets of various sorts, and what would today be called dime-store items. Many of the peddlers saved their money and later established stores in the smaller towns.

In the larger towns and particularly in New Orleans there was a different type of peddler. He walked the streets with his goods on his back or in a cart or hack, or he set up a small stall at the side of the street. He sold coffee, pastries, fruits, meats, vegetables, notions of all types, and other things.

The majority of these town peddlers were Negroes and had special chants, songs, or cries in French or English which they used to advertise their goods. One of the best-known coffee women of New Orleans was named Zabette, and one man wrote that her coffee "was the essence of the fragrant bean, and since her death the lovers of that divine beverage wander listlessly around the stalls on Sunday mornings."

One of the peddler chants went in this fashion:

> *Beautiful rice fritters,*
> *Madame, I have rice fritters,*
> *I guarantee you they are good,*
> *Fine rice fritters, Fine rice fritters.*
> *Madame, I have rice fritters,*
> *If you have no money*
> *Taste, it's all the same,*
> *Madame, I have rice fritters*
> *Quite, quite hot.*

Fine rice fritters
All hot, all hot, quite hot.

Another ran:

Blackber—reeees! Fresh and fine,
Fresh from th' vine,
Three glasses fo' a dime.
Black—berrieeeeeeeeeeeees.

However, the trading boats and peddlers began to disappear after 1900 and few were still operating by 1920. A few stalls are still found in New Orleans, but only during fruit and vegetable seasons can one hear occasionally the cry of the old street peddler.

Banks and Banking. Finances in Louisiana were at a low ebb when the state was returned to Home Rule in 1877. The state debt was enormous and taxes were high. Agriculture was in a bad condition and farmers had little money. Business generally was poor. The result was that in 1879 there was a business and financial panic. Banks closed throughout the state and three large banks in New Orleans could pay their depositors only 15 to 50 per cent of their deposits.

In 1882 the Legislature passed a new banking act. This act permitted the organization of banks with only a small amount of capital, $10,000 in towns with a minimum population of 2,000 and $100,000 in cities of over 25,000 persons. This act did not completely relieve the financial situation, and until late in the period many small communities were without banks. Marksville, for example, did not have a permanent bank until 1897.

However, the situation steadily improved. While in 1881 there were only seventeen banks in Louisiana with total resources of about $23,500,000, by 1899 the number had increased to over seventy-five banks with resources of nearly $55,000,000. In 1898 the new constitution created the office of Bank Examiner, and in 1916 a legislative act ordered him to report to the Legislature every two years. This greatly aided banking conditions.

Throughout this period many people did not trust the banks to keep their money, burying it instead in the yard or under the fireplace, or hiding it in other places. One man bored a deep hole in the leg of a chair, inserted his money, and put a stopper in the hole.

As the state was heavily in debt in 1877, public officials economized in every way possible in an effort to pay off the indebtedness. It was not until 1914 that the State Treasurer could report that practically all of the debt had been funded.

Labor. After 1877 there was much competition between white laborers and the newly free Negroes and it was not long before the leaders of both races began to establish labor organizations. Some of these unions lasted only a short time, while others performed good service for a number of years. By 1880 there were twenty unions in New Orleans alone. The years 1880 and 1887 witnessed many strikes, but it was not until the fall of 1892 that a general strike of major importance occurred in New Orleans. Both sides refused to arbitrate their differences and the strike finally failed. It did, however, pave the way for further labor organization after 1900.

In 1879 many Negroes left Louisiana to settle in such northern states as Illinois, Ohio, and Kansas. Henry Adams, a Louisiana Negro, was one of the most important leaders of the movement, and he claimed to have led nearly one hundred thousand Negroes from several southern states into Kansas alone. Within a few years, however, many of the Negroes became dissatisfied in the North and returned home.

One of the most important labor developments was the tremendous increase of women workers. By the 1880's approximately one-fifth of the women of Louisiana were gainfully employed. Slightly less than one-half of them were engaged in professional or personal services, while most of the others were working in agriculture. However, there were also numerous teachers, nurses, boardinghouse keepers, waitresses, restaurant keepers, factory workers, and even a few barbers and professional musicians. These women workers greatly aided the general economy of the state.

Although labor continued to organize and to strike for higher wages and better working conditions after 1900, comparatively little real progress was made until the modern period.

26. EDUCATIONAL PROGRESS AND THE GROWTH OF CULTURE

General Educational Progress. Education made slow progress during the years from 1877 to 1904. As the old contempt for public schools as "charity" institutions gradually passed, many Catholics also began to regard public education with more favor than formerly. The complications which had arisen between whites and Negroes during the military occupation were effectively removed, and the people, who had been aroused by the waste of educational appropriations, watched funds closely.

The Constitution of 1879, however, was not sufficiently liberal and authorized only small appropriations. In 1887, Professor Henry E. Chambers of New Orleans made a stirring speech to a convention of school leaders, urging the provision of adequate, permanent school funds and the training of qualified teachers, principals and parish superintendents. The next year a new State Board of Education was established, with authority to regulate education throughout Louisiana.

In 1898 the educational provisions of the new state constitution made possible the beginning of more rapid progress in public education. Examination and certification of teachers began shortly afterwards. The movement for school libraries started in 1905 and was followed the next year by the Library Act directing parish school boards to furnish funds for school libraries. In 1907 the State Department of Education established special departments, including the High School Division, the Elementary Division, the Agricultural Division, and the Home Economics Division. Seven years later the practice started of basing teachers' certificates on the number of college credits earned. The State Department of Education was reorganized by the Johnson Act of 1916, which also made other educational improvements.

The Louisiana State Educational Association was organized at Minden in 1884, being reorganized under a new name, the Louisiana State Teachers' Association, during the 1890's. The association held annual meetings in different cities and discussed educational topics and problems. The publication of educational magazines began in 1879 when Robert M. Lusher and W. O. Rogers founded the *Journal of Education.* During the entire period, school institutes were held in the various parishes and annual educational assemblies called chautauquas met at Ruston.

While in 1880 only slightly over 50,000 children were enrolled in Louisiana's schools, by 1903 the number had risen to nearly 210,000, and by 1920 to nearly 355,000. During those years the state gradually increased its educational budget, from $450,000 in 1885, over $840,000 in 1889, nearly $6,000,000 in 1912, to over $16,000,000 in 1920.

James B. Aswell, who successfully initiated and publicized an improved educational program, became State Superintendent in 1904, but resigned shortly after his re-election in 1908. T. H. Harris, during a thirty-two-year period as State Superintendent (1908-1940), constantly expanded, reorganized and modernized the services of a progressive state educational system.

Elementary and Secondary Schools. Public schools made more rapid progress in New Orleans and in the northern and western parts of the state than in south Louisiana, for many south Louisianians still favored private or church schools. Plaquemine, for example, did not have a public school until 1887, when a two-room school house was built, and its first high school was not erected until 1911. Monroe, on the other hand, had public schools prior to 1880 and began high-school work in 1885. One of the interesting rules of the Monroe High School stated that "neatness of clothing and person will be exacted. A child cannot fulfill his destiny unless he is cleanly. Soap and water are a means of grace. It is impossible to conceive of a pure mind and godly presence clad in unclean vestments."

V. L. Roy, a former school superintendent, recalled the schools of the 1880's and 1890's. The first school he attended had a dirt floor and "we sat at tables and ordinary store counters on hard wooden benches. There were no blackboards, maps, globes, or charts. The only desks were those some of the boys had made themselves for their own use." The best teachers were paid $50 a month and the annual school term ran from two to five months. In many cases a vacant store served as the schoolhouse.

As late as 1896 a teacher at Cottonport complained that he was compelled "to rent an old dilapidated building in a field," for which he had to pay "the sum of $5.00 per month." He reported that "with two exceptions, the parents of the children refused to send wood," and that during winter weather he "was compelled to teach in the cold."

The Legislature passed a compulsory school attendance law in 1877 requiring all children between the ages of six and eighteen years of age to attend school, but the law was never enforced. After 1914 all children between seven and fifteen were ordered to attend school for at least 140 days each year. By 1920, however, only about 70 per cent of the children of school age were actually attending elementary school.

The first high schools were established during the 1880's, most of them including all students of the eighth through the eleventh

From Magruder, *A History of Louisiana*

Central High School, Shreveport, about 1908

grades. The courses offered included languages, grammar and composition, mathematics, history, literature, music, and the sciences. Recitations were generally for forty minutes and there were frequent examinations. Outside activities included literary societies, typewritten school papers, military training, and athletic contests in football, basketball, and baseball. Only about 10 per cent of those who started high school finished the course and less than 30 per cent of the graduates entered college.

After 1900, high schools were improved. Better buildings and equipment were provided, teachers were better trained, and school libraries were enlarged. Numbers of small schools were consolidated into larger ones and supervisors were appointed to help improve the quality of instruction.

In addition to public elementary and high schools there were many private or religious academies and institutes scattered throughout the state. These schools generally accepted boarding pupils who lived at the schools, as well as day students. The Cadeville Normal School and Commercial Institute, about seven miles south of Calhoun in Ouachita Parish, for example, was opened in the middle 1880's. Here students could "get board, including fuel, lights, washing, etc., at the boarding hall at $8 a month." The school advertised that the students were "free from all the evils and distracting influences that corrupt their morals." No "loafers, roughs or dudes" were admitted.

Colleges and Universities. There had been many colleges in Louisiana before 1860, but between that year and 1877 these schools had had difficulty in even staying alive. After 1877, however, the colleges began a period of growth.

In 1886 the Louisiana State University was moved to the old United States military barracks at Baton Rouge and additional buildings were constructed. The university remained at this site until it was moved south of the city during the 1920's.

Several state colleges were organized during the years after 1880, principally for the purpose of training teachers for the public schools. These state colleges included the Louisiana State Normal School at Natchitoches, now Northwestern State College, Louisiana Polytechnic Institute at Ruston, and Southwestern Louisiana Institute, now University of Southwestern Louisiana, at Lafayette. Southern University, the state university for Negroes, was founded in 1880 in New Orleans and was moved to Scotlandville in 1914.

Meanwhile several endowed or religious colleges and universities were founded. Tulane University was established in 1884 through the financial support of Paul Tulane, a wealthy businessman. In 1882, Tulane gave all his New Orleans real estate "for the promotion and encouragement of intellectual, moral and industrial educa-

Department of Archives, Louisiana State University

A class of cadets at Louisiana State University

tion among the white young persons in the city of New Orleans." He also stated that the institution should promote "the advancement of learning and letters, the arts and sciences."

Other private institutions included Loyola University of the South, St. Mary's Dominican College, Dillard University (Negro), Xavier University (the only Catholic college for Negroes in the United States), New Orleans Baptist Theological Seminary, Louisiana College, Leland College (Negro), Sophie Newcomb College (now joined with Tulane), and Centenary College.

Libraries. In addition to the large libraries of Louisiana State University and Tulane University, there were sizable collections of books at the various other state and private institutions. The Louisiana State Museum and the Howard Library, both in New Orleans, acquired large collections of books and manuscripts pertaining to the history of the state. In 1897 the Fisk Free Library in New Orleans was combined with the Lyceum Library, later becoming the New Orleans Public Library. In addition to these, many individuals accumulated large collections of books chiefly concerned with specific subjects, particularly those on the history of the state.

During the 1900's, however, Louisiana fell behind the rest of her sister states in providing for the preservation of the records of her past. Although the neighboring states of Arkansas and Mississippi established departments of history and archives, nothing comparable was done in Louisiana.

Newspapers and Magazines. Only a small number of newspapers and magazines continued publication during the Civil War and military occupation period, the majority being forced to stop publication because of lack of financial support. At this time several Radical newspapers were established, a few of which, including the Opelousas *St. Landry Progress,* were owned solely by Negroes. After 1877 the newspapers began to recover their former prestige through the reporting of such writers as James L. Freaner, Lafcadio Hearn, George W. Cable, Henry Castellanos, José Quintero, Henry Rightor, and others. However, because of consolidation and competition, fewer newspapers were published in 1900 than in 1860, although by 1920 the state's city, town and parish newspapers were adequately reporting the news.

The most representative and best-edited magazine was *De Bow's Review,* which had been founded before the Civil War and which stopped publication in 1880. It urged the industrialization of the South and advancement in all economic and cultural activities. Other magazines generally lived but a few years. In all, about a hundred magazines were published. The *Comptes-Rendus de L'Athénée Louisianais* was an outstanding literary magazine and is still being published. Humorous publications included *Gas,* the

Jolly Joker, and *The Lantern,* while the *New Citizen* was especially for women. None of the Louisiana magazines achieved a national circulation.

Literature. Literature flourished during the period. George W. Cable wrote novels and short stories about the Louisiana Creoles, many of which the Creoles believed did not picture them accurately. *Old Creole Days,* a collection of short stories, is probably his most noted work. For over thirty years another writer, Grace King, published histories, biographies, articles, short stories, and novels which gave a more flattering picture of the Creoles.

Though not a Louisianian, Lafcadio Hearn wrote brilliantly on local subjects, and *Chita,* an account of the Last Island hurricane in 1856, is one of the finest books in all Louisiana literature. Dr. Alfred Mercier described ante bellum life; Ruth McEnery Stuart and Kate Chopin wrote stories and tales; Eliza Ripley recreated the old social life of New Orleans. Mary Ashley Townsend, whose pen name was Xariffa, wrote poetry, as did Elizabeth Nicholson, who signed herself Pearl Rivers, and Helen Pitkin Schertz. Albert Delpit went to Paris where he attracted much attention with his dramas. Frank McGloin wrote highly colored romances. Father Adrien Rouquette, noted missionary to the Choctaw Indians of Bayou Lacombe, wrote poetry of high quality.

Charles Colton wrote humorous little poems, one of which, "A Kitchen Free-For-All," began:

> *The fork said the corkscrew was crooked;*
> *The remark made the flatiron sad;*
> *The steel knife at once lost its temper,*
> *And called the tea-holder a cad.*
> *The tablespoon stood on its mettle;*
> *The kettle exhibited bile;*
> *The stove grew hot at the discussion,*
> *But the ice remained cool all the while.*

The poem ended:

> *You'd not think a thing that's so holey*
> *As the sieve would have mixed in the fuss,*
> *But it did, for it said that the butter*
> *Was a slippery sort of a cuss.*

No one knows how the row would have ended,
Had not the cook, Maggie O'Dowd,
Her work being done, closed the kitchen,
And thusly shut up the whole crowd.

Negro literature declined during this period. Many of the old cultured Negro groups of New Orleans lost their wealth or moved from the state, and most Negroes at this time were more interested in journalistic writing and in political advancement. The last important work in French published by a Negro was *Nos Hommes et Notre Histoire* (Our Men and Our History), written by Rodolphe L. Desdunes and published in 1911. It told the story of the Negroes who had contributed to Louisiana literature, art, and other fields, and was of high quality.

Despite the fact that the state took no official interest in preserving its history, many Louisianians discovered and wrote about its past. Richard Taylor, William Miller Owen, Alfred Roman, Henry Clay Warmoth, Sarah A. Dorsey, William Preston Johnston, and others wrote books on the Civil War period. Charles Gayarré had published his four-volume *History of Louisiana* before 1860, but he revised the work during this period and published many historical articles. John Dimitry, Grace King, John R. Ficklen, and Albert Phelps wrote one-volume histories of the state. Alcée Fortier published a four-volume *History of Louisiana* in 1904 and afterwards wrote other books and numerous articles on Louisiana history. In 1900, Henry Rightor published the first complete history of New Orleans.

Painting and Sculpture. The war-ravaged 1860's and the radical and disordered 1870's gave little encouragement to painting, sculpture, and the other allied arts. A revival of art, however, began during the late 1870's, and painting in particular has flourished until the present time.

Enoch Perry painted portraits. Fabrino Julio painted the noted picture the *Last Meeting of Lee and Jackson*, which now hangs in the Cabildo. George Sullivan and Achille Peretti painted after the style of the great masters. Samuel Walker became noted as a portrayer of Louisiana people. Erasme Humbrecht painted murals for the St. Louis Cathedral and other churches. Alexander Alaux painted a large panorama of *De Soto's Discovery of the Mississippi*. After 1914, Luis Graner became noted for his scenes of rural Louisiana.

Alexander J. Drysdale had a studio in the Board of Trade Building in New Orleans where he operated a one-man picture "factory," turning out paintings of Louisiana lowlands by the dozen, and selling them for small prices. It is said that he lined up his boards and canvases and painted all of the skies, followed by the grasses, the trees, and the water of lakes or bayous. His misty landscapes look as though they were seen during a light rainfall. Since his death his works have become much in demand and now sell for high prices.

Comparatively few sculptors made noteworthy reputations during this period. Achille Parelli made head studies, Joseph Domenget and Romeo Celli lived and worked for many years in the New Orleans French Quarter, as did Florville Foy and Eugene and Daniel Warburg.

Other forms of art included wax figures, finely decorated pottery and china, wood carving, cast and wrought ironwork, and ornamented plantation bells.

Several art associations or leagues which encouraged art and displayed various of its forms to the public were founded in the state, particularly in New Orleans. The Art Union, the Southern Artist's League, and the Arts and Exhibition Club were among those founded in the 1880's. The Art Association of New Orleans came into existence in 1905 and about the same time the Louisiana State Museum, located in the Cabildo, began to gather together the artistic work of the entire state. In 1911 the Delgado Museum was completed in New Orleans through the generosity of Isaac Delgado, a wealthy sugar broker. Meanwhile, the colleges and universities in the state began to offer art courses.

The Drama. New Orleans had been a noted theatrical city during the period before the Civil War, and other cities and towns in the state had witnessed performances of both permanent groups and traveling companies. The state rapidly revived its interest in the drama after the war ended.

During the 1860's and 1870's Negro actors performed at the

Orleans Theater in plays by Negro writers, such as Victor Sejour, Adolphe Duhart, and others. Many of these performances were benefits to help the needy of the city.

Soon the whites started to introduce visiting troupes of performers and to sponsor local groups. By the 1890's the Tulane and the Crescent theaters were among the city's best, where Julia Marlowe, George Arliss, Richard Mansfield, Sarah Bernhardt, Minnie Maddern Fiske, Otis Skinner, Walter Hampden, and many other noted actors of the day could be seen.

After the beginning of the new century the Baldwin, Lyric, Elysium, and other theaters were built. At Welch's Hippodrome, later called the Winter Garden, and at the Schubert, musical comedies, dramas, and vaudeville were presented. These popular theaters charged only ten cents for an ordinary evening's entertainment. The first amateur nights were at the Winter Garden, where, if acts did not satisfy the audience, the people yelled, "Get the Hook," and the actors were pulled off the stage.

Shakespearean dramas were popular with whites and Negroes alike. Early in the 1900's a Negro theatrical troupe brought all-Negro-performed drama to the Pythian Hall, the Lyric, and the Palace.

Meantime other towns in the state welcomed troupes of traveling players. The minstrel show had been popular as early as the 1820's, and after the war the entire state swarmed with professional and amateur minstrel performers. New Orleans was the center of this type of entertainment, and a success in the Crescent City meant a successful tour of the state.

Showboats still cruised the rivers and bayous, giving plays, minstrel shows, and other forms of entertainment. Many showboats had romantic names such as the *Cotton Blossom,* the *River Maid,* or the *Daisy Bell.* The *Golden Rod* had a large stage 24 by 40 feet and an auditorium 40 by 162 feet, and was considered one of the finest showboats ever built. The showboat reached its peak of popularity during the years between 1870 and 1890.

The newspapers usually carried advertisements announcing the coming of a showboat; then, a few hours before it arrived at the river landing of the town, a messenger rode through the streets announcing the exact time of its arrival. The landing was heralded by the music of the steam calliope, and when the boat docked, the band crashed into a fast march and a parade of performers left the boat and marched through the town. That night the troupe usually played to a full house.

Music. The people of Louisiana were always a musical people. They enjoyed attending concerts and the opera as well as singing and playing instruments at home. Before the war New Orleans had been one of the great opera centers of the nation, but after it there was a sharp decline in professional music performances throughout the state. Music theaters closed their doors, music societies disbanded, and even the French Opera Company of New Orleans could only support scattered performances. This lasted until after 1900, when there was a revival of interest in music.

After 1880, German singing clubs were active in New Orleans, community singing became immensely popular in the northern and western sections of the state, and brass bands were organized in many towns and communities. The New Orleans Great Louisiana Field Artillery Brass and Reed Band was one of the most popular, and frequently gave concerts outside New Orleans. The Werlein, Grunewald, and Blackmar music companies continued to publish songs and instrumental music.

Louisiana composers began to attract recognition. Ernest Guiraud at the age of fifteen composed his first opera, *Le Roi David* (King David), and later went to Paris, where he achieved a notable reputation. After 1900 numerous Louisiana composers added new vitality and new Louisiana folk themes to the world of music. The New Orleans Philharmonic Society was organized in 1906, and a few years later Dr. Leon Ryder Maxwell became the director of the Newcomb School of Music. These and other men led the music movement in the state.

But it was the Creole who dominated Louisiana music; it was his songs and dances that helped to keep alive the old customs and habits, and when the Creole soldiers from Louisiana marched through French towns during World War I, they astonished the inhabitants by singing old French songs.

27. LIFE IN "OLD LOUISIANA"

Slow Passing of the Old Ways. The years from 1877 to 1920 have been called by many writers and historians the period of "Old Louisiana." It was a leisurely time when no one was in too much of a hurry. People seldom traveled, and when they did, it was generally for short distances, either in a buggy, hack, or wagon, or on horseback. They still retained most of their old customs and living habits, for modern conveniences did not come into everyday use until the later years of the period.

Many of the older Louisianians remembered the days before the War for Southern Independence and believed that life then was better than it had been since. There is a story which illustrates this about a young New York lady visiting Louisiana who remarked: "What a wonderful moon you have down here!" The old grandmother to whom she spoke, replied: "Ah, bless yo' heart, honey. But you ought to have seen that moon befo' the Waw!" As the New South and the New Louisiana gradually developed, Louisianians agreed with historian Alcée Fortier when he wrote: "Let us not scorn the Old South, for the New South . . . is but the continuation of the Old South; the New is possible only because the Old has existed."

The memories of the Civil War and the years of military occupation lingered long in Louisiana. One man wrote that he did not really feel his allegiance to the United States until his sons volunteered during World War I. It was a common sight during those days to see old men wearing suits of "Confederate Grey," the little buttons of the "Southern Cross of the Confederacy" on the lapels of their coats.

During the first half of the period towns and villages kept their old appearance; not until after 1900 did they begin to show signs of progress. One man wrote that New Orleans "was rubbing the dream of her old-time glory from out her eyes and turning proudly to her new role as mistress to the swelling host of stout, black, rusty, prosaic ships panting upon the Spanish Main or breasting the Atlantic."

Creole home. Note the picket fence

Louisianians still retained their individuality; they worked hard but they loved the pleasures of living. When other Americans said: "Anyone who can forgo a certain amount of pleasure can become rich," Louisianians said: "Anyone who can forgo a certain amount of riches can have pleasure." Throughout the years Louisianians retained their love of a good time.

The old Louisiana ways of life were kept by many families, and family duty was still conscientiously performed. One author has written about the young judge who used to sit on the balcony with his two mothers-in-law, two sets of children, and one wife: "After the death of his first wife, his mother-in-law came to live with him and take care of his children. He married again, an only daughter, and her mother couldn't live alone, so she too joined the family

271

circle. Then came more babies and there they all were, quite united and happy together."

The Creoles lived much as they had always lived. They were law abiding and quiet, generally conservative, and slow to change their habits. The family was the center of life, and families were large. One Creole who had a musical ear named his five sons Valmir, Valmore, Valsin, Valcour, and Valerien. Another family did better; Perpetuée and Lastie Broussard had sixteen children, all of whose names began with an "O." There was Odile, Odelia, Ovide, Onesia, Otta, Omea, and so on, until the last baby, whom they named Opta.

Americans from other states began settling in Louisiana in increasing numbers after 1880; they were more aggressive than the Creoles, and the French language became unpopular. Even in the public schools Creole children refused to speak French because other children taunted them or because teachers showed their displeasure at the use of the language. In 1886 the Creoles organized the Creole Association to help preserve their old ways of life, but it was not effective and soon passed out of existence. The old Creole houses of New Orleans, with their balconies of wrought iron, their winding stairs, and their flower-filled patios, began to show signs of age: the day of the Creole was almost over. Of late years, interest has reawakened and Louisianians are now reviving many of the old Creole ways, and St. Martinville is once more the Creole capital of Louisiana.

Improvement of Everyday Living Conditions. The modern conveniences of living which are accepted without thinking today were unheard of at the beginning of this period. During the 1880's William Edwards Clement, who lived on a plantation, learned to read by coal-oil lamps. His home had no plumbing: "The first bathroom, too, was quite a curiosity. Somehow I at first looked upon that new innovation as 'sissy,' encouraging softness." Drinking water, which generally came from an unscreened cistern or shallow well, sometimes contained wiggle tails (mosquito larvae) and small snakes. As there were no door or window screens to keep out flies and mosquitoes, mosquito bars of fine gauze were placed over the beds. People either stayed hot in the summer or cooled themselves with palmetto fans. In winter, rooms were warmed by huge fireplaces, and on Saturday night "we did not turn on the hot and cold water. Instead we luxuriated in the embrace of a big tin bathtub, carried into the bedroom for that purpose— the portable kind, with a raised, roundish back and curved arm rests."

Improvements in everyday living came slowly after 1877 and new inventions provided more comfort, especially in cities and towns which installed city-wide utilities. Though rural life changed too, it was a very much more gradual development.

At the beginning of the period none of the Louisiana cities had underground sewage systems, the first such system being installed in New Orleans in 1880, and in the great majority water was secured from individual cisterns or open wells. "Fire-wells," which were public wells from which water could be drawn in case of fires, were common in most towns. In 1886, for example, Napoleon- ville had six fire-wells and was about to dig a seventh, whereupon the Donaldsonville *Chief* announced: "Donaldsonville has none and ought to be ashamed of herself." A large city like Carrollton, now a part of New Orleans, had over two dozen fire-wells. By the 1890's many towns were beginning to drill deep wells and establish city water systems.

Some of the larger cities had horse-drawn street railways. Though gentlemen paid before taking their seats, ladies sat down and gave their fare to the nearest man, who passed it forward to the coin box or to the driver. Along the ceiling was a cord, at- tached to a bell, one stroke of which meant "stop at the first crossing," while two strokes ordered the driver to "stop at once." The New Orleans and Carrollton Railroad was the first to run its cars with electricity, in 1893. The first electric trolley car was the occasion for a celebration and thousands of people lined the streets as the spic-and-span green cars moved along Baronne Street. "Now," as the people said, "New Orleans rides by wire."

Towns were still lighted by coal-oil street lamps which had to be lit every night by a lamplighter. In 1896 the Donaldsonville lamplighter cared for more than fifty street lamps, and one of the newspapers complained: "Through what is supposed to have been the carelessness of James Jones, the lamp on the corner of Mississippi street and Railroad avenue caught on fire last evening at about 9:30 o'clock. . . . There is a complaint that the lamplighter fails to properly trim the wicks." Two months later the same newspaper urged the installation of electric lights: "We are too big to remain in the dark any longer." Shortly after this it was announced that an electric company was soon to be organized. Crowley, Opelousas, and other cities began to install electric lights, but many towns

Department of Archives, Louisiana State University

No. 3 Fire Company, Baton Rouge, 1887

followed their coal-oil lights first with artificial gaslights, then with natural gaslights after 1916, and finally with electric lights.

Most towns still depended upon volunteer companies of firemen to fight fires. These companies took great pride in their organizations, each company becoming a sort of social club. The men wore bright uniforms, kept their fire engines shining brightly, and paraded their equipment at every opportunity. The Hope Hook and Ladder Company of Plaquemine was organized in 1882 and built a large hall, the upper floor to be used for dances, social gatherings, and theatricals, and the lower floor to house the company's fire truck. Until 1885 the bells of the Catholic church in Plaquemine were used to sound the alarm of fire; after this the fire companies installed bells at their headquarters.

Sidewalks went through four stages of development, starting with a low levee-like banquette, which was afterwards topped with wooden planks, usually laid lengthwise. The third stage was the brick sidewalk. Modern concrete sidewalks did not make their appearance in many towns until after 1920.

Before this period Louisiana had depended during the winter months upon shipments of northern ice which was packed away in icehouses in towns and on plantations to await the uses of summer. Frequently this supply was exhausted before the coming of cool weather in the fall. During the 1880's most Louisiana towns still received their ice supply from New Orleans in barrels packed with sawdust, but by the 1890's many of them had "ice factories."

Special delivery of mail in towns was started in 1885 and free rural delivery in the 1890's. In 1912 the second official airmail flight in the United States brought mail from New Orleans to Baton Rouge in one hour and thirty-two seconds.

Telephones made their appearance during the 1880's. William Edwards Clement has written: "I remember the erection of the first poles in front of our plantation and the stringing of the wires. All this was quite a curiosity, of course, and we greeted it with the doubt and contempt any such fool enterprise should properly merit. People like us, with swift horses always ready could send messages, or visit around at will. We were getting along fine, saw no use for crazy innovations such as telephones. It was just a fad and would soon die out." But the "talking telegraph" stayed and became a part of ordinary daily life.

Motion pictures did not make their appearance until about the time of World War I. In Marksville, for example, "the pictures" or "picture slides" were first shown in 1918, an old building facing the courthouse square being used as a "picture house" until 1920 when "The Palace" theater was built.

Lingering Customs. The old time-honored customs of the people lingered on, however, despite modern mechanical improvements to everyday living.

Courtship was not as easy and simple as it is today. If a young man wished to call on a young lady he sent a friend to ask permission of her father. Couples were seldom left alone, and many a young man spent the entire evening playing dominoes with the girl's father, while her mother and all her aunts questioned him about his family and his financial and social assets.

If he continued to call, papa asked him what his intentions were. This was to save the young lady's time, which she could not afford to waste on a young man who "had a heart like an artichoke," meaning "a leaf for everyone," for she would be considered an "old maid" at the age of twenty-five.

In south Louisiana, becoming engaged was a serious matter. The young man and his father called on the girl's father, all the "family skeletons" were properly explained, and when everyone was satisfied a formal "marriage contract" was drawn up and signed by the young couple and a host of witnesses. This document listed the boy's and girl's financial assets. The girl's father named her dowry, those gifts which he would give her on her wedding day.

This was followed by the engagement breakfast, which was attended by all the aunts, uncles, cousins, and other relatives of the betrothed pair. The engagement ring was presented to the young lady after the breakfast and was usually a ruby in a flat, yellow-gold setting. The groom-to-be presented her with a "wedding basket," filled with articles of lace, shawls, gloves, and pieces of jewelry. She could not wear or use any of the things, of course, before the wedding, neither could she leave her home for more than three days at a time.

Mondays and Tuesdays were considered the best days for weddings; Saturdays and Sundays were considered "common" days on which no one would consider being married, and Friday was "Hangman's Day," when criminals were executed.

A Catholic couple who wanted a really fashionable wedding went to New Orleans and were married in the St. Louis Cathedral; otherwise the wedding was in the bride's church. Protestant weddings caused less fuss and bother; the groom simply went to the courthouse, got the license, and the wedding was performed, either at the church or at the home of the bride. But everyone got excited just the same. On one occasion at Delhi a young Irishman had considerable trouble. He rode sixteen miles to Rayville, got the license, and returned to his waiting bride-to-be. However, the license did not have the last name of the young lady on it, only her first name; so back he went to the parish seat. While he was gone the news leaked out, and he returned to find the whole town gathered to witness his wedding.

The wedding ring was called the "alliance ring" and was usually engraved with the initials of the bride and groom and the date of the wedding. Wedding rings were worn by both bride and groom. After the ceremony Catholic couples signed the register while Protestants signed their names in the family Bible. Rice was never thrown, nor did the bride try to toss her bouquet to her best unmarried friend. The flowers were sent to the cemetery or if she were a Catholic, to the convent where she had been educated.

When someone died all the clocks were usually stopped, the mirrors were covered, and crape was hung on the front door. Older people were usually buried in black coffins, while lavender or gray coffins were used for the middle-aged, and white for children. Everyone dressed in special black mourning costumes, and in many homes the night before the funeral there was a "wake," at which the family provided food and drinks for all the neighbors, relatives, and friends who would call.

A black hearse, drawn by horses draped with black and decorated with black plumes, was used for old and middle-aged people, while white horses and decorations were used for children. Everyone was buried from his home. If his family was in poor or even moderate financial circumstances, the undertaker redecorated the parlor with carpets and coverings for the chairs and sofas and hung black or white curtains and drapes. Sometimes a band playing funeral music went with the procession to the graveyard, and some of the horses drawing the hearse were trained to keep step with the music.

The home, throughout the period, was the center of life. Not long ago an old man said: "Nowadays people are born in hospitals, get married in hotels, buried from the undertaker's. All they use their homes for is a place to change clothes."

Old Superstitions. The people of that day were superstitious, and though not everyone believed all the current superstitions, many believed in at least some of them.

They thought the future state of the weather could be determined by certain signs: gulls flying excitedly in circles meant that bad weather was coming; fogs were on the way if the light of the moon and stars reflected clearly in water. On the lower Mississippi heavy rains were thought to come from Morgan City, so the appearance of a cloud in the southwest caused steamboatmen to say: "Morgan's gonna take the lid off the well."

There were superstitious cures for every kind of human ill: babies were given mud-dauber-nest tea to make them strong and healthy; aching joints were treated with an ointment made from mashed lightning bugs; sassafras tea taken in the spring was supposed to thin the blood which had become thick during the winter; weakly children slept on mattresses of moss gathered from cypresses, in order that the strength of the trees might flow into them. Boils were cured with mixtures of sugar and egg yolks or charcoal and lard, while snake bites could be cured if the wound were immediately dipped in water, causing the snake to die instead of the person.

Bad luck or death was foretold by many signs. Sneezing at the table meant that someone would soon die. To have a haircut on Friday would certainly bring some sort of illness. To prevent losing money, a person burned onion peelings or carried a sprig of verbena in his pocketbook; and burned clothing was never patched or repaired, for to do so meant death in the family. Coffin lids were often left unnailed in order that the spirit could get out on Judgment Day. Though dreams warned of approaching bad luck, it could be warded off by carrying the ninth bone of a black cat's tail in a pocket or by tying butterfly wings to the right leg.

Some people of southern Louisiana believed in evil spirits, some of which inhabited the bodies of living persons and animals, especially wolves, snakes, or bats. There were *loup-garous* and zombis, and children were constantly warned to be careful or "the *loup-garous* will get you." As one old man explained it some years ago: "*Loup-garous* is them people what wants to do bad work, and changes themselves into wolves. They got plenty of them, yes. . . .

They got big red eyes, pointed noses and everything just like a wolf has, even hair all over, and long pointed nails. . . . You keep away you see any of them things, hein? They make you one of them, yes." However, all a person had to do to frighten away a *loup-garou* or a zombi was to throw a frog at him, for they were very much afraid of frogs.

It was thought that the Devil roamed south Louisiana constantly, assuming many disguises in order to fool people. When on earth he was called the Evil One and had many assistant evil spirits like the *letiches,* who tormented babies at night. Sailors and river men were often tempted by mermaids and sirens, and to avoid being a victim of one of these many spirits it was necessary to be very careful.

A few Negroes still practiced voodooism, or serpent worship. Their charms were called *gris-gris* and consisted of bones, powders, chants, and dances.

Amusements. Louisianians did not lack amusements at this time. In the country areas there were hay rides, watermelon and bee-tree cuttings, sugar-cane peelings, family dinners and other gatherings, dances, singing parties, amateur theatricals and musicals, and many other forms of entertainment. In New Orleans there were balls and dances, plays, operas, concerts, picnics at Lake Pontchartrain, and numerous other activities. One old man recalled a few years ago how people used to take rides on the "horse-cars," dance at Hopper's Garden or at the Washington Artillery Hall, take walks along the levees to watch the ships, or ride "old Smoky Mary," the railroad train, out to Spanish Fort.

Circuses, animal shows, and trapeze and sleight-of-hand performers toured the state. Medicine shows, some of which were called "kickapoo Indian shows," presented Indian dances and tomahawk-throwing exhibitions before selling their cure-alls. Organ grinders walked along the streets of New Orleans and other towns, cranking their "hurdy-gurdies" for a few coins.

The people of the cities and larger towns gave "balls" while country and village folks gave "dances," which in south Louisiana were called *fais-do-dos.* Country and village dances were usually held on Saturday night, and in the morning the young men rode through the villages and countryside calling out that the dance that night would be at so-and-so's house. At sundown everyone climbed on horses or into buggies, carts, or wagons and went to the dance; the smaller children were put to bed and the dancing began. Supper was served at midnight. In south Louisiana the supper was usually fish gumbo or bisque, while in the northern or western sections of the state it was soup, fried fish, or fried chicken. The dancing continued after supper until the musicians got up, went out into the yard, and fired several pistol shots into the air, yelling that the dance was over.

City and town balls were much more formal, particularly in New Orleans. Everyone dressed in elaborate fashion, the supper was served formally, and deportment and etiquette were carefully observed. It took a newspaper several days to present all the details of one ball given in Tallulah in 1884.

Negro dances were much as they had been during slavery days, when many of the plantations had slave dance halls. The calinda and the bamboula were still danced, though these violent, primitive dances were going out of fashion.

The custom of celebrating the Mardi Gras season had been discontinued during the Civil War years, but was revived in 1866, and by 1870 the various organizations were again giving balls and sponsoring parades. By 1900 the festivities had assumed their modern pattern, and while New Orleans was the center of interest and activity, there were also celebrations in numerous other towns and cities in southern Louisiana.

One of the most unusual amusements was the ring tournament, where mounted men rode along a course at breakneck speed and with the point of a lance stabbed suspended rings. The riders dressed up as knights of old, and the champion named the queen of the grand ball which followed the tournament. Ring tournaments began before 1860 and lasted until about 1900, when they went out of fashion. They have recently been revived in a few communities in the southern part of the state.

There was much home and community singing, and song festivals were not unusual. Many of the old Creole, river, and water-front songs and Negro spirituals and work songs have become a part of the folklore of Louisiana. One of the water-front songs went in this way:

> *The boys in Wisconsin they take their time,*
> *They go to work to make eight and a dime,*
> *The boys in Chicago they gits a draf'*
> *They go to work to make eight and a half.*
> *The boys in Noo Yawk they oughta be rich,*
> *They go to work to make eight, six bits.*
> *The boys in Noo 'Leans they oughta be dead,*
> *They go to work for fish and bread.*
> *They'll work for the rich and they'll work for the poor,*
> *They'll work for a man jest day long so.*
> *They'll work for Saint Peter and they'll work for Saint Paul,*
> *They'll be in Noo 'Leans workin' when the roll is called.*

"Spasm" bands developed in New Orleans during the 1880's, and by the 1890's there were dozens of them. The musicians used violins, kettles, cowbells, gourds filled with pebbles, harmonicas, banjoes, guitars, all sorts of drums, whistles, and anything else that would make a noise. About 1900, one of these bands began to advertise itself as the "Razzy Dazzy Jazzy Band." The music, with its syncopated beat, gradually became known as "Jazz" and by 1915 had been introduced to Chicago. Thereafter it spread over the nation.

Sports. Louisianians have always enjoyed sports. Boys learned to fish and hunt as soon as they were strong enough to shoulder a fishing pole or a gun. With so many streams and bayous no one was out of reach of a place to fish; even the Gulf of Mexico was not far away. Men hunted bear, bobcats, deer, small game, and all kinds of wild fowl. Wild-hog hunting became so popular in the swamp areas west of the Mississippi that the "hog dogs of Catahoula" were developed, one of the finest breeds of hunting dog in the world. Theodore Roosevelt hunted in the Catahoula country and wrote vividly of one of the guides. "Holt Collier," he wrote, "could not read or write, but he had all the dignity of an African chief, and for half a century he had been a bear hunter, having killed, or assisted in killing, over three thousand bears."

In 1890, Louisiana became one of the first states to legalize prize fighting, and New Orleans became a center for the sport. A "round" lasted until one of the fighters was knocked down. In 1893, Andy Bowen and Jack Burke fought a 110-round fight which lasted for 7 hours and 19 minutes. The fight ended in a draw.

After 1877 the "baseball fever" hit Louisiana and it was not long before every village and town had its team. Rules were different from those of today and huge scores were common, the Donaldson-ville *Chief* reporting in 1877 a game that was won by a "majority of nineteen runs."

Bicycles appeared in 1884, clumsy, large-wheeled affairs which often had a third smaller wheel on the side to help the rider balance himself. Automobiles began to make their appearance shortly after 1900, and in 1909, Ralph DePalma set a world's record at New Orleans with a speed of 60 miles per hour. In 1910 an "international aviation tournament" was held at New Orleans. One of the planes rose to over 7,000 feet and recorded a mile in 57 seconds. The featured event of this tournament was a race between an automobile and an airplane. The Packard car defeated the plane, which was piloted by John Moisant, for whom present-day Moisant Airport was named.

Foods. Everyone ate well during those days, for Louisiana furnished all forms of foodstuffs. The classics of Creole cookery included jambalaya, *daubes glacées,* grillades, fricassees, brochettes, gumbos, bisques, court boullions, as well as the more common red beans and rice. Sunday dinners and banquets took much time because of the endless procession of dishes.

One British traveler reported the dinner menu of a New Orleans hotel as follows:

Soups.—Ox-joint; vermicelli.
Fish.—Baked red snapper, with brown oyster sauce.
Boiled.—Leg of mutton, with caper sauce; sugar-cured ham; corn beef.
Cold dishes.—Corned beef; roast beef; mutton; ham.
Roasts.—Beef; loin of lamb; pig, with apple sauce; loin of pork; loin of mutton; loin of veal.
Entrees.—Beef à la mode; calves head, with brain sauce; croquettes of rice, with lemon sauce; calves feet à la Pascaline; veal and ham

scalloped with mushrooms; maccaroni, with Italian sauce; oyster patties.

Vegetables.—Irish potatoes, mashed or boiled; hominy; rice; beans; spinach; cabbage.

Relishes.—Worchestershire sauce; mushroom catsup; walnut and tomatto catsup; pickled beets; mixed pickles; pickled cucumbers; Cumberland sauce; lettuce; cheese; Harvey sauce; beef-steak sauce; John Bull sauce.

Pastry and Pudding.—Gooseberry pie; bread pudding, with brandy sauce; Pethivier pie; Genoese perlies; Biscuits Milanais; annisette jelly; English cream.

Desert.—Raisins; filberts; almonds; pecans; oranges.

Coffee.

The Englishman wrote that he would have to have the stomach of one of the old Greek Gods in order to enjoy all the dishes.

PART EIGHT

MODERN LOUISIANA

28. POLITICS SINCE 1920

Characteristics of the Period. Following the end of military occupation in 1877, the major political issues had been economy in government, conservative legislation, and the maintenance of white leadership. Political campaigners had promised liberal reforms but after their election had accomplished little, and though some progress had been made, Louisiana, like the other southern states, had failed to progress as much as it should have.

After 1920 the people became intensely interested in political issues, joined political factions, and actively campaigned for their chosen candidates. Political candidates were beginning to promise more and more reforms, the majority of which were of the type which would improve the living standards or the welfare of the farmer and of the working classes of society.

During the past thirty-five years many of these proposed reforms have become realities. They include better roads and bridges, better elementary schools, high schools, and colleges, better hospitals and institutions for the deaf, dumb, and blind. There are superior mental and penal institutions, and public health and welfare conditions have been improved.

Constitution of 1921. The Constitution of 1921, the last to be adopted by the state, is the ninth constitution adopted since that of 1812. Only three other states have ratified more recent constitutions. The Louisiana Constitution of 1921 is the longest constitution in the nation and in 1954 ran to over 560 pages, with over 125 pages of index. This is because 326 amendments have been added since 1921. Amendments have been proposed by every Legislature except that of 1940.

284

No one had been satisfied with the Constitution of 1913, for in general it followed that of 1898 and contained many provisions which had no place in a constitution. Almost immediately after its adoption, there was agitation for a new document. In 1920 the Legislature called a new constitutional convention which met the following year and was unusual in that it had three women members. The most important items considered by this convention were the severance tax, the income tax, education, and roads. The severance tax was one levied on all natural resources such as salt, natural gas, or oil, severed or taken from the ground. After more than three and a half months, the constitution was finally completed.

Some people believed that it was too conservative, others that it was too progressive. Despite its length, the unusual number of amendments which have been necessary, and its weaknesses, it has served Louisiana well. Many political leaders today, however, believe that the state should now have a new constitution.

Political Issues. The chief political issues since 1920 have been roads, education, social welfare, labor, taxes, the proper use of natural resources, and the relative power and authority of the Governor, the Legislature, and local government officials. Political leaders and factions have disagreed about these things, and over them bitter battles have been fought; because of them, political leaders have risen to positions of influence which not all of them were able to retain.

At times the people have become very excited over these issues, while at other times they have seemed to take little interest and their campaigns have been quiet. Louisiana has, on the whole, however, been a politically active state.

Governors Parker, Fuqua and Simpson. John M. Parker became Governor in 1920. It was an exciting term, for the Governor worked actively for many projects to which there was opposition. Plans were made for the Constitutional Convention of 1921; problems arose over the planning of a state highway system; and the illegal activities of the newly reorganized Ku Klux Klan caused trouble, particularly in northern Louisiana. While there was public approval of the Governor's plans for a new state university, the proposed Civil Service law caused controversy. Though only a part of Governor Parker's program succeeded, much progress was made. Louisiana was rapidly shaking off the old-fashioned past.

Parker was followed by Henry L. Fuqua. Fuqua's chief opponent in the 1924 election was a young lawyer named Huey P. Long who was Chairman of the Public Service Commission. Fuqua died in office in 1926 and was succeeded by Lieutenant Governor Oramel H. Simpson. It was during this administration that the first buildings at the new university campus south of Baton Rouge were completed. The Ku Klux Klan problem continued, so legislation was passed outlawing all sorts of hoods, masks, or robes, excepting only those which were worn at Mardi Gras time or at masked balls or parties. A toll bridge east of New Orleans across a part of Lake Pontchartrain was authorized. In 1927 a terrible flood caused Louisiana, Arkansas, and Mississippi to league together to secure Federal aid for flood prevention. The State Highway Commission was reorganized.

Huey Long in Control of Louisiana Government. In the campaign of 1928, Huey Long again ran for the governorship. This time, however, he had the support of many New Orleanians who had not supported him in 1924. Long was an ardent progressive. He promised a free bridge east of New Orleans so that the people would not have to travel over the toll bridge which was being built across Lake Pontchartrain. He promised free textbooks, better roads and other new bridges, improved schools, more care for unfortunates who were poor, blind, deaf, dumb, aged, or sick. He promised natural gas for the city of New Orleans.

Long constantly toured the state, speaking and organizing the farmer and working classes against the wealthy and politically powerful groups which had formerly been in control of the state government. He spoke the language of the country people when in the country districts and the language of the city dwellers when in the cities and towns. His most noted speech was supposedly given at St. Martinville, at the Evangeline Oak, where he attacked the old governing groups:

Where are the schools that you have waited for your children to have that have never come? Where are the roads and the highways that you spent your money to build, that are no nearer now than ever before? Where are the institutions to care for the sick and the disabled? Evangeline wept bitter tears in her disappointment. But they lasted through only one lifetime. Your tears in this country, around this oak, have lasted for generations. Give me the chance to dry the tears of those who still weep here.

He spoke in small communities where a speech by a candidate for Governor had never been heard. He called people by their first names, and developed an art of speechmaking which delighted the people by its humorous attacks on his opponents. Everyone laughed when he walked mincingly across the stage, explaining that he had finally saved enough money to buy a new pair of shoes and that his feet hurt. Parish and local leaders began to join him. He won the election.

He was a Governor who did not forget his campaign promises. He built a free bridge eastward from New Orleans across Chef Menteur and the Rigolets. Free textbooks, better roads and bridges, improved schools, a great state university, and more care for unfortunates soon became realities. A new Governor's mansion was built, and a new state capitol.

In 1929 there was an attempt to impeach him which failed, and the next year he was elected to the United States Senate. He remained Governor until January 25, 1932, when Alvin O. King, the president pro tempore of the State Senate, officially succeeded him.

During these years Long built up a political machine which controlled every phase of the state government and many of the parish governments. In so doing he made many enemies who either opposed his policies, argued that he was moving too fast, or were envious of his power. His opponents said that he had become the "Dictator of Louisiana," but he paid little attention to them and continued with his programs. Senator Long was assassinated in the state capitol in September, 1935.

Meantime, in 1932, Oscar K. Allen, who had been one of Long's first supporters, had been elected Governor. He continued Long's program until his own death in 1936. His term was completed by the president pro tempore of the Senate, James A. Noe, Lieutenant Governor John B. Fournet having been elected to the State Supreme Court.

Department of Commerce and Industry

Louisiana State Capitol

The election of 1936 saw the beginning of the period in Louisiana politics in which we live today. The political factions were lined up on two sides, one group composed of former followers of Huey Long, the other of those who had opposed him. These two large groups have campaigned in each election since 1936; in many first primary elections, however, they have split into smaller groups, led by one candidate or another.

Governors of the last quarter century. Five men have served as governor of the state since 1936. Long faction candidate Richard W. Leche was elected in that year and served until his resignation at the outbreak of the "Louisiana Scandals" in the summer of 1939. He was succeeded by Lieutenant Governor Earl K. Long, who completed his term of office. Sam Houston Jones, a member of the anti-Long faction, was elected in 1940 and was followed by James H. Davis, a member of the same political group, in 1944. Since 1948 the following men have served as the state's chief executive: Earl K. Long (1948-1952), Robert F. Kennon (1952-1956), Earl K. Long (1956-1960), and James H. Davis since 1960.

Modern political trends and issues. Since 1920 Louisianians have been actively interested in state-wide political issues, have supported their chosen political factions, and have aided in the campaigns of their favorite candidates for public offices. Candidates have promised more and more reforms, the great majority of which would improve the living standards and general welfare of the farmers and other working classes of society. Many of these proposed reforms have become realities. There are better roads and bridges, better elementary and secondary schools, colleges and universities, better hospitals, better institutions for the deaf, dumb, and blind, and improved mental and penal institutions. Large sums of money have been appropriated for public health and welfare and pensions for the aged. The movement which began in the early 1920's is still in active progress, and the state is performing services never dreamed of a generation ago.

The most important political issues have included education, social welfare, roads, labor, taxes, civil service, the conservation of natural resources, the development of industry, and the relative authority of the governor, the legislature, and local government officials. Political leaders have disagreed over these issues and over them waged their campaigns.

Major functions and agencies of state government. Based on the expenditure of public funds, the major functions of modern Louisiana state government are concerned with education, public welfare, highways, and hospitals and institutions. More than 80 per cent of the state's total expenditures during the fiscal year 1957-1958 were used for these functions of government.

The reason for the state's intense interest in its educational system is obvious, since an educated and informed citizenry is the foundation of the American democratic form of government and the American way of life. Louisiana supports a very broad educational program, which includes elementary and secondary education, trade and vocational schools, special schools for the blind, deaf, and other physically handicapped children, and colleges and universities.

The Board of Public Welfare is the agency charged with establishing the policies, rules and regulations of the Department of Public Welfare. The most important categories of public assistance include old age assistance, aid to the needy blind, aid to dependent children, disability assistance, general assistance and foster care.

The State Department of Highways is supervised by the Board of Highways and is responsible for the regulation, construction, maintenance, and use of the state highway system. Each parish is responsible for parish roads but receives financial assistance from the state. Towns and cities regulate and maintain their street systems, but the State Department of Highways maintain streets which are extensions of state highways.

Large sums are spent each year for the health and well-being of the citizens of Louisiana. The State Hospital Board is the supervising agency of the Department of Hospitals, which operates all state hospitals except the Charity Hospital of Louisiana at New Orleans, the Confederate Memorial Medical Center at Shreveport, and the State Colony and Training School at Pineville, which are under separate boards. The Department of Hospitals also administrates the Hot Wells Health Resort near Alexandria and other health agencies. The State Board of Health supervises the activities of the State Department of Health. This department administers state funds and federal funds allocated to Louisiana for many basic public health services.

There are numerous other state boards, commissions, and agencies which protect and assist the people of the state in living normal and contented lives. Unlike citizens of many other states, Louisianians believe that these services are functions of the state government rather than of the parishes, cities and towns.

The administration of state government is the responsibility of several elected state officials, headed by the Governor, who has broad executive and appointive powers. Other elected executive officials include the Secretary of State, the Lieutenant Governor, the Commissioner of Agriculture and Immigration, the Attorney General, the Comptroller, the State Superintendent of Public Education, the Commissioner of Insurance, the Register of the State Land Office, and the State Treasurer.

Taxation and the Cost of Government. In 1921 the total income of the state was only a little over $17,000,000; in 1954–55 it was almost $500,000,000. In 1954–55 nearly 23 per cent of the state's income came from mineral leases and royalties, about 17 per cent from Federal government grants, and a little over 12 per cent from taxes on natural resources taken from on or from under the ground. The sales tax brought in over 12 per cent; other taxes, including those on gasoline, tobacco, incomes, beverages, licenses, and fees of various types, made up the balance of the state's income.

In 1954–55 the state spent nearly $450,000,000, of which $91,000,000 had been received from the Federal government. Of this amount over 32 per cent went for education, 24 per cent for public welfare, and 16 per cent for highways. The rest of the money was spent for hospitals and institutions, homestead exemptions, paying off the state debt and the interest on it, and the costs of government and other services.

Government and the operation of governmental services cost a great deal of money. Louisiana governmental services have been greatly extended since 1920, and therefore their cost has greatly increased. In 1955 the state government employed nearly 35,000 persons and the municipal and parish governments nearly 60,000 persons. Of the state employees, for example, nearly 10,000 served in the health, welfare and hospital divisions, and over 5,000 in the Highway Department. During this period many agencies of government, such as the departments of Agriculture and Immigration, Public Works, Conservation, Public Safety, Commerce and Industry, Labor, Education, and the boards of Institutions, Forestry, and Civil Service, have been established or have greatly expanded their facilities and functions. These and other state agencies, rather than parish, city, or other local agencies, now perform services for citizens of the state not dreamed of a generation ago.

Summary of the Period. The period from 1920 to the present has been called "The Progressive Age of Louisiana," and also "The

Severance 33.1% *

Vehicle Licenses 2.86%

Other State Taxes 3.63%

Sales 21.52% -

Beverages 5.18%

Petroleum Products 16.23%

Corporate Franchises 3.48%

Income 7.5%

Tobacco 6.5%

*Includes old gas gathering tax

From Department of Revenue, "Annual Report, 1959-60"

Sources of tax revenue, 1959-60

Age of Huey Long." Huey Long was the dominant figure in Louisiana politics from the time of his election to the governorship in 1928 until his death in 1935. Since that time the Long faction and the anti-Long faction have battled for the leadership and control of state affairs, and the majority of state officials have held their offices for short periods. A few of them, however, have drawn support from both factions and have served through changing administrations of government.

Louisiana's representatives and senators have generally taken little part in state political battles and have represented the people of their districts or the entire state rather than a political faction. Senator Allen J. Ellender has served continuously since his election in 1936 and Senator Russell Long, the eldest son of Huey Long, since 1948.

Much liberal legislation has been passed by the legislatures since 1920, and Louisiana has emerged as a progressive state. Just how much of this can be credited to Huey Long no one can say, but it must be realized that other leaders would have forged ahead too, for progress was a sign of the times. How much of a political dictator was Huey Long? One critic has charged that he had the

From Department of Revenue, "Annual Report, 1959-60"
Distribution of tax revenue, 1959-60

"highest degree of state control ever recorded under America's democratic form of government." Was his over-all leadership of Louisiana government good or bad? A historian recently admitted that "he may have done a lot to jerk the state into the 20th century." One writer on the period wrote that "he gave the people what he had promised them and this was unique in Louisiana history." Another said that "probably the best evaluation of him is to say he was not half as good as his friends would have you believe, and not half as bad as his enemies would want you to believe." The Louisiana voters of Huey Long's day made their own decisions, voting either for or against him. The final decision can be made only by the long test of history.

No one will deny that much progress has been made in Louisiana since 1920 and that since World War II a New Louisiana is rapidly developing. Great strides forward are being made in all fields of life—in agriculture, business, manufacturing, trade, education, and in welfare services to the unfortunate. Today Louisiana faces the future with confidence.

29. ECONOMIC DEVELOPMENT, 1920–1955

General Observations. The economic life of Louisiana since 1920 can be divided into four distinct periods. The state made steady progress until 1929, when the entire United States was hit by a depression during which Louisiana suffered as did the other states. After the nation entered World War II in 1941 the state's entire economy was geared to meeting wartime emergencies. Since 1946, Louisiana has made rapid strides in all phases of economic life.

The population of the state and its cities has grown rapidly. In 1920 the population of Louisiana was approximately 1,800,000; by 1950 it had grown to nearly 2,700,000; and in 1960 was almost 3,250,000.

During recent years Louisiana's people have begun to move from the rural areas to the towns and cities in greater numbers than ever before, most of them moving to small towns rather than to cities. Now rather more than half of the people of the state live in urban centers. New Orleans is still the largest city, with a population of nearly 700,000, while Baton Rouge and Shreveport have been running a very close race for the second position. Many of the villages of 1920 are now sizable towns, and many of the towns have grown into cities.

Agriculture. Modern Louisiana is still primarily an agricultural state. Over 500,000 people live on farms and produce crops, live-

A. J. Rybiski, Jr.; Lake Charles Association of Commerce

Harvesting rice in southwestern Louisiana

A field of cotton in northeastern Louisiana

Madison Parish Chamber of Commerce

stock, and poultry which in 1954 were valued at over $360,000,-000. These farms occupy almost 40 per cent of the total area of Louisiana, the average farm having 103 acres. In 1954 there were over 110,000 farms and the average value per acre was $111.16. More than half of these farms are operated by families who own the land.

Many different crops are grown, ranging from cotton, sugar cane, and tobacco to rice, sweet potatoes, strawberries, pecans, and truck-garden products, and include even lily bulbs and vetiver, a grass whose roots are used in making perfume. Some crops, particularly rice, have to be irrigated, but the great majority depend upon natural rainfall. Louisiana has a particularly long growing season, which in some cases makes possible the growing of two or more crops a year. The state ranks first in the nation in the production of sugar cane, sweet potatoes, and early spring strawberries, second in rice and tung nuts, sixth in cotton and velvet beans, and eighth in cowpeas.

Cotton is the most important crop, and in 1954, Louisiana ginned 555,000 bales valued at nearly $100,000,000. Franklin, Richland, Caddo, St. Landry, and Morehouse are the leading cotton-producing parishes. Rice is grown principally in southwest Louisiana, where the growing plants are irrigated from bayous or wells. In 1954, Vermilion, Jefferson Davis, Acadia, Calcasieu, and Evangeline parishes were the principal rice producers, yielding over 33,000,000 bushels valued at nearly $66,000,000. While Louisiana ranks first among the states in the production of sugar cane, this crop ranks third in Louisiana. In 1954 the production of over 5,500,000 tons was produced chiefly in Iberia, St. Mary, Terrebonne, Assumption, and Lafourche parishes and was sold for nearly $35,000,000.

The minor crops include sweet potatoes from St. Landry, Lafayette, Acadia, St. Martin, and Evangeline parishes; strawberries from the Florida Parishes; and truck crops from the lower Red River and lower Mississippi River valleys. Corn is grown over the entire state and is used chiefly for the production of corn meal and cereals and for the feeding of livestock; hay and forage crops for livestock are also grown on a state-wide basis. Perique tobacco is grown only in St. James Parish and is used for flavoring purposes. Vetiver is

grown in Tangipahoa Parish and Creole Easter-lily bulbs in Plaquemines Parish. Comparatively small quantities of oats, peanuts, soy-
beans, peas, and other crops are produced by farmers engaged in
general farming. The pecan is the principal orchard tree, though

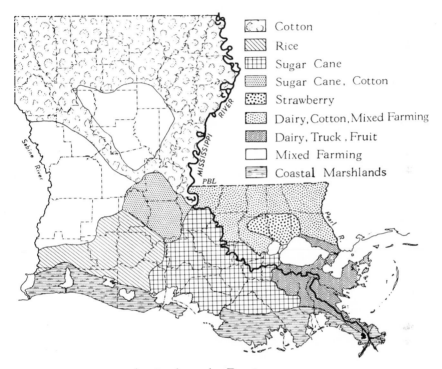

Cotton
Rice
Sugar Cane
Sugar Cane, Cotton
Strawberry
Dairy, Cotton, Mixed Farming
Dairy, Truck, Fruit
Mixed Farming
Coastal Marshlands

Agricultural   Regions

peaches, oranges, and other fruits are grown. Among the truck
crops are cabbage, cauliflower, broccoli, turnips, onions, lettuce,
spinach, okra, and cucumbers. The area surrounding New Orleans
is an immense truck-gardening district which supplies the markets
of the north and east during the winter and early spring months.

During recent years Louisiana has developed into an important
livestock-producing state. Over two-thirds of the farmers raise
cattle, hogs, and sheep for sale to city markets and packing houses.
Dairying is an important part of Louisiana agriculture, and in
1954 over 300,000 dairy cows produced milk, cream, and butter

valued at more than $40,000,000. Early in 1955 a livestock census was taken and it was found that the cattle population was nearly 1,800,000, the hog population was 410,000, and the sheep population was 132,000. These animals, together with poultry, were valued at over $115,000,000.

Many factors have aided in the improvement of agriculture since 1920. There have been inventions and improvements in agricultural machinery, as for example the cotton-picker and the sugarcane harvester. The State Department of Agriculture and Immigration, together with the United States Department of Agriculture, has greatly aided agriculture through various livestock, poultry, plant, and other programs. A relentless attack has been declared against pests and diseases of all varieties. The Louisiana Agricultural Extension Service now operates in all parishes, and farmers are taught how to operate their farms more efficiently. A few years ago Bicniar Prioux of Iberia Parish wrote that "the Extension Service is the best thing that ever happened for the farmer who has to make a living from his farm." Agricultural fairs and festivals have encouraged farmers to take greater pride in what they raise or grow. Today the Louisiana farmer is a businessman engaged in the raising of plants and animals which are needed by the people of the state or the nation.

Lumbering and Forest Products. Louisiana has over 16,000,-000 acres of forested land, practically all of which is of commercial value. On about two-thirds of this total acreage grow oak, ash, hickory, and other hardwoods, while the remaining third grows several varieties of pine. In 1954 over 40,000 people were engaged in the various wood-products industries, and their production totaled nearly $500,000,000.

The lumbering and forest industries are greatly assisted by the State Forestry Commission. This commission helps enforce laws, guards against forest fires and pests, replants cutover areas, and conducts experiments for improving the various types of trees.

Wood products include lumber of all types, shingles, barrels and hogsheads, veneers and plywoods, boxes, railroad ties, telephone and telegraph poles, furniture, wooden fixtures, pulp for paperboard and containerboard, and other articles.

A north Louisiana lumber mill

Oil, Gas and Minerals. Louisiana has been blessed with large deposits of oil, gas, and nonmetallic minerals. There are no metallic minerals in the state. In 1955 these underground resources were valued at more than a billion dollars by the United States Bureau of Mines.

There are oil or gas wells in practically all the state's sixty-four parishes. While several fields were already in production in 1920, large-scale drilling did not begin until after this date. By 1926 the state had over thirty oil fields, and the number of gallons pumped each year had more than tripled; in 1960, Louisiana produced nearly 2,400,000,000 million cubic feet of natural gas, and over 290,000,000 barrels of crude oil. The state ranks third in the nation in crude oil production.

In 1947 drilling was begun in the offshore or tidelands areas off the southern coast of Louisiana in the Gulf of Mexico. This has led to a controversy with the Federal government over the ownership of this offshore water and land, which has not yet been settled by the Federal courts.

Salt was discovered in south Louisiana a hundred years ago

299

but did not become industrially important until after 1920. It is now mined in twenty-five sections of the state but principally in Iberia, St. Mary, and Winn parishes, Iberia Parish being the largest producer. The Louisiana salt is of high commercial value because most of it is over 98 per cent pure, and in 1955 over 3,000,000 tons of it, valued at over $9,000,000, was produced.

The Calcasieu sulphur field was exhausted in 1924, but in 1932 the Jefferson Island field was opened and the year following another field at Grande Écaille. A new system of mining sulphur had been developed during the 1890's by Herman Frasch. Water, heated to a very high temperature, was pumped through pipes into the sulphur beds deep underground and the molten sulphur was then forced up to the top of the ground by compressed air. This system greatly increased production, and by 1955 Louisiana's annual sulphur production was over 2,000,000 tons, valued at nearly $60,000,000.

Other important Louisiana minerals include stone, lime, sand and gravel, and various clays. All these play an important part in modern industry and in 1955 were valued at over $25,000,000.

Manufacturing. Louisiana has made gigantic strides in the field of manufacturing since World War II and is now one of the leaders of the South. In 1954 there were over 3,000 industrial plants employing over 150,000 persons.

Much of this progress is due to the work of the State Department of Commerce and Industry in advertising Louisiana's natural resources and in encouraging manufacturers to build plants in Louisiana. Since 1936 the state has permitted new industries to apply for a tax exemption for a period of ten years. In 1954, for example, plants valued at more than $200,000,000 were built under this plan.

Another of the major reasons why Louisiana has developed its manufacturing industries so greatly is the fact that the state has a tremendous water supply. Water, in very large quantities, is necessary for many types of manufacturing processes. Louisiana has an average daily raw-water flow of over 600,000,000,000 gallons. Over 300,000,000,000 gallons of this total is in the Mississippi River, which has enough water to supply about 2,000 gallons a

Part of the large concentration of industry along the Mississippi River

day to every man, woman, and child in the United States. The Esso Standard Oil Company's refinery at Baton Rouge in 1960 used daily more water than did the city of Cleveland, Ohio.

In 1954 the manufactured products of Louisiana were valued at nearly one and one-fifth billion dollars. Chemicals and chemical products ranked first; foods and foodstuffs, second; petroleum and coal products, third; and pulp, paper, and wood products, fourth. Other classifications of goods produced included transportation equipment, metal products, stone, clay, and glass products, machinery, furniture, leather goods, and many others. It would take many pages to list all of the individual goods made in Louisiana today: candies, fertilizers, soda, boxes, mattresses, boats, vinegar, perfumes, chocolate, wigs, sails, beer, tombstones, oil tanks, and numerous others.

Among the southern states, Louisiana ranks first in the production of paper pulp, second in petroleum-coal products, fifth in food manufacturing, sixth in chemicals, and sixth in lumber and wood products.

Owing to the fact that Louisiana has many basic raw materials —oil, gas, salt, sulphur, water, wood, stone, and clay—it seems destined to become a great manufacturing state. It is predicted that the section along the Mississippi River between Baton Rouge and New Orleans will become one of the greatest industrial centers of the nation.

301

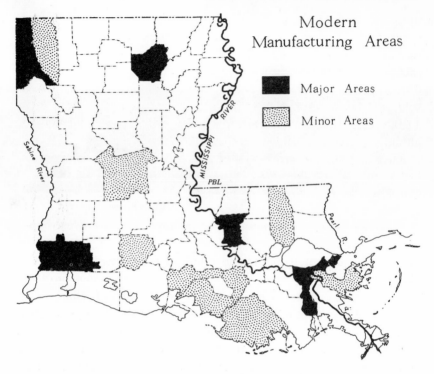

Modern
Manufacturing Areas

■ Major Areas

▨ Minor Areas

Economic Importance of Wild Life and Fisheries. The wild
bird and animal life and the fish of Louisiana's lands, streams,
and Gulf waters are of much economic value; and the State Department of Wild Life and Fisheries regulates, aids, and helps preserve
these natural resources. Louisiana's wildlife preserves are among
the world's largest. Its bird and migratory-waterfowl sanctuaries
were the first established by any of the states and were the result
of a movement led by Edward Avery McIlhenny of Avery Island.
There are over a score of these sanctuaries and preserves, of which
the largest are the Sabine Migratory Waterfowl Refuge, the Delta
Migratory Waterfowl Refuge, and the Pass à Loutre Game and
Fish Preserve. In addition, there are several sanctuaries maintained
by foundations, companies, and private citizens. The Louisiana
Wild Life Federation, a nonprofit, nonpolitical organization, was
organized in 1940 to assist in preserving the wildlife of the state.
    Among the fur-bearing animals are nutria (which were brought
from South America in 1938), raccoon, squirrel, muskrat, mink,

opossum, otter, fox, and even wildcat. The muskrat is first in importance and over 1,380,000 pelts were taken during the 1954–55 season. Nutria was second with approximately 375,000 pelts, raccoon third with nearly 85,000 pelts, and mink fourth with 65,000 pelts. In all nearly 2,000,000 pelts of various animals were sold, and they were valued at nearly $3,500,000. More than 11,000 alligators were killed for their hides and meat in 1954–55, although only 38 of them were over 10 feet in length.

The catching and processing of fresh- and salt-water commercial fish is one of the important industries of present-day Louisiana. Commercial fresh-water fish include catfish, buffalo, gaspergou, garfish, and other varieties, while the salt-water fisheries catch shrimp, oyster, turtle, crab, Gulf menhaden, trout, redfish, flounder, red snapper, sheepshead, and mullet.

The first commercial canning of shrimp was done in 1867 by the Dunbar family at Grand Terre Island, but the shrimp-packing industry did not really begin until 1918. At that time seines were discarded in favor of huge nets called "trawls," which were handled by motors on board large shrimp boats. The marketing of headless shrimp began in 1934. Today shrimp are packed in many ways, and in 1955 the production totaled over 365,000 barrels valued at over $20,000,000.

In 1955 oyster production reached almost 740,000 barrels; hard-shelled crab, over 10,000,000 pounds; and soft-shelled crab, 1,500,000 pounds. Louisiana produces about 80 per cent of the crawfish sold in the United States, over 775,000 pounds in 1955. The same year she also produced 125,000 pounds of frogs and over 130,000 pounds of turtle meat. Fresh- and salt-water fishing brought the fishermen an income of over $25,000,000 in 1955.

In addition to direct state income, the wildlife and fishing lands and waters brought fine sport to thousands of citizens and provided many a zestful meal for their tables. Nearly half a million hunting and fishing licenses were sold by the state in 1955.

Transportation. There are nearly 50,000 miles of highways, roads, and streets in modern Louisiana. Almost 16,000 miles are under state control; approximately 28,000 miles are under parish control; and about 5,000 miles of streets are under the supervision of cities and towns. These highways were used in 1955 by 750,000 automobiles, almost 200,000 trucks, and nearly 75,000 buses, trailers, and other types of licensed vehicles.

There are over 4,000 miles of railroad track in the state which are used by over thirty different railroads. The largest lines include the Southern Pacific, the Texas and Pacific, the Missouri Pacific, the Louisiana and Arkansas, and the Yazoo and Mississippi Valley. But all of Louisiana's railroads are not large systems. The Tangipahoa & Eastern Railways Company's track from Fluker to Ogden is only three and one-half miles in length, and the shortest railroad, the Washington-Western Railways Company, from Jenkins to Green, has only one mile of track.

More than a dozen airlines serve the state. The Louisianian can now fly to practically any town or city within the borders of his state, or to New York, San Francisco, Mexico City, Havana, or other American or foreign cities. The state has 175 airports and airstrips, over 20 seaplane bases, and three heliports for helicopters.

The navigable waters of Louisiana, on which boats may operate during all or part of the year, total about 4,800 miles. Some of these streams, bayous, and rivers are long and carry heavy boat and barge traffic; the Mississippi River flows over 550 miles in Louisiana and the Red River a little over 500 miles. On the other hand, some rivers and bayous are very short. The Tangipahoa River can be navigated for only fifteen miles, Petite Anse Bayou for only eight miles, and Dorchite Bayou for only six miles. Over a dozen large barge-lines ship various kinds of goods over the streams of Louisiana.

Commerce. Louisiana imports and exports many different types of raw materials and manufactured goods. The business of commerce and trade gives employment to many thousands of persons and plays an important part in the general economic life of the state.

The chief imports, named in order of their weight in tons, are: sugar, molasses, bananas, bauxite, coffee, petroleum, minerals and metals, phosphates and fertilizer, rubber, burlap, and bagging. Sugar, molasses, bauxite, petroleum and other products are imported into Louisiana for manufacturing purposes. The most important export commodities produced in Louisiana, or in other states and shipped from Louisiana ports, included wheat, corn, flour, cotton, oils and greases, sulphur, and feeds. These imports and exports annually weigh over 10,000,000 tons and are valued at over $2,000,000,000.

One reason for the growth of New Orleans as a shipping center

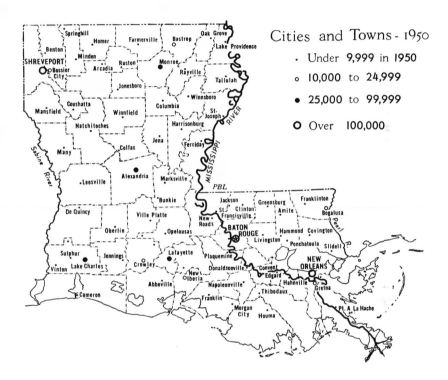

Cities and Towns - 1950

. Under 9,999 in 1950

o 10,000 to 24,999

● 25,000 to 99,999

O Over 100,000

is that it has a Foreign Trade Zone, one of four such zones in the United States. This zone is a fenced-in area where foreign goods may be stored, processed, and repackaged without having to pay American customs, duties, excise, or other taxes. These goods may then be shipped to other countries or imported into the United States.

New Orleans is Louisiana's largest port, Baton Rouge and Lake Charles ranking second and third respectively. During the twelve months preceding July 1, 1955, nearly 3,700 ocean vessels and nearly 2,300 inland waterway and river boats and barges docked at New Orleans, handling nearly 50,000,000 tons of cargo. During the same period, Baton Rouge handled about 16,500,000 tons, and Lake Charles nearly 15,500,000 tons. New Orleans ranks second in the United States in the value of goods imported and exported there and third in the tonnage of these goods, while Baton Rouge is the nation's largest inland port.

However, not all of Louisiana's commercial business is the handling of manufactured goods. One of its most important businesses is the entertaining of tourists who visit the state. In 1954 three million tourists visited Louisiana, and it was estimated that they spent nearly $300,000,000 while in the state. The three most important tourist attractions were New Orleans, Baton Rouge (home of the state capitol and the state university), and the Acadian Country.

The State Department of Commerce and Industry maintains several tourist stations to assist these visitors and to furnish them with information on the interesting attractions of the state.

Banks and Banking. Prior to the present era Louisiana frequently had to borrow money from outside the state to promote its agricultural and other resources. While business firms still borrow huge sums from outside the state, many of their financial transactions are now with local banks.

In 1902 the state began to modernize its banking system, and in 1918 additional legislation helped place Louisiana banks on a more sound financial basis. These and subsequent laws, aided by Federal legislation, have greatly strengthened the banks of the state.

During the depression of 1929, Louisiana banks faced many financial difficulties, but the state and national governments came to their assistance, enabling the great majority of them to weather the financial storm. At the present time the people of Louisiana have more than $2,500,000,000 deposited in their banks. They own more than $50,000,000 worth of United States Savings Bonds and have more than $400,000,000 of savings in various homestead associations.

Labor. Although Louisiana had many labor unions prior to 1920, it was generally considered to be a nonunion state. Labor Day was not officially recognized until 1928.

The modern organization of labor unions had begun during the period from 1910 to 1914 when the Brotherhood of Timber Workers succeeded in securing better wages and a nine-hour day. The State Federation of Labor made its appearance in 1916, and the movement continued until 1929, when the number of labor unions began to decline. Since 1938, however, hundreds of unions representing different labor groups have been organized.

The Legislature has passed numerous laws regulating labor. Women's and children's labor laws regulate the labor of these two groups, while the Workmen's Compensation Law protects those who are injured while on the job. Employers must furnish reasonable medical, surgical, and hospital service and most employers provide these services through workmen's compensation insurance. The State Department of Labor has a division of Employment Security, which works with the Federal government in taking care of laborers during periods of unemployment.

The state maintains over twenty employment offices located throughout the state to assist people in finding work. In 1954 jobs were secured for over 200,000 people, nearly 125,000 of whom were agricultural workers.

Today working conditions and wages are good in Louisiana. In 1954 in the field of manufacturing, for example, wages averaged $65.25 per week. Petroleum refining ranked first, with average weekly wages of $98.25. Despite this, many workers were dissatisfied with wages or working conditions, or had other complaints, and during the same year there were forty strikes, involving nearly 17,000 laborers.

30. CULTURAL PROGRESS

General Educational Progress. Louisiana's modern educational system—broad in concept and massive in operation, with a goal of "total education"—has steadily gained momentum during the years since 1920. T. H. Harris continued to serve as State Superintendent until 1940; John E. Coxe served from 1940 to 1948, and Shelby M. Jackson since 1948.

In 1920 there were 336,000 white and 229,000 colored children of school age in the state, only a comparatively small percentage of whom were attending school. By 1959 these numbers had risen to 561,500 and 319,700 respectively, and over 95 per cent of the children between the ages of six and eighteen years were enrolled in public or private schools. In 1920 there were less than 10,000 school teachers; by 1959 the number of teachers in the public schools numbered more than 25,000. In 1920 less than half of the teachers had gone to college more than two years; by 1959 more than 90 per cent had received four or more years of college training. In 1920 less than 20,000 pupils were transported to school; by 1959 more than 350,000 students were being transported daily to public and private schools.

These statistics amply demonstrate the progress which has been made in public education during the past forty years. Education has become one of the most important activities of Louisiana government, on which approximately 30 per cent of the state's income is now spent. The total operating cost of education during the fiscal year 1958-1959 amounted to over $187,000,000.

Public Elementary and Secondary Schools. The State Department of Education, headed by an elected State Superintendent, is responsible for elementary and secondary education in Louisiana. The Superintendent and the Department serve in a professional capacity for the administration of policies set forth by the eleven members of an elective State Board of Education.

The State Department of Education is composed of six divisions; Elementary and Secondary Education, Higher Education, Vocational Education, School Administration, Special Services, and Vocational Rehabilitation and Veteran's Education.

The voters in each of the sixty-four parishes elect a parish board of education. The cities of Bogalusa, Lake Charles, and Monroe also have independent city-school systems. The parish boards and city boards of these three cities appoint parish or city superintendents of education and supervise elementary and high-school education in their districts. They are, however, under the State Department of Education in regard to textbooks, the certifying of teachers, courses of study, and other matters.

Educational progress implies improvement in each aspect of education: various courses of study, teacher training, supervision of teaching, teacher-benefit laws, consolidation of schools, transportation of pupils, school attendance, school finance, libraries, textbooks, and lunch programs, all of which come under the authority of the State Department of Education.

Courses of study have gradually been improved and broadened. While years ago the student frequently studied only arithmetic, reading, and writing, today he studies also many other subjects, all of which help in fitting him for modern life.

Much has been done to improve teacher training, and as a result teachers today are better qualified than they were twenty or even ten years ago. In the past, prospective teachers had to pass qualifying examinations; today they also receive training in the theory of education and in teaching methods. Their salaries have greatly increased in the course of the past several years. As late as 1948 the average annual salary was only $2,213, but by 1958 it had grown to $4,560.

In past years there was no classroom supervision of instruction. Today classroom supervisors, especially trained in teaching methods and in definite fields of subject matter, help teachers to give the most effective possible instruction to their students.

In 1921 there were over 3,400 public schools in Louisiana. Through consolidation and school-bus transportation, this number was reduced until in 1948 there were only about 2,250 schools. By 1959 the number had been further reduced to 1,384.

Prior to 1928 the textbooks were not supplied to the pupils. It was in that year, however, that the Legislature passed the first Free Textbook Law, and additional laws have been passed since then, so that today the pupil is furnished free textbooks, library books, paper and pencils, audio-visual aids, and much other special equipment. The Louisiana school-lunch program was begun in 1932, received its first legislative appropriation in 1939, and by 1959 there were over 1,400 such programs serving an average of nearly 540,000 pupils daily.

While education has made much progress during the past thirty-five years, there is still room for additional advancement, and educational leaders are constantly working to provide better facilities.

Higher Education. There are twenty-three colleges and universities in Louisiana, of which ten are supported by the state and thirteen by funds from private endowments and religious institutions. In 1954–55 over 35,000 students were enrolled in these colleges and universities.

Louisiana State University is the largest university, and is governed by a fifteen-member Board of Supervisors. The Governor is a member of this board, and he appoints the other members for overlapping terms of fourteen years. The university moved to its present 4,700 acre campus in 1925, although some classes were still held on the old campus at the site of the present state capitol until 1932. Its buildings and equipment are presently valued at over $50,000,000. The university's medical and nursing schools are located in New Orleans. Its library is the largest in Louisiana, containing over 750,000 books and pamphlets and many thousands of manuscripts on the history of the state.

All the other state colleges are governed by the State Board of Education. The largest of these colleges are Southern University at Scotlandville, the Negro state university which is the largest Negro college in the United States, and the University of Southwestern Louisiana at Lafayette. The state institutions are well distributed over the state to serve better the young men and women who wish to secure college educations.

Tulane University and Loyola University at New Orleans are the largest private institutions of higher learning. Sophie Newcomb College is the women's division of Tulane.

Louisiana is well supplied with academic institutions, her colleges and universities offering training in practically all fields of learning. Louisiana State University, Tulane, and Loyola offer graduate and professional degrees which rank with those of the best universities of the nation.

Libraries. The Louisiana State Library provides information and book services to the people of the state, to state and local officials, and through book loans to other libraries. It has a large collection of films on various subjects and these are loaned to other libraries, groups, and individuals. Its collections total over 350,000 books and other library materials, and in 1952–53 it mailed over 38,000 packages of books and made nearly 2,000,000 book loans. During the same period it supplied various types of information to nearly 100,000 people.

Most of the parishes have their own libraries, located at the

New State Library, Baton Rouge

parish seats, East Baton Rouge Parish having the largest, followed by Ouachita and Calcasieu parishes. Some of the cities also have large collections of books, the New Orleans Public Library loaning over one million volumes a year and its holdings including many valuable magazines and other library materials.

Louisiana's libraries are fortunate in having had some noted librarians who were much interested in collecting material on the history of the state. James A. McMillen was the Librarian at Louisiana State University for a number of years and was largely responsible for the building of the university's great collection of books, pamphlets, newspapers, magazines, and government documents pertaining to the history of Louisiana. William Beer was the head of the Howard Memorial Library of New Orleans (now a part of the Tulane University Library), and he was one of the nation's greatest book collectors. One of his friends wrote that he "collected everything from sugar reports to rare Louisiana imprints, and plenty of both. Quite right he was, too, for there was no branch of knowledge upon which he was not called upon, at some time or other, to furnish books."

In 1906 the state established the Louisiana State Museum, appointing Dr. Robert Glenk as the first Director. Dr. Glenk served for over thirty years and during that period accumulated a great collection of published materials on the history of Louisiana. The museum was opened to the public in the old Spanish Cabildo building, adjacent to the St. Louis Cathedral in New Orleans, in 1911.

The Department of Archives at Louisiana State University was organized by Edwin A. Davis, a member of the History Department, in 1935. He secured passage of a law in 1936 permitting the department to receive the old official records of the state, parishes, and cities which were no longer needed in government. During the next ten years he collected the personal papers and records of over six hundred Louisiana families, as well as thousands of business, state, and parish records. Today Louisiana State University's Department of Archives is one of the major university departments of the South engaged in this type of work.

Louisiana's network of parish, city, and college and university libraries makes available to the citizen practically any type of information which he may wish to secure, and if he does not live near a library, the state library or one of its branches will mail him the book he desires.

Museums. Louisiana's museums may be divided into three groups: there are art museums, those which collect historical relics, and medical museums which show various types of medical exhibits.

The most important museums possessing objects of art are the Delgado Museum in New Orleans, which houses a noted collection of paintings and sculpture, the Louisiana State Museum at the Cabildo, and the State Exhibits Building at Shreveport.

The largest historical museums are the Louisiana State Museum and the Louisiana Historical Association's Confederate Memorial Hall, also in New Orleans. Louisiana State and Tulane also have museums containing historical relics. The Acadian House at the Longfellow-Evangeline Memorial Park near St. Martinville exhibits furniture, utensils, and other home furnishings used by the Acadians, while the Barringer House in Monroe and the Marksville Prehistoric Indian Park Museum display collections of Indian relics.

Noteworthy medical collections are owned by the Louisiana State University and Tulane University medical schools.

Newspapers, Magazines, Radio, and Television. Louisiana is well equipped to furnish news and other information to its people through printed materials, radio, and television. In 1955 the state had nineteen daily newspapers and over a hundred weekly newspapers.

The most important New Orleans newspapers are the *Times-Picayune* and the *States and Item.* In Baton Rouge are published the *Morning Advocate* and the *State-Times,* and in Shreveport the *Journal* and the *Times.* The *Louisiana Weekly,* published in New Orleans, is one of the leading Negro newspapers of the South; the *Federationist* is a labor publication of the Louisiana Federation of Labor.

During the two decades following 1920, New Orleans had a group of newspaper reporters who attracted national attention, and some of whom later published literary or historical books on New Orleans or Louisiana. Among these journalists were John McClure, Lyle Saxon, Bruce Manning, Hamilton Basso, Hermann B. Deutsch, and Meigs O. Frost.

At the present time Louisiana has many magazines and journals of various types. A few Spanish-, Italian-, French-, and German-language journals are published, and also labor, trade, commercial, and professional publications such as the *American Cotton Grower,* the *Daily Journal of Commerce,* the *New Orleans Medical and Surgical Journal,* and rice, sugar, and coffee journals, all published in the interest of their special fields.

Radio appeared in Louisiana in 1922, shortly after the first radio programs were broadcast from KDKA in Pittsburgh, Pennsylvania. The same year WAAB, owned by the Coliseum Place Baptist Church, and WWL, of Loyola University, began broadcasting in New Orleans. During the 1920's newspapers began to operate radio stations in conjunction with their publications. KWKH of Shreveport became the first Louisiana radio station to attract national attention when W. K. Henderson, a retired businessman, publicized his fight against chain stores. WDSU was the first station to make direct broadcasts from ships and airplanes and to broadcast Southern League baseball games. Today there are more than sixty radio stations in Louisiana.

Several hundred citizens have amateur transmitting and receiving stations and communicate with other radio amateurs. Many Louisianians also have short-wave receiving sets and hear programs from Havana, Mexico City, and other foreign cities.

Television made its appearance in 1948 when station WDSU-TV was opened at New Orleans. By 1960 in over 60 per cent of Louisiana's households there were more than 500,000 television sets, which were receiving general and educational programs.

Literature. Though Louisiana had occupied a high place in literature during the last twenty-five years of the nineteenth century, from 1900 to 1920 little was written in or about Louisiana. Beginning in the early twenties, however, there came a "reawakening," when writers discovered that the fabulous and romantic history of Louisiana offered many themes and plots for novels, short stories, plays, biographies, historical fiction, and other forms of writing.

The movement began in New Orleans where more than a dozen young writers, who were later to gain national recognition, lived in the Vieux Carré, studying Louisiana's colorful past and present and from it gaining inspiration for their writing. Sherwood Anderson, William Faulkner, Ernest Hemingway, and others contributed to a little magazine called the *Double Dealer,* as well as to other publications, and began to make reputations. Walter Coquille became known for his dialect "Bayou Pom Pom" stories. James J.

McLoughlin, wrote fascinating newspaper stories, also in dialect, under the name of "Jack Lafaience."

Before long the movement spread over the entire state. At Louisiana State University two English faculty members, Robert Penn Warren and Cleanth Brooks, Jr., began the publication of the *Southern Review,* which gained international fame. There also historian Wendell H. Stephenson edited the *Journal of Southern History,* first assisted by Edwin A. Davis and later by Fred C. Cole, who succeeded Stephenson as editor. These two journals were sponsored by the university and continued publication for some years until the university withdrew its sponsorship.

Several Louisianians won national renown through their books, Lyle Saxon becoming the state's most beloved author with his *Father Mississippi, Fabulous New Orleans, Old Louisiana* and other works. His *Children of Strangers* is one of the most sensitive novels ever written about the modern Negro.

John Smith Kendall wrote *A History of New Orleans,* and Stanley C. Arthur became noted for his works on New Orleans and Louisiana history. Hewitt L. Ballowe, a retired doctor who had lived all his life near the mouth of the Mississippi, wrote *The Lawd Sayin' the Same* and *Creole Folk Tales,* which have become famous in American folk literature. Harnett Kane's *The Bayous of Louisiana* beautifully described the country and people of south Louisiana, but his subsequent work has not measured up to his early promise.

Lyle Saxon died in 1946 and his place as Louisiana's most beloved author and her best writer on the Louisiana theme was taken by Robert Tallant. Tallant wrote more than a dozen novels and other works on Louisiana, of which his *The Romantic New Orleanians, Mardi Gras,* and *Mrs. Candy and Saturday Night* are probably the most widely known. Tallant died suddenly in the spring of 1957 and his death was a great loss to Louisiana literature.

Meanwhile Gwen Bristow, and her husband Bruce Manning, E. P. O'Donnell, and others were writing Louisiana novels which earned national approval. Roark Bradford wrote penetrating and humorous stories and books on the plantation Negro, his most noted books including, *This Side of Jordan, John Henry, Kingdom Coming,* and *Ol' Man Adam an' His Chillun.*

During the modern period many authors have visited or lived in Louisiana in order to get material for articles, short stories, and books. The Teche Country, the Barataria area, the Vieux Carré of New Orleans, the Delta Country of the lower Mississippi, and the Natchitoches area have become favorite scenes of stories, articles, and books.

As yet the great authors of a few years ago have not been challenged; no one has replaced Lyle Saxon, Roark Bradford, Hewitt Ballowe, E. P. O'Donnell, or Robert Tallant. However, romantic and historic Louisiana offers many opportunities, and today more than a hundred Louisianians are actively engaged in some form of writing. The future is promising.

The Arts. Since 1920, both New Orleans and other sections of Louisiana have attracted numerous painters, some of whom have been natives of the state while others have become adopted sons for at least a period.

Though Alexander J. Drysdale, the painter of misty, hazy Louisiana swamp scenes, continued his work after 1920, it declined in quality. P. M. Westfeldt was a noted water colorist, and Robert B. Mayfield is remembered for his sketches of New Orleans. Ronald Hargrave spent several years in New Orleans, painting portraits and making notable etchings of Vieux Carré scenes. It is for his paintings and artistic photographs that Weeks Hall, of "The Shadows" at New Iberia, is remembered. E. H. Suydam sketched throughout the state, and illustrated the books of Lyle Saxon. Conrad Albrizio executed murals for many public buildings and Olive Leonhardt published a book of drawings called *New Orleans, Drawn and Quartered*.

William Spratling, who now lives in Mexico, taught art at Tulane University for a number of years and became a noted painter of Louisiana houses and people. Charles W. Bein, a water colorist, for a time headed the New Orleans Art School. The Baroness de St. Mart, a miniature painter, had a studio in one of the Pontalba Buildings on Jackson Square. She was frequently bothered by tourists, some of whom thought that she was the original Baroness de Pontalba who had the buildings constructed in 1848.

Louisiana's most noted present-day artist is Caroline Wogan Durieux, a member of the Department of Fine Arts at Louisiana State University. She has worked with all known media of painting and has recently developed new processes for the atomic reproduction of paintings and drawings. She is best known as a humorous painter, and her work has attracted national and even international recognition.

The most noted cartoonist of this period was Trist Wood, who drew sharp and critical political cartoons for Huey Long's political newspaper the *Louisiana Progress*. A. V. Hall, Roy Aymond, and Keith Temple of the New Orleans *Picayune*, John Chase of the *States*, and Jack Sparling of the *Item* also made reputations in this field.

There has been considerable activity in the field of photography. Arnold Genthe published *Impressions of Old New Orleans*. Grace de la Croix Daigre, of Plaquemine, who took notable pictures of places and people along the lower Mississippi, once wrote humorously: "A hundred faces he has, dat Ol' Man Ribber," and she tried to capture all of them on film. Elemore Morgan, of Baton Rouge, has the best collection of photos on present-day Louisiana.

Arthur Morgan is the state's most important present-day sculptor and the first native-born Louisianian to make an international reputation in this field of art. Born in Ascension Parish in 1904, he achieved his first success at the age of twenty, when he was hailed by the New York press as a young prodigy. His most noted work is his statue of Chief Justice Edward Douglass White now in the national capitol at Washington, D. C.

Although not a native, Armin Scheler of the Louisiana State University Department of Fine Arts is represented in books featuring the work of modern American sculptors. Duncan Ferguson has done bas-reliefs and Enrique Alferez has executed figures for several of the state's public buildings. Juanita Gonzales, until her death in 1935, was thought to be a young sculptress of great promise; her heads of Governor Francis T. Nicholls and General Richard Taylor at the state capitol are considered excellent work. Richmond Barthé, a Negro sculptor who was reared in New Orleans, is nationally recognized.

Drama. Professional drama has declined in importance in Louisiana since the appearance of motion pictures, radio, and television. While the major cities of the state are occasionally visited by traveling companies of players, only New Orleans regularly presents stage plays.

The amateur or little-theater movement, on the other hand, has made rapid progress. Le Petit Théâtre du Vieux Carré of New Orleans was founded in 1916 and soon became one of the best-known little theaters in the nation. Le Petit Théâtre du Reveil Française was started in 1930, for the purpose of reviving the French language in New Orleans, and four years later The Group Theater came into existence. Civic theaters, Town and Gown Players, Players' Guilds, and Little Theaters have been established in many towns and communities, and though the actors of these groups are all amateurs they employ professional directors for their plays. All the colleges and universities have speech departments which sponsor the production of plays. *The Cajun,* written by Ada Jack Carver of Natchitoches, won second place in the 1926 National Theater Competition.

Music. Music had declined after the Civil War, but revived strongly after 1900. The New Orleans Philharmonic Society was founded in 1906, and by the 1920's it was giving concerts and bringing noted musical artists to New Orleans. Dr. Henry W. Stopher brought nation-wide recognition to the state university's music department when he brought ex-Metropolitan baritone Pasquale Amato and the noted conductor Louis Hasselmans to the institution to produce operas. In 1936 the New Orleans Civic Symphony was organized and some years ago was merged with the Philharmonic Society to become the New Orleans Philharmonic Symphony.

Other college and university departments of music have also made contributions through their bands and orchestras, and their other musical programs. John Morriessy, Director of the Tulane University band, has become a band-music composer of national recognition through his compositions on Louisiana and Latin-American themes. Dwight Greever Davis, Director of Bands at Northwestern State College, has achieved a wide reputation as a conductor, band-music arranger, and organizer of a central music organization for the states of Arkansas, Louisiana and Texas. Dillard University sponsors the Lower Mississippi Valley Musical Festival, and when it was inaugurated in 1937 more than three hundred singers participated.

In more recent years music has become highly developed in the public schools, junior-high schools, and high schools, and annual contests are held between the various bands and orchestras.

Recent musical compositions by Louisianians, or about Louisiana, have aroused public interest. Ferde Grofé portrays the feeling of the state in his *Mississippi Suite,* as does Virgil Thompson in the *Louisiana Story.* Jacques Wolfe's *Swamp River Suite* and his musical score for Roark Bradford's *John Henry* are highly descriptive of Louisiana. In 1920, Mortimer Wilson's *New Orleans,* a composition based on the New Orleans Mardi Gras, won the prize for the best original American overture.

31. EVERYDAY LIFE IN MODERN LOUISIANA

Modern Louisiana. Everyday life in Louisiana has witnessed many changes since 1920. The state has made rapid progress, and many features of the "Old Louisiana" are now but memories of the older generation. Louisianians live in better houses, equipped with more household conveniences and with radio and television sets. Their work has been made much easier by all the labor-saving devices of today, and the improved schools, colleges, and libraries have given them better educations. They have more and better automobiles, travel over superior roads, and use bridges instead of ferries to cross bayous and rivers. A few years ago Frederick W. Williamson wrote that an automobile trip from Monroe to Alexandria took all day and was "accompanied by flat tires and 'boggings-up' in the marshy places." The many inconveniences of the "old days" are being rapidly forgotten.

Louisianians no longer live in the past and talk about the "good old days before the war." They live in the present and look forward to the future, and if they occasionally talk of "Yankees" and Yankee ways it is in jest and in the pride of the state and the South. Talk of the days "before the war, or during the war, or right after the war," is now a part of the Louisiana heritage.

Improvements in Living Conditions. Until recent years many south Louisiana small towns looked more like European than American villages, and north Louisiana towns were old-fashioned. Since 1920, however, these towns have come to look like any other American town. Abbeville, St. Martinville, Thibodaux, Natchitoches, and a few others, however, are trying to preserve some of their Old World atmosphere. The 1920's saw so many changes in the Vieux Carré of New Orleans that civic-minded citizens organized an association for the preservation of its old Spanish appearance.

Country life has become much more attractive by the installation of rural electrical systems, indoor plumbing, and natural or bottled gas. The farmers have built new homes, barns, and farm buildings. In 1930 only about 1½ per cent of the farms used electricity, while in 1954 over 92 per cent of the farms were electrified. Of the nearly 112,000 farms in the state, over 50,000 have electric washing machines, over 30,000 have electric water pumps, and over 15,000 have electric freezers. Some Louisiana farmers are even beginning to heat and cool their homes with electricity. The day of the walking plow and the old palm-leaf fan has passed.

Today rural and city dwellers alike get the day's news over radio or television. They hear and see plays, concerts, baseball, and other athletic sports; they become acquainted through radio or television with the people and countries of the entire world; and they can be guests at political conventions, at sessions of the Legislature, or at the National Congress. They can drive or walk along paved streets to the nearest motion-picture theater, and if they need additional information or entertainment, by going to the nearest library they can secure books, magazines, and newspapers.

Passing of the Old Creole Civilization. The old Creole civilization of south Louisiana is rapidly fading. A generation ago there were comparatively few roads in the region, none of them being paved or hard surfaced for easy travel in rainy weather. Many of the larger towns and cities were accessible only by boat. In those days people traveled between farms, plantations, or communities on horseback, or in buggies or *pirogues*. While buggies and *pirogues* are still seen in south Louisiana, they have almost disappeared from general use.

The south Louisiana Creoles are traveling as never before; they are being educated in good schools; they are living in superior homes —today mention is seldom made of a *bousillage* house, a camelback house, or a shotgun house. Their daughters are going to college along with their sons and are not chaperoned as once they were. Their views on religion have broadened as Protestants have moved into their communities, and their children have largely stopped learning the French language, now speaking only English.

However, many of the old Creole customs and folkways have been preserved and rightly so, for these, with the French language, are all part of a Louisianian's heritage. Some of the old proverbs remain: grandmothers and grandfathers still tell their grandchildren, "when the cat's away the rats give a ball," or "grab for too much and it slips away from you," or "when we come close to a giant, he often turns out to be only a common man on stilts." Many Creoles call a modern clothes closet an "armoire"; they still drink *café noir,* strong and black, or *café au lait,* with hot milk. Occasionally when you make a large purchase at a store or pay your monthly bill the proprietor will give you a little gift as "lagniappe."

During the past few years Louisianians have come to realize that many of their old heritages should be preserved. Today the Louisiana Folklore Society and other organizations are trying to preserve many old customs, buildings, and historic landmarks.

Amusements. Modern Louisiana probably has more different types of festivals than any other state in the Union. These fairs and festivals are generally staged for three purposes: to educate the people, to advertise a particular natural resource or product, and to provide recreation. In the State Fair the entire state participates, while the area fair is primarily for a particular section. A joint-parish fair is one in which two or more parishes join, whereas a parish fair is supported by only one parish. A community fair is for the benefit of a certain town or community, the product fair or festival is for the advertisement of rice, oranges, peaches, yams, or other products.

More than a hundred fairs and festivals are held yearly in modern Louisiana. Over fifty parishes stage parish or joint-parish fairs; there are nearly twenty product festivals, almost a dozen area fairs, and several community fairs. As late as 1910 the Legislature made no appropriations for the benefit of these fairs and festivals. In 1920 a little less than $50,000 was appropriated, whereas in 1955 the Legislature appropriated nearly $3,500,000 for the two years 1955 and 1956. During recent years there has been criticism of the large sums given by the Legislature to these fairs and festivals, some people believing that the citizens of the various communities should finance their own projects.

In 1956 the state celebrated the two-hundredth anniversary of the coming of the Acadians to Louisiana. A group of citizens from all sections of the state organized a program of activities for the entire year. The celebration closed at St. Martinville, the Acadian capital of Louisiana, with a great festival which attracted thousands of tourists.

One of the most interesting Louisiana celebrations is the Natchitoches Christmas Festival, which is completely supported by the Natchitoches community. It originated in 1927 when Max Burgdorf suggested that Natchitoches put on a lighting and fireworks display, and has developed until today, at Christmas time, the entire city is lighted. The business section of town receives special treatment with over $75,000 worth of lighting equipment, including over 125,000 light bulbs. People from many states, as well as thousands of Louisianians, visit Natchitoches each year at Christmas time to see the display of lights and to witness the fireworks exhibition.

Even more widely known outside the state is the Louisiana carnival season which ends on Mardi Gras day. The center of the carnival activities is New Orleans, where there are over a dozen regularly scheduled day or night parades and literally dozens of balls held by the various carnival organizations. The King of the Carnival on Mardi Gras day is Rex, the Lord of Misrule, while Comus is the Lord of Mirth and Laughter. New Orleans is jammed

A typical parade float passes in front of City Hall in New Orleans on Mardi Gras day

with masked revelers, but the police have little trouble with the crowds and join in the fun. At six in the evening masks are removed but the fun making continues until midnight ushers in Ash Wednesday. The Lenten Season has begun, and the revelry must cease.

Some years ago a visitor wrote: "And though New Orleans can strike a serious note, it is a gay-hearted city. New York is too hurried even to smile, London on a sunny day can only look complacent and cheerful, but New Orleans can riotously laugh. During the carnival, Rex, its king, is the merriest, maddest, gayest of all living monarchs. Mardi Gras makes even the most melancholy citizen cheerful. The people love the carnival and never grow tired of it, for it means colour, light, music and movement."

Although New Orleans has the most important carnival in Louisiana, many other towns, cities, and communities have their own Mardi Gras carnival parades and balls.

In addition to modern commercialized entertainment, Louisianians still enjoy many of the old amusements. Families and friends still gather for dinners, parties, and visiting. There is still the old practice of the *gumbo ya-ya,* where people get together and just talk, and on Saturday nights, particularly in south Louisiana, the old *fais-do-do,* ball or dance, is still held.

Louisianians are still a fun-loving people, and newcomers to the state rapidly develop an enjoyment of those amusements which the natives of the state have enjoyed for generations.

Sports. One of the state's greatest assets is its wide variety of recreational facilities. Its mild climate, numerous streams, bayous, and lakes, rolling hill country, broad prairies, and great forests offer outdoor sporting opportunities possessed by few states. Hunting and fishing are universally enjoyed, the coastal marshes, streams, and lakes being combed for ducks, geese, and other wild fowl; the upland areas for quail, squirrels, and rabbits; and the interior ridge-lands and swamps for deer, wild hog, and even bear. The sportsman can fish in the fresh-water bayous and streams for bass, crappie, and perch; in the Gulf of Mexico for shark, king mackerel, flounder, or tarpon; and in the coastal lagoons for trout, sheepshead, and redfish.

The state maintains more than a dozen state parks, of which Lake Bistineau State Park in Webster Parish, Chicot State Park in Evangeline Parish, Fontainebleau State Park in St. Tammany Parish, and Sam Houston State Park in Calcasieu Parish are a few. These parks have various types of recreational facilities, including vacation cabins, picnic shelters, beaches, small game courts, and group-camp buildings. Outdoor Louisiana offers many opportunities for camping, swimming, boating, and hiking.

Louisianians love competition in their sports, and all types of racing are popular: pirogue racing, horse racing, power-boat and sailboat racing. Racing meets and regattas are held annually at various race tracks and on various waters.

Attempts are being made to revive the former popularity of two

Leon Trice; courtesy Louisiana State University Sports Publicity Office

*Louisiana State University 1958 National Champions in action against
Tulane*

sports, the ring tournament and the game of raquette. Ring tournaments are again being held in Ville Platte and other southern Louisiana towns, where mounted knights try to run their lances through the suspended rings. Less success, however, has been achieved in reviving the old Creole game of raquette, which is very similar to lacrosse. A small ball is tossed up in the center of a large playing field, and the two teams, which may have any number of players, try to carry or throw the ball with small rackets toward their opponent's goal. The goal is a small piece of tin, which makes a loud noise when struck by the ball. In olden days when a game was won the winning team carried its captain around the field, while giving the victory cry, which sounded like a modern football yell. One of these victory crys went:

325

He, he, he, mo drapo,
Li, li, ouap, ouap, gi, li, li,
Boum, boum.

Louisiana, of course, has all the modern scholastic and college competitive sports, such as football and basketball, and these contests attract many thousands of spectators annually. The Mid-Winter Sports Carnival is held annually at New Orleans in the last week in December and ends with the Sugar Bowl football game on January 1. The cities and towns have recreational parks, golf courses, tennis courts, and picnic grounds where the young and old find excellent sports and recreational facilities.

Foods and Fashions in Cookery. An English visitor to New Orleans once wrote that it was the one city in the world "where you can eat and drink the most and suffer the least"; another traveler said that New Orleans was the "only city in America where street quarrels may be heard over the respective merits of certain restaurants and dishes." These comments need not have been restricted to the city of New Orleans, for the whole state of Louisiana is renowned for its excellent food.

Louisiana cookery is basically of two types: the Southern cookery of northern and western Louisiana inherited from English-speaking ancestors from the eastern states of the South, and the Creole or southern Louisiana cookery, which combines the French love of delicacies with the Spanish taste for strong, hot seasonings. However, the members of every national group living in Louisiana have contributed to the great variety of dishes, and today the Louisianian eats everything from French and Spanish bisques, gumbos, and jambalayas to Hungarian *kapostas* and goulashes.

Roy Alciatore, the owner and proprietor of Antoine's Restaurant in New Orleans, has given a good explanation of Louisiana's excellent foods. He wrote: "I consider myself most fortunate in having been born in that most extraordinary heaven of natural resources. . . . Where else in the world will one find such a variety of seafood," and he continues to list Louisiana's great food resources. One visitor described the New Orleans market, where "the fish stalls were shimmering mounds of silver, purple and blue, with strings of red snappers hanging above, seemingly carved out of pink coral. Grey trout, speckled with orange and scarlet, were flanked with enormous lobsters and greenish grey crabs."

Many of the old-time dishes are still prepared by Louisiana cooks. *Maquechou* is a dish made of sweet corn cut from the cob and smothered with onions, *congri* is a combination of kidney beans and rice and is sometimes still called *moros y cristianos* (Moors and Christians), and *daube glacée* is a jellied veal made with calves' and pigs' feet. *Riz au lait* is a dessert made of rice boiled in milk, *pain-patate* is a small cake made of sweet potatoes, while *calas tout chaud* are rice cakes fried in deep fat, liberally sprinkled with sugar, and served hot. *La Cuite* is a heavy cane syrup filled with pecans. Gumbo is still a favorite and one still hears the old jingle which used to be recited:

> *Poor crawfish ain't got no sho,*
> *Frenchmen catch 'em and make gumbo.*
> *Go all 'round the Frenchmen's beds,*
> *Don't find nothing but crawfish heads.*

Coush-coush (sometimes spelled kush-kush), corn meal soaked with milk and fried in a little fat, is still eaten for breakfast. Bouillabaisse, which British novelist William Makepeace Thackeray said was "a sort of soup, or broth, or stew, or hotchpotch of all sorts of fishes," is yet found on many Louisiana tables.

Over the entire state "pot liquor and corn pone" is an old favorite, pot liquor being the water in which any type of greens have been cooked with a piece of salt meat or ham. Huey Long once took time out in the United States Senate to explain how it should be made properly.

Some Louisianians, particularly the Negroes, have given nicknames to their dishes. The "Sunday breakdown" is fried chicken and grits, "Flat cars" are pork chops, while "Red and white" is red beans and rice, and a "Coal yard" is a cup of strong, black coffee.

Religion. In 1956 a survey of the National Council of Churches revealed that Louisiana had the highest percentage of church-going people in the United States, with over 80 per cent of the white population attending Protestant, Catholic, or Jewish churches. Slightly over 50 per cent of these people are Protestant, a little more than 43 per cent are Catholic, and the rest are either Jewish or belong to some other faith. About 80 per cent of the colored population are Protestant, a majority of whom are Baptist.

There are over 2,500 churches in the state, New Orleans alone having over 750 churches. The largest religious denominations are the Baptist with over 1,200 churches, the Methodist with over 600, and the Catholic with over 400.

The Catholic Church is of course the oldest church in the state. Until recently south Louisiana had few Protestants, and north Louisiana had few Catholics, but now Catholics and Protestants alike live in all sections of the state. Many old Catholic customs are still observed, though others are passing from common use. In New Orleans, in particular, the custom of offering public thanks to some saint by way of a newspaper advertisement is still practiced. The celebration of All Saints' Day with the gathering of people in the cemeteries, with hundreds of candles lighting the graves, is still to be witnessed in south Louisiana. Fishing boats and fleets are still blessed, the most important of these ceremonies being the annual blessing of the shrimp fleet. Funerals are still sometimes announced on a black-bordered poster giving the name of the deceased and the time and place of the funeral.

The little Catholic Chapel of the Madonna located about nine miles south of Plaquemine has the distinction of being the smallest church in Louisiana. The building is only eight by eight feet and just large enough for a small altar, a priest, and his assistant.

Three fraternal orders are allied with religion, the Masonic Order, the Knights of Columbus, and B'nai B'rith. The Masonic Order is open to all persons who believe in God and the immortality of the soul, regardless of faith; the Knights of Columbus is a Catholic organization; and B'nai B'rith is for Jews. The colored counterpart of the Knights of Columbus is called the Knights of Peter Claver. In 1955 there were almost 50,000 Masons in Louisiana, nearly 20,000 Knights of Columbus, and almost 6,000 members of B'nai B'rith.

Popular Music. Her Negro and Creole folk songs are Louisiana's most characteristic music. The Negroes have contributed much of both melody and rhythm to American folk music. To this day the old Creole peddler's songs are occasionally heard, particularly in New Orleans, and the religious songs of several generations past are still sometimes sung, as for example:

Tell yuh 'bout a man wot live be-fo Chris'—
His name was Adam, Eve was his wife.
Tell yuh how dat man he lead a rugged life,
All be-cause he tak-en de 'ooman's ad-vice.
She made his trou-ble so hard—She made his trou-ble so hard—
Lawd, Lawd, she made his trou-ble so hard.
Yas, indeed—his trou-ble was hard.

Jazz originated in New Orleans near the end of the last century, spreading from there over the entire world, and new forms of it are constantly developing. Originally small bands playing on the streets or in the dance halls used no printed music, but composed it as they went along. These bands developed what they called "ear" music. Jazz did not become popular in the nation until about the time of World War I, and until that time the word "jazz" was considered vulgar and not to be used in front of a lady. Louisiana has produced many famous jazz musicians among whom, of the modern period, are Louis Prima, Jelly-Roll Morton, Sidney Bechet, Louis Armstrong, and King Oliver.

Music is inborn in the Louisiana Creole. As an infant he slept to the old cradle songs, the singing of which was family tradition. Some of these are still sung, as for example "Comper Lapin" ("Gossip Rabbit"), "O Mi Sieu Banjo" ("O Mister Banjo"), and "Cher, Mo L'Aime Toi" ("Dear, I Love You So"). As he grew older he heard others, songs for games, songs of love, war, and joy, and the dance songs played and sung at the *fais-do-dos.*

The old Creole music is rapidly passing. Many people no longer speak French, and the radio and television songs are usually sung in English; but the Louisianian, be he Creole or not, still loves music with the enthusiasm of his fathers. He frequently studies music in elementary and secondary school or in college, sometimes learns to play a musical instrument or to sing, and becomes acquainted with operas and symphonies.

32. MODERN LOUISIANA

Modern Louisiana. The romantic and historic past, the bustling, industrial present, and the boundless future are happily combined in modern Louisiana. The speech, customs, and other heritages of many nationalities give extra color to a land where the old rubs shoulders with the new. One of the most self-sufficient of the states, its varied resources have brought to Louisiana many new citizens during the past few years. The old civilization, coupled with the warm climate and the numerous recreational opportunities, makes the state a great attraction for tourists. The native Louisianians, together with the new citizens born in other states, can take pride in their rich heritage and confidently face the future.

Its many aspects make Louisiana one of the most interesting states of the Union. Between Opelousas and Morgan City lies the heart of the romantic Bayou Teche and Creole country, while in the Feliciana parishes are many old ante bellum homes. Grand Isle is a picturesque fishing and resort village located on the Gulf of Mexico, and there are orange groves in the Delta Country of the Mississippi River. Here too are the villages of fishermen and trappers of varied nationalities who retain many of their native customs. Examples of early French architecture, and plantations once held by slave-owning Free Negroes long before the Civil War are found near Natchitoches. New Orleans is one of the most "different" cities in the United States, its modern shopping center of Canal Street just a stone's throw away from the aged and graceful buildings of the Vieux Carré.

The Flags of Louisiana. Many flags have flown over Louisiana. Until 1762 the golden lilies of the French kings, the yellow fleur-de-lis flecked on a white shield, waved from the capitol at New Orleans. It was followed by the red, white, and yellow flag of Spain, with golden castles and red lions on a white field. In 1785 the flag of Spain was changed and the bars of the province of Aragon were added. For a time the present-day Florida Parishes belonged to England, and this section flew the crosses of St. George and St. Andrew.

During the first twenty days of December, 1803, the tricolor of Revolutionary France was Louisiana's flag, being succeeded by the flag of the United States. In 1810 the people of the Florida Parishes revolted against Spain and organized an independent republic whose flag bore a large white star on a blue field. The western boundary of the Louisiana Purchase had not been decided in 1812 when the state entered the Union, and Spain claimed the southwestern section of Louisiana. Before the matter was officially settled Mexico had won her independence from Spain, and some historians claim therefore that the flag of Mexico flew over the narrow section of land just east of the Sabine River called the Sabine Strip.

After Louisiana seceded in 1861 and before she joined the Confederate States of America, she was an independent nation and her flag was similar to that of the United States except that it had a single yellow star in a red field. It was followed by the Stars and Bars of the Southern Confederacy, and after the end of the Civil War, by the flag of the United States again.

Official Emblems of Louisiana. Louisiana's State Seal was officially adopted in 1902. The description is as follows: "A pelican, with its head turned to the left, in a nest with three young, the pelican, following the tradition, in the act of tearing its breast to feed its young; around the edge of the Seal to be inscribed 'State of Louisiana.' Over the head of the pelican to be inscribed 'Union, Justice'; under the nest of the pelican to be inscribed 'Confidence.'"

There has been some argument over this seal, and the exact meaning of the words "with its head turned to the left." Did this mean to the bird's left or to the left of the person looking at the picture? Only recently the Secretary of State decided that it meant to the pelican's left and to the right of the person who looks at it.

The official State Flag which was adopted in 1912 has a blue field, on which is a white pelican feeding its young, as in the State Seal. Below the pelican is a white ribbon on which is written in blue the State Motto, "Union, Justice, Confidence."

The State Bird is the Eastern Brown Pelican.

The State Flower is the white blossom of the magnolia tree, and though many people consider the magnolia as the state tree, it has never officially been so designated.

The State Song, which was adopted in 1932, is titled the "Song of Louisiana," with both music and words by Vashti Robertson Stopher. The State March Song, "Louisiana, My Home Sweet Home," was adopted in 1952, the music by Castro Carazo and the words by Lou Levoy and Sammie McKenzie.

Louisiana has several nicknames of which "The Pelican State" seems to be the most popular; less common are "The Bayou State," "The Sugar State," and "The Creole State." Louisianians themselves also have nicknames, being called "Pelicans," "Creoles," and sometimes "Tigers." The name "Tigers" comes from a famous Louisiana military unit which fought in the Civil War.

A Land of Tales and Legends. Louisiana is a state about which legends have been woven and tall stories told. Many of these legends and tales have been deliberately made up by Louisianians.

The story is told that the Custom House at New Orleans has cotton bales for its foundations, though cotton bales would hardly serve this purpose. The real foundation of the Custom House consists of cypress pilings, topped by heavy cypress logs and then covered with an extra thick layer of concrete.

It is legendary that Louisiana was named for Louis XIV of France and his mother, who was Anna of Austria. In fact, La Salle named the country "Louisiane," which meant literally the "land of Louis." The Spanish changed the spelling to "Luisiana." After the area was purchased by the United States, Americans combined the two words using the French spelling of "Louis" and the Spanish ending "iana."

There is a story that when the French Prince Louis Philippe visited Valcour Aime, a wealthy planter, in 1798, that the dishes of gold which were used at a banquet were afterwards tossed into the Mississippi. There are only two things wrong with this fine story: first, Valcour Aime was a very sound businessman and would never have thrown away the golden dishes; second, he was not born until 1798 and would scarcely have been old enough to have entertained the prince.

There are plenty of "mosquito" stories, many of which were first told by travelers and later adopted by Louisianians. There are "one set of mosquitoes who sting you all day and another set which sting you all night." In northeast Louisiana two mosquitoes can whip a dog and four can hold a man down and hog-tie him; along the lower Mississippi one never kills a mosquito, one "butchers" him. A person living near Lake Providence never buys life insurance, he buys "mosquito insurance." In many places mosquitoes "torment alligators to death, and sting mules right through their hoofs."

Citizens of New Orleans enjoy telling tourists about the house which Louis Philippe, Lafayette, and Marshal Ney, one of Napoleon's generals, are supposed to have visited on one occasion. It is a wonderful story, but, in fact, Louis Philippe visited Louisiana in 1798, Lafayette in 1825, Marshal Ney was never there at all, and the house was not built until 1832.

Louisianians still repeat legends of the noted slave outlaw, Bras Coupé, who had superhuman strength, or the true tale of Coulon de Villiers, who captured George Washington when he surrendered at Fort Necessity. There are "fishy" tales about the *choupique* which is able to live out of water, and northern statesman John Hay, who was Secretary of State of the United States, once wrote a poem about Jim Bludso whose steamboat exploded. The poem ends:

The fires bust out as she clar'd the bar,
And burnt a hole in the night,
And quick as a flash she turned and made
For that willer-bank on the right.
There was runnin' and cursin', but Jim yelled out
Over all the infernal roar,
"I'll hold her nozzle again the bank
Till the last galoot's ashore."
Through the hot, black wreath of the burnin' boat,

Jim Bludso's voice was heard,
And they all had trust in his cussedness
And knowed he would keep his word.
And, sure's you're born, they all got off
Afore the smokestacks fell,
And Bludso's ghost went up alone
In the smoke of the Prairie Belle.

The best of all Louisiana legends, however, was "invented" one afternoon by two joke-loving Louisiana authors, Lyle Saxon and Roark Bradford, and told to a northern writer who believed the tale and put it into a book as a "real Louisiana legend." It has been copied and recopied by many other writers. It is the legend of Annie Christmas, a gigantic Negro woman with a mustache and a voice as loud and deep as a foghorn. She could whip a dozen river boatmen with one hand tied behind her back and carry a hogshead of sugar under each arm and another on top of her head. She once towed a barge up the Mississippi from New Orleans to Natchez so fast that the boat skipped over the water like a swallow, and she never once got out of breath. Though she usually dressed as a man, she sometimes wore red satin gowns and scarlet plumes, and her necklace was thirty feet long, each bead representing eyes she had gouged out or noses and ears she had bitten off in her fights. Once when a flood threatened New Orleans, she grabbed a shovel and in one day built a levee all around the city. Annie finally fell in love with a man named Charlie, but instead of having twins or triplets they had twelve sons, who were over seven feet tall by the time they were six years old. When Charlie died Annie gave him a fine funeral. Then she and her twelve sons placed his body on a barge, and together they floated down the Mississippi and out to sea, and were never seen again.

Languages of Louisiana. Many languages are spoken in modern Louisiana, including English, French, Spanish, Italian, and German, and a few Indians still speak their old languages. Sometimes two languages are mixed in the same sentence, and such phrases as *"beaucoup* persimmons," meaning "many persimmons," are heard.

Modern Louisianians, particularly those of French descent, deliberately mix up their words as a little joke among themselves or for the benefit of newcomers or tourists. They will say "he lives in that house which is white, him," or they will end the sentence with "Yes?" or "No?" or "Hein?" If you tell a girl that she is pretty she may say, "You is tell me something what I is already know." And if you talk of leaving Louisiana, a man may ask you: "For why you want to go to She-cow-go, you? See how the sun she shine on the bayou, hein? If you was in She-cow-go you would not see the sun like those, no? In She-cow-go when the sun come up, the smoke from Pittsburgh he pass all over She-cow-go." And he will laugh with you at his little joke.

Louisianians are proud of their Creole heritage. A Creole will tell you: "General Jackson? Certainly we know of him. He fought at Chalmette. He helped Jean Laffite and the Creoles lick the British." Today many Louisianians who have no French ancestors are learning to speak French, and some of them say *"Je suis Français, Français de la Louisiane,"* "I am French, Louisiana French."

A State with a Fabulous History. Many books have been written about Louisiana, not all of which present the true story. Grace King wrote that Louisiana had been the "spoiled child of American historians, who have treated her more as some charming character of fiction than as a sister in the sedate family of states." A critic said of one author: "She has not only given us back our past, but has stuck a rose in its teeth, and a pomegranate bloom behind its ear!"

Louisiana history needs no added glamour; the names of her parishes, for example, indicate their own romantic story. Some, like Avoyelles, Natchitoches, Ouachita, or Caddo are named for Indian tribes; others were given Indian names: Calcasieu (crying eagle), Catahoula (beloved lake), and Tangipahoa (ear of corn). Others recall the French period: Baton Rouge (red stick), Terrebonne (good earth), Plaquemines (persimmons). La Salle, De Soto, Iberville, and Bienville are named after explorers or colonial leaders, while Iberia, Concordia, East Feliciana, and West Feliciana reflect the Spanish period. St. James, St. John the Baptist, and St. Martin have a religious origin. Some were named for American statesmen like Washington, Franklin, or Jefferson, others for such Confederate leaders as Jefferson Davis or Beauregard.

Louisiana history is filled with gallant incidents. Think of the romantic story of the Casket Girls, and the dramatic Battle of New Orleans. There is humor in this letter written by Wylie Micajah Barrow, a young Civil War soldier: "This morning I was up early

"Oak Alley," near Vacherie

as there was no use to attempt to sleep. We had nothing to eat until nine o'clock when they brought us a barrel of crackers and some bacon. We fried the bacon on sticks. Lord deliver me from such hardships; sitting on the ground, trying to keep warm, our eyes filled with smoke, and no handkerchief to blow my nose on. Sky cloudy."

A young student writing just before the Civil War showed a patriotic sense of duty: "I intend to remain & study until my Country calls me home; & if she does, I will lay aside my law books; and shoulder my musket." Young James Stubbs very conscientiously endeavored to present his personal honor: "I have tried hard all the time to conduct myself soberly & quietly; I have not had a cross word with any one at all. I have treated everybody as politely as possible."

Louisiana Has Done Little to Preserve Its History. Despite the fact that Louisiana's historical past is one of the most colorful of all the states, she has done less than any other state to preserve her records.

The French were careless in the keeping of records, but the Spanish, realizing their historical importance, kept and preserved carefully the records of their government. The early state-government officials had good intentions but lost many important documents. A century ago Charles Gayarré pleaded for the establishment of a state department of history, but nothing was done. During the periods of the Civil War and military occupation many state, parish, and local records were destroyed or lost.

The Louisiana Historical Society, which had had active and inactive periods since its organization in 1836, was reorganized in 1893 and it began to publish historical material and to hold meetings where Louisiana's history was discussed. The *Louisiana Historical Quarterly* was founded in 1917. During the past twenty years, however, the society has become chiefly a New Orleans organization and is no longer active throughout the entire state. Its *Quarterly* went out of existence in 1958, despite the efforts of Dr. Joseph Tregle, then of Loyola University, to keep it alive.

The Louisiana Historical Association was organized in New Orleans by a group of Civil War veterans in 1889 for the purpose of preserving the records and relics of that conflict. It established Confederate Memorial Hall in New Orleans and for a number of years was very active in its work. In 1958 the association was reorganized at Alexandria on a state-wide and broader historical basis and early in 1960 began publication of its journal, *Louisiana History*. Membership in the association is open to all persons interested in Louisiana history, with special rates for students.

A state agency for the preservation and better organization of Louisiana's historical and present-day archives and records, officially called the State Archives and Records Service, was created by the Legislature in 1956 but received no appropriation. The 1958 Legislature made a small appropriation, which has enabled the Service to begin operations in a modest way.

Some years ago Henry P. Dart, a noted New Orleans lawyer,

pleaded for the preservation of Louisiana's historical records. He wrote: "Let us put our archives in shape for the children who will soon take our places, that they may study the past and plan for the future."

The Peoples of Modern Louisiana. Gilbert L. Dupré of St. Landry Parish once wrote of Louisiana and its people: "I love its soil. I love its people. We are cosmopolitan to the core. Originally of French and Acadian descent, the American is now with us. My children are descended from a Connecticut Yankee on the mother's side. That's a good cross. Creole on one side, Yankee on the other."

Modern Louisianians are bred from many nationalities and races: Frenchmen, Spaniards, Canary Islanders who were called *Isleños,* European West Indians, English, Germans, Italians, Acadians, Irish, Sicilians, Hungarians, Slavonians; Indians; Chinese; Free Negroes from Santo Domingo, Negro slaves from Africa or the other slave-holding states; and others too. Each of these national and racial groups has contributed to Louisiana's culture and civilization.

In most communities these nationalities are well mixed, but in others one group may remain almost intact, and thereby still preserve many of its native customs; these communities are called "culture islands." Pure Spanish, for example, is still spoken on Delacroix Island in St. Bernard Parish; many Slavonians live in Plaquemines Parish and speak their native Slavic language; and a group of Hungarians is found in Livingston Parish.

It has been suggested that three statues in the state represent the basic national and racial energies which lifted Louisiana from the Mississippi swamps. The statue of Bienville, the "Father of Louisiana," in front of the new railroad station in New Orleans, typifies her heritage from the French. Overlooking Cane River at Natchitoches is the bronze figure of an old Negro who might stand as deputy for his people's contribution to the development of Louisiana. The third statue looks from the formal shrubbery toward the State Capitol—Huey Long represents the energy and drive of the Anglo-Saxon people. Other statues should be erected to the memory of other Louisianians who have worked to make a great state.

A Final Word. Louisianians have always loved their land. Years ago, when French Commissioner Laussat left Louisiana in 1804, he wrote: "It is a hard thing for me, having once known this land, to part from it." A hundred and fifty years later when Louisiana's big-league baseball pitcher Bill Lee retired and returned home, he said: "Baseball doesn't give you much of a chance for home. Man, nothing can beat the feeling when you walk in your own backyard after supper, and the dogs come jumping up on you with rabbits in their eyes."

Modern Louisianians are trying to preserve many of the old values of life, among which one historian lists pride, bravery, honor, courtesy, generosity, and loyalty. Another writer, expressing it differently, speaks of six senses. The sense of place: the strong feeling for the land and community where one lives. The sense of family: respect for ancestors and for what they accomplished. The sense of unity: the closeness which Louisianians feel when they meet away from home. The sense of proportion: the combination of courtesy, leisure, and hard work. The sense of humor: the love of legends and tall tales and the ability to sometimes laugh at ourselves. The sense of religion: the feeling which has caused Louisianians to be the most church-going people in the nation.

Will future citizens of Louisiana be able to retain the good things from their old civilization while continuing to keep in step with cultural and scientific progress? The answer is up to each new generation.

Louisianians might well heed the words of Daniel Webster: "Our proper business is improvement. Let us cultivate the resources of our land, build up its institutions, promote all its great interests, and see whether we also, in our day and generation, may not perform something to be remembered."

INDEX

Ablamowicz, Madame, 195
Acadian Coast, 109; First and Second coasts, 122
Acadian House, 313
Acadians, 109, 110, 125, 141
Acolapissa Indians, 16
Adams, Henry, 258
Adams, John, 130
Adams, Samuel, 129
Advocate, 194. *See also Morning Advocate*
Agricultural Extension Service, 248
Agriculture, 33, 35, 40, 41–42, 45, 53, 58, 60, 61, 62–63, 71, 90, 110–11, 122–23, 139, 147, 176–78, 220, 232, 245, 247–48, 294–98
Aime, Valcour, 332
Airlines, 304
Albrizio, Conrad, 316
Alexandria, 175, 210-11, 213
Alferez, Enrique, 317
Allen, Henry Watkins, 224, 231
Allen, Oscar K., 287
Almonester y Rojas, Don Andres, 102
Amato, Pasquale, 318
American Cotton Grower, 313
American Party, 165
American Revolution, 89, 90–99, 115, 127, 128, 129
Amusements, 20–21, 78–79, 125–26, 128, 142–43, 149, 189–90, 194–96, 236, 267–69, 275, 279–80, 318, 320, 321–26
Anderson, Sherwood, 314
Animals, 3, 11–12, 29, 35, 63, 111, 281, 302–303, 324
Antoine, C. C., 222

Archives, 264; Department of, Louisiana State, 312; State Archives and Records Service, 337
Arliss, George, 268
Armesto, Don Manuel Andres Lopez, 126
Art Association of New Orleans, 267
Art Union, 267
Arthur, Stanley C., 315
Arts and Exhibition Club, 267
Asiento Company, 38
Assinai Indians, 16
Aswell, James B., 260
Atakapa Indians, 15, 16
Aubry, Philippe, 81, 83–84, 116
Aymond, Roy, 317

Bahia de Santa Maria de Galvez, La, 98
Baker, Joshua, 224–25
Ballowe, Hewitt, 315, 316
Bando de Buen Gobierno, 100
Bank, Planters', 147
Bank of Amsterdam, 44
Bank of Louisiana, 147
Bank of Orleans, 147
Banks, Lewis, 32
Banks, Nathaniel P., 208, 210, 213, 218, 219
Banks and banking, 44, 147, 168, 179, 232, 257–58, 306
Banks' Arcade, 171
Baratarians, 151, 153, 159, 170
Barbé-Marbois, François, 133
Barcelona, Father Cirilo de, 124
Barnum, P. T., 195
Barthé, Richmond, 317
Baseball, 282, 339

Basso, Hamilton, 313
Bastrop, Baron de, 109
Baton Rouge, 70, 81, 93–95, 98–99, 101, 120, 122, 141, 170, 175, 194, 208–209, 250, 253, 313; naming of, 30; fort built at, 52; Republic of West Florida set up at, 146; as capital, 169, 215, 253
Baton Rouge Agricultural Society, 178
Battle of December 23, p. 156
Battle of Lake Borgne, 155–56
Battle of Mansfield, 211
Battle of New Orleans, 159–62
Battle of New Year's Day, 159
Battle of Pleasant Hill, 211
Bayou Sara Mounted Riflemen, 157
Bayougoula Indians, 16, 29
Bayous of Louisiana, The, 315
Beale's Rifles, 157
Beaubois, Father Ignatius de, 50
Beauregard, Gen. P. G. T., 219
Bee, New Orleans, 171, 194, 202
Beer, William, 312
Bell, John, 197–98
Beluche, Oncle, 159
Benjamin, Judah P., 198, 201
Bernhardt, Sarah, 268
B. F. French Library, 194
Bienville, Jean Baptiste le Moyne Sieur de, 28, 30–34, 37, 41–47, 50–57, 63, 64, 68, 81, 338
Billouart, Louis. *See* Kerlerec
Biloxi, 30, 34, 36, 45, 49, 62, 70
Biloxi Indians, 29
Birds, 3, 11–12, 302, 324, 331
Bishop, Anna, 195
Black Code, 50, 64, 69
Blackburn, W. Jasper, 233
Blanc, Father Antoine, 193
Blanchard, Newton C., 239
Bludso, Jim, 333
Blunt, Raford, 229
B'Nai B'Rith, 328
Board of Trade Building, 267
Boats, 18, 64–65, 74, 102, 104, 105, 114, 180–82, 250, 255–57, 304, 306, 321
Boisbriant, Pierre Dugué de, 45

Bonaparte, Joseph, 133
Bonaparte, Lucien, 133
Bonaparte, Napoleon. *See* Napoleon
Booksellers, 194
Booth, Edwin, 195
Booth, Junius Brutus, 195
Boré, Étienne de, 63, 106, 111
Bowen, Andy, 282
Boyd, David F., 213, 234
Bradford, Roark, 315, 316, 319
Bradly, Henry, 118
Braud, Denis, 127
Breckinridge, John C., 197–98
Bridges, 68, 118, 168, 239, 284, 286, 287, 319
Bristow, Gwen, 315
Brokenburn Plantation, 231
Brooks, Cleanth, Jr., 315
Brotherhood of Timber Workers, 307
Brown, William G., 233
Buckner, Simon B., 213
Bulletin, New Orleans, 194
Bullitt, Alexander C., 194
Burke, Jack, 282
Burr, Aaron, 146
Butler, A. J., 218
Butler, Benjamin F., 208, 216–18

Cabildo, 102, 116–17, 136, 137, 138, 266, 267, 312, 313
Cable, George W., 264, 265
Cadillac, Antoine de la Mothe, 38–43
Caddo Gazette, Shreveport, 194
Caddo Indians, 14, 16, 168
Caddo Lake Boys, 207
Caldwell, James H., 195
Calvery, E. G., 255
Cambell, Alexander, 11
Campbell, Gen. John, 98
Canals, 180–81
Canby, E. R. S., 219
Capitals of Louisiana, 168–69, 215, 253
Capitol, 288, 338
Capuchins, 45, 60, 71, 77–78, 80, 102, 124–25
Cajun, The, 318
Carmelites, 45, 77
Carondelet, Baron de, 104–107, 112

Carpetbaggers, 222, 225, 233, 238
Carver, Ada Jack, 318
Casa Calvo, Marquis de, 107, 139
Casket Girls, 49–50, 335
Cassidy, H., 203
Castellanos, Henry, 264
Cat Island, 29–30, 60, 155
Catahoula Guerrillas, 207
Celle, Romeo, 267
Cenelles, Les, 196
Centenary College, 192, 263
Chalmette Plain, 161
Charity Hospital, 57, 245
Chandeleur Islands, 28
Charlevoix, Father Pierre, 52
Chartres Street, 78, 171
Chase, John, 317
Chepart, 51
Chickasaw Indian War, 55–57
Chickasaw Indians, 51, 54–58
Chief, Donaldsonville, 241, 252, 282
Children of Strangers, 315
Chita, 265
Chitimacha Indians, 16
Choctaw Indians, 21, 119, 157, 168, 265
Choiseul, Duke de, 81
Chopin, Kate, 265
Christmas, Annie, 324
Civil Service, 286, 289, 290–92
Civil War, 204–220, 245, 260, 264, 266, 270, 332, 335–36
Claiborne, William C. C., 136, 138, 139, 142–43, 145–46, 148, 149, 150, 151, 153, 155, 164, 165, 168
Clapp, the Rev. Theodore, 193
Clark, George Rogers, 92
Clay, Henry, 165
Clement, William Edwards, 272
Climate, 3–6, 61, 111, 187, 296, 324
Clinton and Port Hudson Railroad, 180
Clothing, 64, 74–75, 113, 128, 141, 186–87, 213, 232, 255
Cochrane, Sir Alexander, 152, 161–62
Code Noir. See Black Code
Code of 1769, 116
Cole, Fred C., 315

College of Franklin, 192
College of Jefferson, 192
College of Orleans, 148, 192
College of St. Charles, 192
College of the Immaculate Conception, 192
Colleges and universities, 148, 192, 262–63, 310, 318
Collell, Francisco, 92, 95
Colton, Charles, 265
Commerce, 41, 64, 80, 90, 102, 104–105, 107, 147, 181–83, 250, 304–306. *See also* Trade
Company of the Indies, 45–50, 53–54, 58, 63, 66, 67
Company of the West, 44–45, 54
Comptes-Rendus de L'Athénée Louisianais, 264
Concordia Intelligencer, Vidalia, 194
Confederate Memorial Hall, 313
Confiscation Law, 217
Conservative Party, 223
Constitutional, Alexandria, 200
Constitutional Union Party, 197
Constitutions. *See* Government
Conway, T. W., 233
Coquille, Walter, 314
Corn, 36, 41, 62, 63, 68, 76, 111, 119, 129, 178, 187, 296, 305
Cotton, 58, 63, 152, 176, 178, 181, 210, 218, 295–96
Cotton Trade Journal, 248
Coupé, Bras, 333
Coureurs de bois, 31, 34
Courier, New Orleans, 194
Courier, Opelousas, 194
Courier du Vendredi, Le, New Orleans, 127
Coxe, John E., 308
Creole Folk Tales, 314
Creoles, 62, 87, 88–89, 92, 99, 102, 105, 113, 116, 119, 125, 126, 138, 141–42, 147, 148, 152, 153, 164, 165, 167, 168, 240, 265, 269, 271, 272, 282, 315, 320–21, 329, 335
Crescent, New Orleans, 194, 201
Crescent Theater, 268
Criminals, 42, 47–48, 69, 118, 171, 243–44

Crowley, founding of, 246
Crowley, Patrick, 246
Crozat, Antoine, 37–43
Culture, 127–28, 148–49, 194–96, 265–69, 312–19, 320, 329. See also Education; Libraries; Newspapers
Cushman, Charlotte, 195
Custer, George A., 221, 222
"Custom of Paris," 39, 68
Customhouse, 47, 102–103, 332

D'Abbadie, Jean Jacques, 80–81
D'Abrado, Marquesa, 82
Dagobert, Father, 77, 89, 124
Daigre, Grace De la Croix, 317
Daily Crescent, 204. See also Crescent
Daily Journal of Commerce, 313
Daily Picayune, 288. See also Picayune
Daily Topic, New Orleans, 194
Daily True Delta, 204. See also True Delta
Dart, Henry P., 337–38
D'Artaguette, Pierre, 55–56
Dauphin Island, 33, 34, 39, 41, 45
Davis, Dwight Greever, 318
Davis, Edwin A., 312, 315
Davis, James H., 289–90
Davis, John, 195
Deane, Charles, 195
De Blanc, Alcibiade, 226
De Bow's Review, 194, 264
De León, Ponce, 25
Delgado, Isaac, 267
Delgado Museum, 266, 312
Delpit, Albert, 265
Delta, New Orleans, 194
Democratic Party, 165, 166, 197, 226, 237
De Moscoso, Luis, 25
De Narváez, Pánfilo, 25
De Palma, Ralph, 282
De Pauger, Adrien, 46
De Pineda, Alonso, 25
Derbigny, Pierre, 165
Desdunes, Rodolphe L., 266
Deslonde, P. G., 222

De Soto, Hernando, 25
De Soto's Discovery of the Mississippi, painting of, 267
D'Estréhan, Félice de St. Maxent, 92
Deutsch, Hermann B., 313
De Vaca, Álvar Cabeza, 25
D'Iberville, Pierre le Moyne, Sieur, 27–34, 36, 37, 88
Dickson, Alexander, 93
Dillard University, 263, 319
Dimitry, Alexander, 191
Dimitry, John, 266
Disease, 22, 34, 65, 78, 168, 188–89, 245. See also Leprosy; Medicine; Yellow Fever
District of Louisiana, 143
Domenget, Joseph, 267
Donaldsonville, as capital, 168–69
Dorsey, Sarah A., 266
Double Dealer, 314
Douglas, Blanche, 250
Douglas, Stephen A., 197–98
Dow, Dr. Robert, 127
Dred Scott Decision, 197
Drysdale, Alexander J., 267, 316
Dubourg, Father Louis, 193
Dubuclet, Antoine, 222
Duclot, Louis, 127
Duelling, 167–68
Duhart, Adolphe, 267
Duke of Orleans, 44. See also Phillipe, Louis
Dumas, Francis, 222
Dunn, Oscar J., 222, 225
Du Pratz, Le Page, 46
Durieux, Caroline Wogan, 317
Durnford, Capt. Elias, 96
Duson brothers, 246

Eads, James B., 250
Earthquake, 142
Education, 57, 126, 148, 168, 190–92, 229, 233–34, 239, 242, 245, 259–63, 284, 285, 287, 294, 306–310, 319, 321; of Indians, 20; in French Colonial period, first school opened, 78; in Louisiana, first public school, 89; State Superintendent's office created, 170, 191;

medical schools and college medical training, 188; for deaf, dumb, and blind, 244; State Board of Education established, 259
Electric lighting in towns, 274
Electricity in rural areas, 320
Ellender, Allen J., 293
Ellsler, Fanny, 195
Emblems of Louisiana, state bird, flag, motto, seal, 331; state flower, song, march song, 332
Employment Security, division of State Department of Labor, 307
English settlement, 26–27, 37–38
English Turn, 60
Enterprize, steamboat, 153
Epidemics, 36, 37, 78, 126, 168, 188, 235
Esso Standard Oil Refinery, 301
Evangeline Oak, speech of Huey P. Long at, 286–87

Fabulous New Orleans, 315
Fairs, 321–22
Farmer's Union Banner, 248
Farragut, David G., 208
Father Antoine. *See* Sedella, Father Antonio de
Father Mississippi, 315
"Father of Louisiana," 37, 57, 338
"Father of Louisiana Elementary Education," 191
Faulkner, William, 314
Federationist, 313
Ferguson, Duncan, 317
Ferries, 168, 181, 239
Ficklen, John R., 266
Filhiol, Don Juan, 101
Filibustering expeditions, 146, 170–71
Filiosa, Sylvain, 51
Filles à la Cassette. See Casket Girls
Firemen, volunteer companies of, 274
Fires, in New Orleans, 102, 106, 121
Fish, 11–12, 187, 249, 302–303, 324
Fisheries, 42–43, 129, 249, 302
Fisk Free Library, 194, 264
Fiske, Minnie Maddern, 268

Flags, 69, 98, 201, 203, 204, 220, 330–31
Flanders, Benjamin F., 224
Fleur-de-lis, 69
Flood, of 1927, 286
Food and foodstuffs, 18–19, 36, 42, 48, 49, 62, 67, 68, 73, 75–76, 103, 111, 114, 119, 176, 187–88, 211, 213, 255, 256, 282–83, 326–27
Forests, 3, 13–14, 298, 324. *See also* Timber; Timberlands; Trees
Fort Bourgogne, 52
Fort Bute, 93–94
Fort Charlotte, 96
Fort de la Boulaye, 32, 34
Fort De Russy, 211
Fort Jackson, 200
Fort Jesup, 171
Fort Macomb, 203
Fort Maurepas, 30–31, 33, 34, 45
Fort Miro, 122
Fort New Richmond, 93–94
Fort Panmure, 93, 95, 98–99
Fort Pike, 203
Fort Rosalie, 41, 51
Fort St. Charles, 52
Fort St. Jean, 52
Fort St. Louis, in New Orleans, 52
Fort St. Louis de la Louisiane, 37
Fort St. Louis de la Mobile, 33–34. *See also* Fort St. Louis de la Louisiane
Fort St. Philip, 105, 162, 200
Fort San Carlos, 121
Fort San Fernando, 121
Fort San José, 121
Fort San Juan, 121
Fort San Luis, 121
Fortier, Alcée, 36, 225, 246, 266, 270
Foster, Murphy J., 239
Fournet, John B., 287
Franchmastabbia, 119
Freaner, James L., 264
"Free Men of Color," 113
Free Negroes, 50, 113, 139, 141, 173, 184, 194, 196, 230–31, 330
Free State Party, 223

Free Textbook Law, 309
French and Indian War, 60–61
French explorations, 25
French Market, 103
French Opera Company, 269
French Revolution, 105, 124
French settlements, 26–27, 59, 108
Frost, Meigs O., 313
Funerals, 76, 78, 277
Fuqua, Henry L., 286
Furs and fur trade, 34, 36, 40, 42, 248–49

Galvez, Don Bernardo de, 89–100, 127
Galveztown, 92, 94, 122
Gas, humorous publication, 264
Gas, natural, 13, 139, 248–49, 299, 301
Gayarré, Charles, 32, 148, 192, 196, 266, 337
Gayoso de Lemos, Manuel, 107, 119
General Bank of France, 44
Genevaux, Father Hilaire de, 124
Genthe, Arnold, 317
Geography, 3, 324
Gergaud, Esther, 235
German Coast, 49, 94, 109; First and Second coasts, 121
German settlement, 48–49
Gibbs, Sir Samuel, 161
Glenk, Dr. Robert, 312
Gonzales, Juanita, 317
Gottschalk, Louis, 196
Government, 37, 39–40, 43, 45–46, 54–55, 57–60, 62, 67–69, 80–91, 99–104, 106–107, 108, 115–20, 131, 136, 138–39, 142–46, 149–50, 163–73, 215–16, 218, 220, 222–29, 237–44, 284–94
Government constitutions, of 1812, pp. 149–50, 163, 170, 284; of 1845, pp. 170, 192; of 1852, pp. 170, 224; of 1864, pp. 224–25, 238–39; of 1868, pp. 225, 233, 238–39; of 1879, p. 239; of 1898, pp. 239–40, 285; of 1913, p. 240; of 1921, pp. 240, 284
Graaf, Laurent de, 28

Grace, Albert L., 251
Grand Pré, Carlos de, 98, 128
Graner, Luis, 267
Grant, Gen. U. S., 209, 225, 227, 228
Gravier, Father Jacques, 22, 30
Gray Sisters, 34
Grofé, Ferde, 319
Group Theater, The, 318
Guinea Company, 38
Guiraud, Ernest, 269

Hahn, Michael, 223–24
Hall, A. V., 317
Hall, Luther E., 239
Hall, Weeks, 316
Hampden, Walter, 268
Hancock, Winfield S., 224
Hargrave, Ronald, 316
Harris, T. H., 260, 308
Hasselmans, Louis, 318
Hay, John, 333
Hayes, Rutherford B., 227
Health, 78, 126, 168, 189, 284. *See also* Medicine
Heard, William W., 239
Hearn, Lafcadio, 264, 265
Hebert, Paul O., 166
Hector, Don Francisco Luis. *See* Carondelet
Hemingway, Ernest, 314
Henderson, W. K., 314
Hennepin, Father Louis, 27
Hennessey, David C., 243
Highway Department, 291
Highways, 303–304. *See also* Roads
Hinds, Maj. Thomas, 157
Historical museums, 313
History, of Louisiana, 87–88, 196, 264, 266, 312, 315, 335–38. *See also* Archives
History of Louisiana, by Fortier, 266
History of Louisiana, by Gayarré, 266
History of New Orleans, A, 315
Holidays, 76–77, 125, 322
Home Rule, 227–28, 236, 243, 257
Homes, 71–73, 122, 184–86, 271
Horn Island, 43

Hospitals, 57, 78, 103, 245, 284
Houma Indians, 16, 30
Howard Association, 189
Howard Library, 264, 312
Hubert, Father Darius, 201
Hull, Gen. Isaac, 150–51
Humble, James, 167–68
Humbrecht, Erasme, 266
Hurricanes, 57, 111, 265

Iberville. *See* D'Iberville
Ice supply, 275
Illegal trade. *See* Smuggling and illegal trade
Immigrants, 47–49, 89, 91, 93, 101, 103, 108–110. *See also* Settlers
Impressions of Old New Orleans, 317
Indians, 3, 14–24, 25, 28, 40, 42, 48, 50–51, 53, 54–58, 60, 65, 69, 89, 90, 101, 106, 118–19, 145–46, 150–51, 157, 164, 168, 265, 279, 313, 334, 335; groups and tribes of, 14–16; as slaves, 63, 86
Indigo, 40, 41, 61, 63, 65, 66, 111
Industry, 64, 113, 178–79, 220, 245– 46, 248–50, 300, 303. *See also* Manufacturing
Inquisition, 103
Insects, 74, 111, 248. *See also* Mosquitoes
Irazabel, Don José Calbo de, 97
"Iron Hand," 26
Isle of Orleans, 10, 61, 77, 80, 139
Isleños, 92, 141, 338
Item, New Orleans, 313, 317

Jackson, Gen. Andrew, 142, 151–62, 165, 335
Jackson, Shelby M., 308
Jackson Square, 70, 78, 137, 316
Jazz, 281, 329
Jefferson, Thomas, 132, 135–36, 150, 182, 220
Jennings Cavalry, 241
Jesuits, 45, 50, 60, 77, 80, 124
Jetty system, 250
John Brown's Raid on Harper's Ferry, 197

John Henry, 315, 319
Johnson, Andrew, 224
Johnson, Henry, 165
Johnson, Isaac, 166
Johnston, Gen. Joseph E., 213
Johnston, William Preston, 266
Johnstone, George, 93
Jolly Joker, 265
Jones, Elliott, 248
Jones, Sam Houston, 289–90
Journal, Shreveport, 313
Journal of Education, 260
Journal of Southern History, 315
Journals, 313
Julio, Fabrino, 266

Kane, Harnett, 315
Keane, Gen. John, 161
Kellogg, William Pitt, 225–26
Kelly, "Captain," 254
Kendall, George W., 194
Kendall, John Smith, 315
Kennon, Robert F., 290–91
Kerlerec, Chevalier de, 59–61, 79– 80
King, Alvin O., 287
King, Grace, 34, 47, 265, 266, 335
King, Rufus, 132
Kingdom Coming, 315
Knapp, Seaman A., 247
Knights of Columbus, 328
Knights of the Border, 207
Knights of the White Camellia, 222, 225
"Know-Nothing" Party. *See* American Party
Koasati Indian, 23
Koroa Indians, 16
Ku Klux Klan, 222, 225, 285–86

Labor, 50, 90, 111, 183–84, 229, 258, 285, 307, 313
Labor organizations, 258, 307
Lafaience, Jack. *See* McLoughlin
Lafayette, 263, 310
Laffite, Jean, 151, 158–59
Lake Charles, 305, 306
L'Album Littéraire, 194

Lambert, Gen. John, 161
La Montagne, Alexis, 111
La Morandière, Roberto de, 99
Land, 3, 6–8, 62–63, 109–110, 139, 302; titles to, 87, 118, 146; grants of, 89, 91, 101, 109; records of, 241
Language, 24, 89, 120, 145, 148, 168, 194, 313, 318, 321, 334–35, 338
Lantern, The, 265
Lanterne Magique, Le, 149
Lanusse, Armand, 196
La Salle, Robert Cavelier, Sieur de, 26, 27, 30, 33, 332
La Salle's Last Discoveries in America, 27
Last Meeting of Lee and Jackson, painting of, 266
La Tour, Le Blond de, 46
Latour, Maj. Arsene, 157
Laurens, Henry, 129
Laussat, Pierre Clement de, 120, 131, 135–39
Law, John, 44–45, 53–54
Lawd Sayin' the Same, The, 315
Laws, 38, 39, 50, 64, 68–69, 86, 100, 106, 112, 113, 115–16, 120, 145, 168, 172–73, 179, 216, 217, 218, 222, 243–44, 257, 261, 286, 291, 306, 307, 309
Leathers, T. P., 250
Le Camp, Jean, 35
Le Camp, Jean François, 35
Leche, Richard W., 289
Lee, Bill, 339
Lee, Richard Henry, 129
Lee, Gen. Robert E., 213, 219
Legends, 21, 332–34
Leland University, 234, 263
Lemos, Manuel Gayoso de, 107, 119
Le Moyne, Charles, 28
Le Moyne, Charles, sons of, 28
Le Petit, Mathurin, 55
Lepinay, Chevalier de, 43
Leonhardt, Olive, 316
Leprosarium, established at Carville, 245
Leprosy, 245

Le Sueur, Pierre, 32
Levees, 8, 9, 10, 47, 68, 76, 118, 144, 168, 238, 242
Liberal Republicans 226
Liberals, 226–27
Libraries, 194, 264, 309, 310, 311–12, 320
Lincoln, Abraham, 197–198, 221, 223
Lind, Jenny, 195
Linfield, The Rev. W. E. N., 201
Literature, 127, 194–96, 265–66, 314
Livestock, 35, 48, 63, 71, 111, 176, 178, 182, 210, 232, 247, 294–96, 297–98
Livingston, Robert, 132–133, 135
Lockett, Samuel H., 254
Long, Earl K., 289–91
Long, Huey P., 286–88, 290, 317, 338
Long, Dr. James, 171
Long, Russell, 293
Lopez, Gen. Narciso, 171
Lotteries, 238
Louis, Jean, 57
Louis XIV, 27, 125
Louis XV, 60, 81
Louis XVI, 105
Louisiana Agricultural Extension Service, 298
Louisiana Agricultural Society, 178
Louisiana and Arkansas Railroad, 304
Louisiana College, 263
Louisiana Farmer and Rice Journal, 248
Louisiana Federation of Labor, 313
Louisiana Gazette, 149
Louisiana Historical Association, 313, 337
Louisiana Historical Quarterly, 337
Louisiana Historical Society, 337
Louisiana History, 337
Louisiana Infantry Regiments, First and Second, in Spanish-American War, 240
Louisiana Lottery Company, 238
Louisiana Monitor, The, 106, 127, 148

Louisiana Planter and Sugar Manufacturer, 248
Louisiana Progress, 317
Louisiana Purchase, 129–38, 145, 150, 182, 330
Louisiana Purchase Treaty, 133, 171
"Louisiana Scandals" and Governor Leche, 289
Louisiana State Educational Association, 259
Louisiana State Library, 311
Louisiana State Museum, 264, 267, 312–13
Louisiana State Normal School, 262
Louisiana State Seminary of Learning and Military Academy, 192, 234
Louisiana State Teachers' Association, 259
Louisiana State University, 192, 234, 262, 264, 310, 311, 312, 315, 317
Louisiana Story, 319
Louisiana Tigers, 207, 332
Louisiana Weekly, New Orleans, 313
Louisiana Wildlife Federation, 302
Louisianian, New Orleans, 231
Lovell, Gen. Mansfield, 208
Loyola University, 263, 310, 314, 337
Ludlow, Noah, 195
Lumber and lumbering, 58, 64, 66, 248–49, 298–99
Luxemburg, Father Raphael de, 78
Lyceum Library, 264

Macarty, Marie Celeste Elenore de, 92
McClure, John, 313
McEnery, John, 226
McEnery, Samuel D., 239
McGloin, Frank, 265
McIlhenny, Edward Avery, 302
McLoughlin, James J., 314–15
McMillen, James A., 311
Macready, Charles, 195
Madison, James, 135, 138, 149, 150
Maestri, Robert S., 290
Mafia society, 243–44

Magazines, 193–94, 264–65, 313, 314
Magic Lantern, The, 149
Mail, 147, 183, 275
Maison Rouge, Marquis de, 109
Manning, Bruce, 313, 315
Mansfield, Richard, 268
Manufacturing, 58, 64, 105, 113, 178–79, 232, 249–50, 294, 300–302. *See also* Industry
Mardi Gras, 315
Mardi Gras, 189–90, 280, 319, 322–24
Marest, Father Gabriel, 22
Marigny, Bernard, 167–68
Marlowe, Julia, 268
Marriage, 23, 76, 276–77; courtship leading to, 276
Marshall, R. B., 253–54
Martin, François Xavier, 196
Martin, Wade O., Jr., 292
Martyr Patriots, The; or, *Louisiana in 1769,* p. 67
Masonic Order, 328
Maspero's Exchange, 171
Massacre Island, 33
Maxent, Antonio, 119
Maxwell, Dr. Leon Ryder, 269
Mayfield, Robert B., 316
Medicine, 126–27, 188–89, 245; and Indians, 21–22; in French Colonial period, 78; college medical training, 188; medical schools, 188; superstitious cures for ills, 278; medical collections, schools, 313; medical publications, 313
Medicine shows, 279
Mercier, Dr. Alfred, 265
Metropolitan Brigade, 226
Mexican Gulf Railroad, 180
Mexican War, 172
Mid-Winter Sports Carnival, 326
Milhet, Jean, 81–82, 84
Milhet, Joseph, 92
Military Occupation, by Federals, 216–18, 220–36, 264, 270
Miro, Don Estevan, 92, 98, 100–104, 110, 119, 125, 245
"Mississippi Bubble," 53

Mississippi Dragoons, 157
Mississippi River, 3, 6, 7, 8–9, 10, 11, 13, 15, 16, 25, 26, 27, 29–32, 34, 93, 94, 111, 121, 132, 139, 251, 300–301, 304; De Soto buried in, 25; D'Iberville finds, 29; as artery of commerce, 64–65, 182; navigation of, 107; trade, 114, 129–30; control of, 129
Mississippi Suite, 319
Missouri Pacific Railroad, 304
Mobile, 30, 41, 45, 46, 62, 70, 93, 98; founding of, 33; population of, in 1704, pp. 34–35; present site located, 37; settlers land at, 49; first hospital established in, 78; captured by Galvez, 95–96
Money, 36, 41, 44, 45, 53, 62, 83, 108, 115, 116, 131, 218, 228, 239, 256, 257–58; types of in Louisiana, 67–68
Moniteur de la Louisiane, Le (The Louisiana Monitor), 106, 127, 148
Monroe, 109, 122, 141, 260; established, 101
Monroe, James, 132, 133, 135
Monroe, John F., 201
Montez, Lola, 195
Moore, Thomas O., 166–67, 197–204, 207–208, 224
Morgan, Arthur, 317
Morgan, Gen. David, 160–161
Morgan, Elemore, 317
Morgan, Lewis, 289
Morning Advocate, Baton Rouge, 313. *See also Advocate*
Morriessy, John, 318
Morrison, deLesseps S., 290
Morro Castle, 105
Mosquitoes, 53, 74, 214, 272, 333
Moss, Spanish, 249
Mount Lebanon University, 192
Mounted Wild Cats, 207
Mouton, Alexandre, 166, 208
Mouton, Gen. Alfred, 208, 210
Mrs. Candy and Saturday Night, 315
Mulattoes, 173–74
Museums, 312–13

Music, 20–21, 127, 128, 149, 195–96, 269, 280–81, 318–19; boat songs, 251; bands, 269; German singing clubs, 269; jazz, 281, 329; Creole music, 329; Negro music, 329
Muskhogean Indians, 15

Naming of Louisiana, 332
Napoleon, 124, 130, 132–33, 135, 333
Natchez, 41, 45, 62, 70, 81, 93, 95, 98, 146, 180, 250
Natchez Indian War, 50–51
Natchez Indians, 15–16, 50–51
Natchitoches, 45, 53, 70, 110, 119, 120–22, 141, 145, 320, 338; St. Denis appointed Commandant of the fort at, 40
National groups; Indians, 3, 23–24; white people, 3; Creoles, 62; French Creoles, 88–89; at end of Spanish period—Acadians, French, Spaniards, Canary Islanders, Germans, Swiss, Englishmen, Scots and Irish, Americans from Pennsylvania, Virginia, Carolinas, or other states, Scandinavians, gypsies, 121; French, Spanish, Acadian, 125. *See also* People; Settlers
National Republican, 231
Neckere, Father Leo de, 193
Negro Insurrection of 1791, in Santo Domingo, 103, 112, 120
Negro slaves, 42, 50, 62, 63–64, 91, 173; as laborers, 183. *See also* Slaves
Negroes, 69, 112–13, 126–27, 141, 173, 189, 196, 217, 218, 220, 222–23, 225, 226, 227, 229, 230–31, 233, 234, 235, 238, 239, 256, 258, 263, 266, 267, 268, 279, 310, 313, 315, 317, 329, 338. *See also* Free Negroes; Slaves
New Biloxi, capital moved to, 45; hospital established in, 78
New Citizen, 265
Newcomb School of Music, 269

New Orleans, 58, 60, 62, 70, 81, 83, 86, 93, 94, 98, 101, 104–105, 107, 111, 113, 120, 126, 127, 140, 180, 199, 202, 209, 216, 236, 237, 246, 250, 256, 266, 269, 270, 280, 294, 312, 314, 316, 330; capital moved to, 45; founding of, 46–47; settlers land at, 49; Jesuit Plantation established at, 50; growth of, 52, 54; arrival of Vaudreuil at, 57; crime and drunkenness in, 69; hospitals built in, 78; population of, 100, 139; fire in 1788, p. 102; fire of 1794 and 1798, p. 106; Cabildo organized in, 116; fires of 1788 and 1794, p. 121; right of deposit at, 130; in War of 1812, pp. 151–62; as capital, 168–69; growth of population, 175; as commercial city, 182–83; Mardi Gras in, 189–90, 322–24; newspapers in, 194, 313; occupation by Butler, 208; picture of, during period of military occupation, 235; Morrison elected mayor of, 290; as port and shipping center, 305–306; journalists of, 313; works on, 315
New Orleans, 319
New Orleans and Carrollton Railroad, 180, 273
New Orleans and Pacific Railroad, 253
New Orleans Baptist Theological Seminary, 263
New Orleans Civic Symphony, 318
New Orleans Lawn Tennis Club, 236
New Orleans Library Society, 194
New Orleans Medical and Surgical Journal, 313
New Orleans, Mobile, and Chattanooga Railroad, 252
New Orleans, Opelousas, and Great Western Railroad, 253
New Orleans Opera House, 195
New Orleans Philharmonic Society, 269, 318
New Orleans Public Library, 264, 311
New Orleans University, 234

Newspapers, 106, 148–49, 171, 172, 183, 193–94, 199–200, 201–202, 227, 231, 264, 313, 317; first in Louisiana, 127
Ney, Marshall, 333
Nicolls, Col. Edward, 152
Nicholls, Francis T., 227–28, 239, 317
Nicholson, Elizabeth, 265
Nicknames, of Louisiana, 332
Noe, James A., 287
Northwestern State College, 262
Nos Hommes et Notre Histoire (Our Men and Our History), 266
Nouvelle-Orléans, 47
Nuñez, Vincente José, 102

O'Donnell, E. P., 315–16
Oil, 13, 139, 248–49, 299, 301, 305
Old Creole Days, 265
Old Louisiana, 315
Old Square, 47. See also Vieux Carré
Ol' Man Adam an' His Chillun, 315
Opelousas, 70, 94, 110, 120, 122, 141, 210; as capital during Civil War, 169, 215
Opera, 195, 199, 236, 269, 279
Order No. 28, of Gen. Butler, 217
Ordinance of Secession, 200–201
O'Reilly, Lt. Gen. Alejandro, 85–88, 98, 112, 114–16, 118, 119, 124
Orleans Theater, 195
Owen, William Miller, 266
Ouachita Indians, 14

Packard, Stephen B., 227–28
Painting, 127, 266–67, 316–17
Pakenham, Gen. Sir Edward, 152, 158–62
Palmer, Bishop Benjamin M., 193, 199,235
Panis, Jacinto, 92
Parelli, Achille, 267
Parker, John M., 285–86
Parks, state, 324
Parties, political, in Louisiana, 165, 197, 223
Patrick, Robert, 165, 214
Peabody, George, 233

Peabody Fund, 233
Pecans, 296–97
Peddlers, 256–57
Pénicaut, André, 18, 19
Pensacola, 93, 151; Spanish settlement of, 28; capture of by Galvez, 96–98
People, 120, 141–42, 176, 271–72, 330, 338–39. *See also* Immigrants; Settlers; National groups
People's League, 226
Père Antoine. *See* Sedella, Father Antonio de
Peretti, Achille, 266
Périer, Étienne, 45, 46, 54
Periodicals, 194
Perique tobacco, 178, 296
Perkins, John, Jr., 200
Perry, Enoch, 266
Le Petit Théâtre du Reveil Française, 318
Le Petit Théâtre du Vieux Carré, 318
Petroleum, 13. *See also* Oil
Phelps, Albert, 266
Phillipe, Louis, Duke of Orleans, 44, 47, 332–33
Photography, 316–17
Picayune, New Orleans, 172, 194, 201, 202, 317. *See also Daily Picayune; Times-Picayune*
Pinchback, P. B. S., 222, 233
Pinckney, Thomas, 129
Pinckney Treaty of 1795, p. 129
Pineville, 52, 70, 122
Pipes, D. M., Jr., 248
Pirates, 151, 170. *See also* Baratarians
Place d'Armes, 47, 70, 85, 94. *See also* Plaza de Armas
"Plantation of the Company," slave-trading station, 50
Plantations, 107–108, 121, 122, 176, 231, 330; development of, 62; in War of 1812, pp. 156, 157
Planters' Bank, 147
Planter's Banner, 194
Planter's Home Journal, 248
Plaza de Armas, 94, 103. *See also* Place d'Armes

Pleasant, Ruffin G., 239
Poetry, 196, 265, 333
Pointe Coupee Slave Plot, 112
Police Juries, 189, 215, 241
Police Jury, 172, 242
Politics, 165–68, 222–29, 237–38, 284–94; national, in Louisiana, 165; election of 1860, pp. 196–98; secession, 196–205; political cartoons, 317
Polk, Bishop Leonidas, 193
Pollock, Oliver, 92
Ponchartrain, Count de, 39, 41; desires to expand French possessions, 27; holds conferences with French and Canadian leaders, 27
Ponchartrain Railroad, 180
Pontalba, Baroness de, 316
Pontalba Buildings, 316
Population, 38, 49, 54, 58, 64, 91, 100–101, 120–21, 139, 147, 173, 175–76, 231, 247, 294, 305; of Mobile, in 1704, pp. 34–35; of Mobile, in 1708, p. 36; of Louisiana, census of 1744, p. 58; in 1756, p. 61; census of 1777, 90-91; census of 1788, taken by Miro, 103; in 1762, p. 107
Porter, Alexander, 142
Porter, Admiral David, 211
Poultry, 296, 298
Powers, Stephen, 229
Poydras College, 205
Poydras, Julien, 127
Primot, Catherine, 28
Printing press, first in Louisiana, 127
Prize fighting, 282
Proclamation of Good Government, 100
Propagateur Catholique, La (*The Catholic Propagator*), 194, 200
Province of Louisiana, created by O'Reilly, 115
Public Service Commission, 286
Punishment, 87, 98–99, 103, 105, 118, 243; of criminals and for small offenses, 69–70; of leaders of rebellion against Spain, 86; of slaves, 112

Queen Anne's War, 36
Queen Isabella, 125
Quinipissa Indians, 16
Quintero, José, 264

Race riots, 222, 225; in Colfax, New Orleans, Coushatta, 226
Race tracks, 190
Radical Returning Board, 226–27
Radicals, 222–23, 225–29, 233; newspapers established by, 264
Radio, 313–14, 320
Radisson, Pierre Esprit, 26
Railroads, 168, 180, 232, 252–54, 304
Randall, James R., 204
Rebellion, against Ulloa; of 1768, pp. 83–85, 87, 98, 109; of 1781, p. 98
Reconstruction Period, 220
Red River Republican, 194
Red River Whig, 194
Regulations. *See* Laws
Religion, 21, 22, 50, 103, 148, 192–93, 235, 321, 327–28; churches, French Colonial, 76; French Colonial Catholics, 76–77; in French Colonial period, 76–77; Catholic, 101, 124–25, 126; under Spanish rule, 124–25; Catholics and Protestants, 125, 141; churches in 1860, p. 193
Remonville, Sieur de, 27
Reptiles, 3, 13; alligator, 12; water moccasin or water viper, "highland moccasin" or "cottonmouth," rattlesnake, coral snake, 13; snakes, 272
Republic of Louisiana, 202
Republic of West Florida, 1810, p. 146
Republican, New Orleans, 227
Republican Party, 197, 237
Resources, 285, 299–301, 330; natural, underground—gas, natural gas, oil, petroleum, sulphur, salt, 13, 139, 248–49, 301; natural—water, fresh, 14, fur-bearing animals, Spanish moss, 248–49; minerals, 32, 43, 139, 299–300

Rice, 58, 62, 63, 65, 76, 111, 178, 187, 295, 296, 313
Rigaud, Pierre. *See* Vaudreuil, Marquis de
Rightor, Henry, 264, 266
Ripley, Eliza, 265
Rising Sun Tavern, 171
Rivers, Pearl. *See* Nicholson, Elizabeth
Rivers and bayous, 3, 8, 63, 175, 180–81, 250, 304, 319, 324; number of, 3; Mississippi, 8–9; Black River, Ouachita, Red River, Sabine, 9; Amite River, Atchafalaya, Bayou Lafourche, Bayou Manchac, Bayou Teche, Calcasieu, Mermentau, Mississippi Sound, Pearl River, Vermilion, 10
Roads, 68, 74, 118, 144, 168, 181, 239, 241, 242, 254–55, 284, 285, 303, 319, 320–21; Texas Road and Nolan Road, 147; "plank" roads, 181; "Shed Road," 255
Robertson, Thomas Bolling, 165
Roi David, Le, opera by Ernest Guiraud, 269
Roman, A. B., 165–66
Roman, Alfred, 266
Romantic New Orleanians, The, 315
Roosevelt, Theodore, 281
Rouquette, Father Adrien, 265
Roy, V. L., 260
Royal Bank of France, 44
Rural Topics, 248
Russ, R. E., 246
Ruston, founding of, 246

Sabine Parish, 172-73
Sabine Strip, 145, 171
St. Denis, Louis de Blanc de, 150
St. Denis, Louis Juchereau de, 40–41, 66
St. Francisville, 81, 122, 195
St. Landry Progress, 264
St. Louis, Avoyelles and Southwestern Railroad, 253
St. Louis Cathedral, 266, 312
St. Louis Church, 70-71, 85
St. Mart, Baroness de, 316

St. Martinville, 122, 141; as Creole town, 246
St. Mary's Dominican College, 263
Salcedo, Juan Manuel de, 107
Salt, 13–14, 58, 248, 299–300, 301
Sanchez y Ramon, Señorita Manuela de, 40
Sanders, J. Y., 239
Santa Rosa Island, 97
Sauvole, Sieur de, 37; becomes commander of Fort Maurepas, 30
Saxon, Lyle, 313, 315, 316, 324
Scalawags, 222, 225, 238
Scheler, Armin, 317
Schertz, Helen Pitkin, 265
Sculpture, 127, 266–67, 317
Secession, 196–204
Sedella, Father Antonio de, 103, 125
Sejour, Victor, 267
Settlers, 45, 47–48, 100–101, 109–110, 121, 185, 338; Canadian, 31, 42; French, 42, 47, 108; German, 48, 62, 92, 141, 173, 184; Irish, 173, 184; land granted to, 91, 109; American, 92, 93, 101; English, 92, 93; Spaniards, *Isleños*—settlers from Canary Islands, 92; from Santo Domingo, 103; western, 129–30; Italian, 243. *See also* Immigrants
Shepley, Gen. George F., 223–24
Sheridan, Gen. Philip, 224–25
Ship Island, 28, 43, 155; naming of, 29
Showboats, 268–69
Shreve, Henry Miller, 153, 250
Shreveport, 175, 211, 215, 230, 248, 253, 294
Sibley, Dr. John, 145–46
Simpson, Oramel H., 286
Skinner, Otis, 268
Slave Revolt in 1791, in Santo Domingo, 103, 112, 120
Slavery, 112–13, 197; development of, 63–64; Indian, abolition of, 86; forbidden by O'Reilly, 118. *See also* Slaves
Slaves, 37, 38, 42, 50, 54, 58, 62, 90–91, 111, 139, 141, 173, 230,

338; Indian, 51, 63, 86; selling of brandy to prohibited, 69; cabins for, 72; ownership of, in Louisiana, 174; clothing of, 183–84
Slave-trading station, Algiers, 50
Slidell, John, 201
Smith, Gen. Kirby, 213, 220, 229
Smith, Sol, 195
Smith, Dr. Sol A., 229
Smuggling and illegal trade, 66, 67, 89, 168
Snakes, 214. *See also* Reptiles
Soil, 8
Sophie Newcomb College, 263, 310
Southern Artists' League, 267
Southern Pacific Railroad, 304
Southern Quarterly Review, 194
Southern Review, 315
Southern University, 263, 310
South-Western, Shreveport, 202
Southwestern Louisiana Institute, 262–63
Spanish-American War, 240
Spanish Cession of Louisiana to France, 130
Spanish explorations, 25
Spanish settlement, in Florida, 26–27, 28
Sparling, Jack, 317
Sports, 20, 189–90, 236, 281–82, 320, 324–26; *papegai,* 190; hunting, 281; prize fighting, baseball, 282
State Board of Education, 259
State Board of Health, 189
State Department of Commerce and Industry, 300, 306
State Department of Education, 259, 308–309
State Department of Labor, 307
State Department of Wild Life and Fisheries, 302
State Exhibits Building, 313
State Federation of Labor, 307
State Highway Commission, 286
State Library, 194
State Superintendent of Education, 170, 260, 308; office created, 191
States, New Orleans, 313, 317
State-Times, Baton Rouge, 313

Steamboat, first to arrive in New
  Orleans, 147
Steamboat era, 180
Steamboats, 175, 183, 232, 250–52
Stephenson, Wendell H., 315
Stopher, Henry W., 318
Stopher, Vashti Robertson, 332
Storm, in New Orleans, 52
Storms, 34, 53, 63, 74, 96
Straight University, 234
Strawberries, 296
Strikes, 258, 307
Stuart, Ruth McEnery, 265
Sugar, 63, 65, 106, 111, 152, 176–
  77, 181, 210, 218, 248, 296, 313
Sugar cane, "tafia" drink made from,
  63
Sullivan, George, 266
Sulphur, 13, 248–49, 300, 301, 305
Superstitions, 278–79
Suydam, E. H., 316
Swamp River Suite, 319
Sweet potatoes, 296

Tallant, Robert, 315, 316
Talliaferro, James G., 201
Tangipahoa & Eastern Railways
  Company, 304
Tangipahoa Indians, 15
Taylor, Gen. Richard, 210, 211, 219,
  266, 317
Taylor, Gen. Zachary, 165, 166, 172;
  as President, 210
Tchoupitoulas Coast, 121
Télégraphe, Le, New Orleans, 148–49
Telephones, 275
Television, 314, 320
Temple, Keith, 317
Territory of Orleans, 143
Texas and Pacific Railroad, 304
Texas War for Independence, 171
Theater and drama, 194–95, 267–68,
  318
Theaters, 149, 199, 268
Theatricals, amateur, 127, 149
This Side of Jordan, 315
Thompson, Virgil, 319
Thornton, Col. William, 156
Tilden, Samuel J., 227

"Timbalier, Le," 51
Timber, 64. *See also* Forests; Lumber
  and lumbering; Trees
Timberlands, 139. *See also* Forests
Times, Shreveport, 313
Times-Picayune, New Orleans, 313.
  See also Picayune
Tobacco, 40, 41, 58, 61, 65, 66, 68,
  89, 111, 113, 152, 176, 181, 296;
  "perique," 178, 296
Tonti, Henri de, 26, 27, 30, 32, 36
Tourists, 306, 330
Townsend, Mary Ashley, 265
Trade, 34, 36, 38, 40, 41–42, 43, 45,
  53, 60, 61, 64–67, 80, 83, 89, 90,
  102, 104, 107, 108, 114–15, 119,
  129–130, 146, 147, 150, 168, 175,
  181–83, 250, 255–57, 294, 304–
  306. *See also* Commerce; Smug-
  gling and illegal trade
Trade and commercial publications,
  313
Transfer of Louisiana; from France
  to Spain in 1762, pp. 61, 80; from
  Spain to France in 1803, pp. 135–
  36; from France to U. S. in 1803,
  pp. 136–38
Transportation, 64–65, 74, 123–24,
  147, 180–81, 232, 242, 250–55,
  270, 273, 282, 303–304, 319. *See
  also* Boats
Travel. *See* Transportation
Treaty of Fontainebleau, 1762, p. 61
Treaty of Ghent, 162
Treaty of San Ildefonso, 107, 130
Treaty of 1795, p. 105
Tree, Ellen, 195
Trees, 11, 12, 13–14, 39, 53, 298.
  See also Forests
Tregle, Joseph, 337
Tribune de la Nouvelle-Orléans, 231
Truck-gardening, 296–97
True American, New Orleans, 194
True Delta, New Orleans, 194, 201
Tulane, Paul, 196, 263
Tulane Medical Unit, 241
Tulane Theater, 268
Tulane University, 263, 264, 310
Tulane University Library, 312

Tung nuts, 296
Tunica Indians, 15–16
Turpin's Coffee House, 171
Tuttle, Gen. James, 219
Twain, Mark, 230

Ulloa, Don Antonio de, 80–84, 85, 110, 115, 119
Uncle Tom's Cabin, 197
Union League, 222, 225
United States Mint and Custom House, 203
Universities. *See* Colleges and Universities
University of Southwestern La., 310
Unzaga y Amézaga, Luis de, 87, 88–90, 100
Ursulines, 50, 52, 78, 124–25, 126

Vacheries, 63
Vaudreuil, Marquis de, 57–59
Vegetation, 10. *See also* Trees; Shrubs and flowers
Victor, Claude, 131
Victor C. Barringer House, 313
Vieux Carré, 47, 70, 103, 157, 314, 316, 320, 330
Villeré, Jacques, 164–65, 168
Villiers, Coulon de, 333
Voltaire, 61
Voodooism, 112, 279

Walker, Gidgeon, 122
Walker, Joseph, 166, 167
Walker, Samuel, 266
Walker, William, 112, 171
War Between the States. *See* Civil War
War for Southern Independence. *See* Civil War
War Hawks, 150
War of the Rebellion. *See* Civil War
War of 1812, pp. 133, 150–62, 170, 171
Warmoth, Henry Clay, 225–26, 229, 266
Warren, Robert Penn, 315
Washington, George, 220, 333
Washington-Western Railways Company, 304
Water supply of Louisiana, 300–301

Watkins, John W., 255
Weathercock, The, 149
Webster, Daniel, 339
Weekly Delta, New Orleans, 199
Weekly Gazette and Comet, Baton Rouge, 199–200
Weitzel, Godfrey, 208
Welfare, social, 188–89, 244–45, 284, 285, 291, 292, 294
Wells, J. Madison, 224
West Feliciana Railroad, 180
West Florida Rebellion of 1810, p. 146
Westfeldt, P. M., 316
Wheat, 62, 111, 129, 187, 305
Whig Party, 165, 166, 197
White, Edward D., 166
White, Chief Justice Edward Douglass, 317
White League, 226
Wickliffe, Robert C., 166, 197
Wild life preserves, 302
Wilkinson, James, 136, 142, 146
Williamson, Frederick W., 319
Willing, James, 93
Wilson, Mortimer, 319
Wiltz, Louis A., 239
Wiltz, Margarethe, 92
Wolfe, Jacques, 319
Women, arrival of, in Louisiana, 34, 49; as workers, 258; Gen. Butler's Order No. 28 against, 217; magazine for, 265; college for, 310
Women and Children Labor Law, 307
Wood, Trist, 317
Workmen's Compensation Law, 307
World War I, 240–41
World War II, 289, 294
World's Industrial and Cotton Centennial Exposition, 247

Xavier University, 263

Yankee Pelters, 207
Yazoo and Mississippi Valley Railroad, 304
Yellow Fever, 33, 65–66, 78, 188–89, 235, 242
'Yo Solo,' 98
You, Dominique, 159

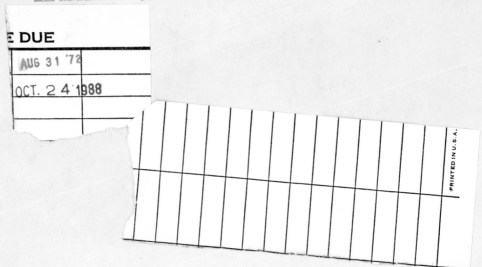

PRINTED IN U.S.A.